Essentials

of Millon Inventories Assessment, Second Edition

Essentials of Psychological Assessment Series
Series Editors, Alan S. Kaufman and Nadeen L. Kaufman

Essentials

of Millon Inventories

Assessment,

Second Edition

Stephen Strack

 John Wiley & Sons, Inc.

CONTENTS

SERIES PREFACE

I n the *Essentials of Psychological Assessment* series, our goal is to provide the reader with books that deliver key practical information in the most efficient and accessible style. The series features instruments in a variety of domains, such as cognition, personality, education, and neuropsychology. For the experienced clinician, books in the series offer a concise, yet thorough, way to master the continuously evolving supply of new and revised instruments, as well as a convenient method for keeping up to date on the tried-and-true measures. The novice will find here a prioritized assembly of all the information and techniques that must be at one's fingertips to begin the complicated process of individual psychological diagnosis.

Wherever feasible, visual shortcuts to highlight key points are utilized alongside systematic, step-by-step guidelines. Chapters are focused and succinct. Topics are targeted for an easy understanding of the essentials of administration, scoring, interpretation, and clinical application. Theory and research are continually woven into the fabric of each book, but always to enhance clinical inference, never to sidetrack or overwhelm. We have long been advocates of "intelligent" testing—the notion that a profile of test scores is meaningless unless it is brought to life by the clinical observations and astute detective work of knowledgeable examiners. Test profiles must be used to make a difference in the child's or adult's life, or why bother to test? We want this series to help our readers become the best intelligent testers they can be.

In *Essentials of Millon Inventories Assessment, Second Edition,* Dr. Stephen Strack brings together a group of talented clinicians to introduce the family of measures based on Dr. Theodore Millon's comprehensive theory of personality and psychopathology. The five instruments covered—Millon Clinical Multiaxial Inventory–III, Millon Behavioral Medicine Diagnostic, Millon Adolescent Clinical Inventory, Personality Adjective Check List, and Millon Index of Personality Styles—were developed for specific client populations and contain scales to assess traits and symptoms unique to those populations. Nevertheless, the shared theoretical base of these tests makes it easy for both novice and experienced users to develop skills with all of them. To assist the reader in this process, authors of each chapter follow the same outline and address key similarities among the instruments as well as the distinctive features of each Millon inventory.

Alan S. Kaufman, Ph.D., and Nadeen L. Kaufman, Ed.D., Series Editors
Yale University School of Medicine

FOREWORD

This valuable synopsis of how to interpret the Millon inventories may be employed as part of an introductory or advanced personality assessment course, as part of a seminar series, or as part of a course devoted to the personality disorders. Because of its more focused character, the first option probably presents the best opportunity for instructors to discuss the issues involved in the development and use of the inventories. This book presents an approach to learning the Millon Clinical Multiaxial Inventory, Millon Behavioral Medicine Diagnostic, Millon Adolescent Clinical Inventory, Personality Adjective Check List, and Millon Index of Personality Styles that the authors have found to be effective over the course of many years, in a variety of different venues, with a variety of time constraints. Particular chapters may be expanded or contracted by instructors depending on the level of students' prior training, their interests or goals, and the focus of the class or seminar. With some practice, the material may be introduced in as little as 3 hours or expanded to fill several weeks.

The focus of this book is not on material of a theoretical nature, for which abundant references are already available. Instead, chapters address themes that challenge students to learn how to employ these inventories as illustrations of the fundamental issues and goals of all assessment and, sometimes, of the entire spectrum of clinical psychology. Unfortunately, space did not permit Dr. Strack to touch on many of the subtleties that might be presented. Teachers may wish to direct students so motivated to original sources for such material.

When learning personality assessment, it may be necessary for students to bring each instrument to life with real cases, by discussing with fellow students the spirit of issues that are actively discussed in the field, the numerous problems that other test authors have thought important to address, and even the personalities of the developers. Just as each individual human personality has its own development path that inclines it toward particular strengths and weaknesses rather than others, so each clinical assessment instrument has its own unique biography. Far from being simply filler, these historical and contextual particularities may be as essential to an informed use of an instrument as history and context are to the individual person to be assessed.

After studying the basic facts of each test's features, the student may wish, depending on the level of the cases he or she sees, to briefly discuss with fellow students profile interpretation in the abstract. The purpose is to evolve an integrated, or multiaxial, conception of the individual. First, there is the most basic level of interpretation, that which deals with the presenting complaints and symptoms. Here we are only interested in determining which scales are elevated and what diagnoses may be made. For each inventory, this involves examining which scale elevations exceed the base rate cutting score across all scales. Together, these form diagnostic hypotheses that can then be considered in the context of other information outside the inventory (presenting complaints, the therapist's "feel" for the patient or client, reports of significant relationships, other instruments, background clinical information, etc.). In view of the end goal, the integrated understanding of the person, this level of interpretation must be considered primary. This is especially true for the personality styles and disorders, which are not disorders at all but instead constructs that act as contexts through which the individual's presenting clinical symptoms must be understood.

It may be useful to consider interpreting the Millon inventory scale elevations either dimensionally or configurally or contextually. A dimensional interpretation is necessary to model degrees of clinical expression in real cases. Individuals may be somewhat anxious, or somewhat depressed, and so on without actually meeting formal diagnostic criteria. On the other hand, even among patients who meet these criteria, some are more severely disordered than others. In contrast, a strictly diagnostic approach results in a loss of information about the person by dichotomizing scale scores into present or absent judgments.

A configural interpretation is necessary for the same reason. Individuals almost never present as pure diagnostic prototypes; instead, each person is likely to combine a unique pattern of personality styles and clinical states. The point to be made is that not all patients with the same formal diagnosis have the same problem. A single diagnostic label rarely if ever provides information specific and comprehensive enough to serve as a sound basis for intervention efforts. Not only do patients differ with respect to the magnitude of their difficulties or pathology, but they also differ in the features with which they approximate a clinical prototype. Whether diagnoses are derived through clinical observation, mathematical analyses, or theoretical deduction, patients differ in how they meet various clinical requirements, a fact institutionalized in the fourth edition of the *Diagnostic and Statistical Manual of Mental Disorders* and its subsequent text revision. In and of itself, then, diagnosis underspecifies pathology, especially with regard to treatment considerations. Moreover, the vast majority of patients represent what I have termed "mixed subtypes." In moving toward an integrated conception of the "real" person, we must ask how each elevated scale interrelates and is relevant to the interpretation of each specific case.

At a final stage of the inventories' interpretation, the proper question to be asked is not whether, but how—how the interaction of individual characteristics and contextual factors, that is, the interaction of personality style and psychosocial stressors, produces classical clinical symptomatology. Instructors will likely wish to point out that this synthesis requires a certain amount of clinical imagination on the part of the student, regardless of which of the five inventories discussed in this text is used. This requires that the symptom complaint and psychosocial history be integrated within the overall biographical and personality context.

That a former student of mine, Stephen Strack, has seen fit to organize this book is an event of great joy for me. As an esteemed clinician, trainer, and test developer himself, he represents the high quality and professional integrity that every professor could wish to find in his former trainees. In this work, consisting of many hands, Strack has arranged to pass along to the next generation of students the rich body and comprehensive knowledge he has acquired of these highly successful inventories in a manner both brief and useful.

Theodore Millon
Coral Gables, Florida

Essentials
of Millon Inventories Assessment, Second Edition

One

ESSENTIALS OF MCMI-III ASSESSMENT

Robert J. Craig

INTRODUCTION

The Millon Clinical Multiaxial Inventory–III (MCMI-III; Millon, 1997a) is a 175-item true-false self-report measure of 14 personality patterns and 10 clinical syndromes for use with adults 18 years of age and older who are being evaluated and/or treated in mental health settings. Since the introduction of this test in 1977, it has become one of the most frequently used assessment instruments for the examination of personality disorders and major clinical syndromes. Only the Rorschach (Exner, 1993) and the Minnesota Multiphasic Personality Inventory–2 (MMPI-2; Butcher, Dahlstrom, Graham, Tellegen, & Kaemmer, 1989) have produced more research within the past 5 years. There are now over 400 empirical studies (Craig, 1993a, 1997) and seven books (Craig, 1993a, 1993b; Choca & Van Denburg, 1996; Jankowski, 2002; McCann & Dyer, 1996; Millon, 1997b; Retzlaff, 1995) based on this measure.

> ### DON'T FORGET
>
> - The MCMI-III is appropriate for use with adults who are being evaluated and/or treated in mental health settings.
> - It was designed to detect personality disorders and a few clinical syndromes.
> - It should *not* be used with persons who are not seeking mental health assistance (i.e., "normal" individuals).

HISTORY AND DEVELOPMENT

The original version of this instrument, the MCMI-I (Millon, 1983a), was developed to operationalize the theory of psychopathology introduced by Millon (1969/1983b) in *Modern Psychopathology*. In that text he proposed three axes—active-passive, pleasure-pain, and self-other—as the basic building blocks of normal and abnormal personality. Conceived in terms of instrumental coping patterns designed to maximize positive reinforcements and avoid punishment, the model crossed the active-passive axis with four reinforcement strategies—detached, dependent, independent, and ambivalent—to derive eight basic personality patterns (asocial, avoidant, submissive, gregarious, narcissistic, aggressive, conforming, negativistic) and three severe variants (schizoid, cycloid, paranoid). Although Millon did not propose a formal model of clinical syndromes along with his personality taxonomy, he asserted that most or all psychiatric conditions (e.g., major depression, anxiety disorders, psychosis) could be best explained as extensions of personality.

Millon's strong theoretical interests led him to a test development strategy that was also grounded in theory. Jane Loevinger (1957) had previously proposed that assessment instruments be built in a three-step process with theory guiding development and validation in every step. Millon used her strategy to create the MCMI-I as well as subsequent editions of the instrument.

The three steps of test development and validation described by Loevinger (1957) were called theoretical-substantive, internal-structural, and external. In the theoretical-substantial phase, items are generated for scales in terms of how well they conform to theory. Here Millon created an initial pool of face-valid items and then split the 1,100-item list into two equivalent forms.

For the internal-structural phase of development, scales are created to match a set of criteria defined by the theory. For example, Millon's (1997a; Millon & Davis, 1996) model posits that personality scales should have high internal consistency, test-retest reliability, and a theoretically consistent pattern of correlations with other scales. During this phase, the two test forms were administered to a variety of clinical samples, and Millon retained items with the highest item-total scale correlations. He then calculated item-scale intercorrelations and item endorsement frequencies and eliminated items with extreme endorsement frequencies (e.g., those below 15% and above 85%). This left 440 items, which were later reduced to 289. Millon gave the experimental form of the MCMI-I to a variety of clinical patients and had 167 clinicians complete a diagnostic form for each patient they had seen for assessment or therapy. The items were then reduced to 150. Three experimental scales were eliminated and three scales were added, and the validation process described above was then repeated until the final version contained 175 items.

For the third stage of external criterion validation, which is analogous to convergent-discriminant validity, Millon had psychiatric patients complete the final form of the MCMI-I along with several self-report measures of personality and clinical syndromes. Based on these data he judged that the scales were faithful to his theory, and the test was then published with norms based on over 1,500 psychiatric patients.

The second edition of the measure, the MCMI-II (Millon, 1987), was created to keep pace with changes in the revised third edition of the *Diagnostic and Statistical Manual of Mental Disorders-III-R* (DSM-III-R; American Psychiatric Association, 1987). An experimental form was developed according to the model previously described totaling 368 items. Scales measuring Self-Defeating and Aggressive (Sadistic) personality disorders were developed. A total of 45 items in the MCMI-I were changed, and Millon introduced an item-weighting system whereby prototype items (e.g., those items essentially related to the disorder) were given higher scores. He also derived three validity scales and increased the number of personality disorder scales from 11 to 13. Validation studies were then conducted as described earlier.

The MCMI-III was developed to bring the test in line with DSM-IV (American Psychiatric Association, 1994). Here 45 of the 175 items in the MCMI-II were changed, two new personality disorder scales—Depressive and Post-Traumatic Stress Disorder—were added to the test, the item-weighting system was changed from a 3-point to a 2-point system, scales were reduced in length, and noteworthy items pertaining to child abuse and eating disorders were added but not scored on any of the scales. Significantly, Millon made sure that most test items directly reflected diagnostic criteria in the DSM-IV. The published version of MCMI-III (see Rapid Reference 1.1 for publication information) contains a three-item Validity Index, three Modifying Indices to assess response bias, 14 personality scales, and 10 clinical syndrome scales. The personality and clinical scales contain 12 to 24 items each. Internal consistency of the scales was estimated to be .67 to .90 using Cronbach's (1951) alpha, and test-retest stability was estimated to be .84 to .96 over a period of 5 to 14 days (Millon, 1997a, pp. 57–59). Rapid Reference 1.2 summarizes the MCMI-III scales.

....

≡*Rapid Reference 1.1*

Millon Clinical Multiaxial Inventory–III

Author: Theodore Millon, Ph.D.

Publication date: 1994

What the test measures: Personality disorders and clinical syndromes

Age range: 18 and above

Administration time: 20–30 minutes

Qualifications of examiners: Graduate training in psychodiagnostic assessment. Users of interpretive reports must meet full membership qualifications for the American Psychological Association, American Psychiatric Association, American Medical Association, or the National Association of Social Workers.

Publisher: National Computer Systems

      P.O. Box 1416

      Minneapolis, MN 55440

      Phone: 800-627-7271

      Fax: 800-632-9011

MCMI-III manual, $46; profile report, $15.25–17.25; interpretive report, $32.50–34.50 (2002 prices).

Item Overlap and Item Weighting

A notable feature of Millon's (1997a; Millon & Davis, 1996) model of psychopathology is that various personality types and clinical syndromes are presumed to be related to one another in a predictable manner. For example, schizoid and avoidant personality styles are believed to share a trait of social detachment. This trait makes both types of individuals appear distant, withdrawn, and uneasy in social situations. In decompensated form, these personalities are thought to be prone to Schizotypal and psychotic disorders.

In accordance with his model, theoretically related personality and clinical scales share certain items. The number of shared items varies across the test, but Millon (1997a) identified the most defining characteristics of a scale by assigning a weight of 2 to these primary, or prototypical items, and giving a smaller weight of 1 to items that are less definitive, or nonprototypical. Thus the central features of a personality style or clinical syndrome are weighted 2, whereas characteristics that are less central and defin-

≡ Rapid Reference 1.2

....

Summary of MCMI-III Scales

Validity Index

Three items measure highly improbable events designed to detect random responding and confusion.

Modifying Indices

X. Disclosure. Scale X assesses the amount of self-disclosure and willingness to admit to symptoms and problems.

Y. Desirability. Scale Y measures examinees' tendency to answer items so that one looks very favorable and without problems.

Z. Debasement. Scale Z assesses examinees' tendency to answer items by accentuating, highlighting, and exaggerating problems and symptoms.

Clinical Personality Patterns Scales

1. Schizoid. Individuals are socially detached; prefer solitary activities; seem aloof, apathetic, and distant with difficulties in forming and maintaining relationships.

2A. Avoidant. Individuals are socially anxious due to perceived expectations of rejection and fearful.

2B. Depressive. Individuals are downcast and gloomy, even in the absence of a clinical depression.

3. Dependent. Individuals are passive, submissive, and feel inadequate. They generally lack autonomy and initiative.

4. Histrionic. Individuals are gregarious, with a strong need to be at the center of attention. They can be highly manipulative.

5. Narcissistic. Individuals are self-centered, exploitive, arrogant, and egotistical.

6A. Antisocial. Individuals are irresponsible, vengeful, engage in criminal behavior, and are strongly independent.

6B. Aggressive (Sadistic). Individuals are controlling and abusive; they enjoy humiliating others.

7. Compulsive. Individuals are orderly, organized, efficient, and perfectionistic. They engage in these behaviors to avoid chastisement from authority.

8A. Passive-Aggressive (Negativistic). Individuals are disgruntled, argumentative, petulant, negativistic; they keep others on edge.

(continued)

8B. Self-Defeating. Individuals seem to engage in behaviors that result in people taking advantage of and abusing them. They act like a martyr and are self-sacrificing.

Severe Personality Pathology Scales

S. Schizotypal. Individuals seem "spacey," self-absorbed, idiosyncratic, eccentric, and cognitively confused.

C. Borderline. Individuals display a labile affect and erratic behavior. They are emotionally intense, often dissatisfied and depressed, and may become self-destructive.

P. Paranoid. Individuals are rigid and defensive. They hold delusions of influence and persecution. They are mistrusting and may become angry and belligerent.

Clinical Syndromes Scales (Axis I Symptom Scales)

A. Anxiety Disorder. Individuals are anxious, tense, apprehensive, and physiologically overaroused.

H. Somatoform Disorder. Individuals are preoccupied with vague physical problems with no known organic cause. They tend to be hypochondriacal and somaticizing.

N. Bipolar: Manic Disorder. Individuals have excessive energy and are overactive, restless, impulsive, unable to sleep, and manic.

D. Dysthymic Disorder. Individuals are able to maintain day-to-day functions but are depressed, pessimistic, and dysphoric. They have low self-esteem and feel inadequate.

B. Alcohol Dependence. Individuals admit to serious problems with alcohol and/or endorse personality traits often associated with abusing alcohol.

T. Drug Dependence. Individuals admit to serious problems with drugs and/or endorse personality traits often associated with abusing drugs.

R. Post-Traumatic Stress Disorder. Individuals reports unwanted and intrusive memories and/or nightmares of a disturbing, traumatic event; they may have flashbacks.

Severe Syndromes Scales

SS. Thought Disorder. Individuals experience thought disorder of psychotic proportions; they often report hallucinations and delusions.

CC. Major Depression. Individuals are severely depressed to the extent they are unable to function in day-to-day activities. They have vegetative signs of clinical depression (poor appetite and sleep, low energy, loss of interests) and feel hopeless and helpless.

PP. Delusional Disorder. Individuals are acutely paranoid with delusions and irrational thinking. They may become belligerent and act out the delusions.

ing are weighted 1. Careful readers will note in the test manual (Millon, 1997a) that items are given a weight of 2 only once, but may be scored 1 for one or more additional scales. This indicates that various traits and symptoms can be central to only one personality or clinical syndrome, but they may overlap with other, related personalities and syndromes.

The result of item overlap on MCMI-III scales is that there are moderately high scale intercorrelations. The test manual gives a matrix of scale intercorrelations that ranges from −.80 to +.85, although most values are more modest (in the range of −.50 to +.50; Millon, 1997a, Table 3.6).

> ### DON'T FORGET
>
> - MCMI-III scales have varying numbers of overlapping items. This creates a moderate amount of correlation between scales.
> - Scale items are given a weight of 2 when they represent central, or prototypical, features of a given personality or syndrome. Less defining characteristics are given a weight of 1.

Normative Sample

The MCMI-III normative sample consisted of 998 psychiatric patients from the United States and Canada, whom Millon divided into two groups for test development purposes. The first group of 600 patients was used to create scales, and the second group of 398 patients was used for cross validation to verify accuracy of the standardized scores. Although modest in size, the normative sample represents a broad range of demographic characteristics. Patients were men (54%) and women (46%) from outpatient (52%) and inpatient (26%) settings, as well as correctional facilities (8%). Age range was 18 to 88, although 80% were between the ages of 18 and 45. Most of the patients had completed high school (82%), and among these 18% also had a college degree (18%). A notable limitation of the sample is that most subjects were White (86%), with only a small number of Blacks (8%), Hispanics (2%), and all others (4%) represented.

Base Rate Scores

MCMI-III personality and clinical syndrome scores were standardized as base rate (BR) scores rather than T scores. T scores were considered inappropriate

Rapid Reference 1.3

What the Base Rate Scores Mean

- MCMI-III scales were standardized as base rate (BR) scores that can range from 0 to 115. BR scores reflect the prevalence of the various personality styles and clinical syndromes in the MCMI-III normative sample.

- BR scores ≥ 74 indicate the *presence* of a clinically significant personality style or syndrome.

- BR scores ≥ 84 indicate that a particular personality style or syndrome is *prominent* for the individual.

- BR scores of 60 represent the *median* for all patients.

by Millon (1997a; 1997b) because they assume an underlying normal population distribution, and the MCMI-III normative sample consists of psychiatric patients. BR scores reflect the diagnoses of the individuals who make up the normative sample. For the MCMI-III, Millon had experienced clinicians provide DSM-III-R multiaxial diagnoses for all of the patients in the normative group. By knowing the scores of these patients on the MCMI-III, and their clinical diagnoses, Millon was able to create anchor points for his scales that would reflect the prevalence, or BR, of each psychiatric condition. BR scores of 60 were set at the median raw score obtained by all patients. BR scores of 75 were assigned to the minimum raw score obtained by patients who met criteria for the particular disorder or condition. BR scores of 85 were given to the minimum raw score of patients who were judged to have a particular disorder or condition as their primary problem.

For the personality scales, BR scores of 75 to 84 signify the presence of clinically significant personality *traits,* while BR scores of 85 or above suggest the presence of a *disorder.* For the clinical syndrome scales, BR scores of 75 to 84 indicate the *presence* of a syndrome, and BR scores of 85 or above denote the *prominence* of a particular syndrome. (See Rapid Reference 1.3.)

THEORETICAL FOUNDATION

Since the publication of *Modern Psychopathology* (Millon, 1969/1983), Millon's model of psychopathology evolved and expanded. In its current form, Millon (1997b; Millon & Davis, 1996) asserts that the structure of a clinical science consists of four main elements: (a) a theory that explains the phenomena un-

	Existential Aim		Replication Strategy		
	Life Enhancement	Life Preservation	Reproductive Propagation	Reproductive Nurturance	
	Pleasure-Pain		Self-Other		
Deficiency, Imbalance, Conflict	Pleasure (low) Pain (low or high)	Pleasure-Pain Reversal	Self (low) Other (high)	Self (high) Other (low)	Self-Other Reversal
Adaptation Mode	Personality Disorders				
Passive: Accommodation	Schizoid (low pleasure, low pain) Depressive (high pain, low pleasure)	Masochistic	Dependent	Narcissistic	Compulsive
Active: Modification	Avoidant	Sadistic	Histrionic	Antisocial	Negativistic
Structural Pathology	Schizotypal	Borderline, Paranoid	Borderline	Paranoid	Borderline, Paranoid

Figure 1.1 Breakdown of Personality Disorders According to Millon's Model

Note. From Millon (1997a) with permission, National Computer Systems.

der observation, (b) a taxonomy that categorizes these phenomena into meaningful dimensions, (c) instrumentation that measures these phenomena, and (d) intervention that remediates problematic cases. Thus the MCMI-III is an instrument that measures Millon's taxonomy of classifying personality pathology, which was derived from Millon's bioevolutionary theory of personality development and pathology (Millon, 1990). Originally, the MCMI was not designed to be in agreement with official psychiatric nosology and nomenclature. However, subsequent revisions of the test have brought it closer to DSM categories.

Millon's theory posits three "survival aims" or polarities in the laws of nature (Figure 1.1). The first is to maintain existence. At the psychological level this polarity translates into activities organized to give pleasure or enhance one's life or to experience pain by merely preserving life. After existence has been ensured, the next organismic task is to adapt to one's environment. At the psychological level the adaptational polarity translates into actively changing one's environment or passively accepting and accommodating to one's circumstances of life. Finally, there is a need to replicate to ensure survival of the species. At the psychological level replication strategies pertain to whether one is focused primarily on one's self or on others through nurturing behaviors. Millon has recently introduced a fourth polarity, abstraction, but has not, as yet, developed this part of his theory.

This theory of personology development translates into a theory-based framework for both personality styles and personality pathology. Millon identified five main sources of reinforcement (independent, dependent, ambivalent, discordant, and detached) and two coping styles (active and passive). This translates into a five-by-two matrix of theory-derived personality disorders that closely corresponds with DSM-IV personality disorder categories but is not identical to it. For example, Millon's Self-Defeating and Aggressive (Sadistic) personality disorders are not found in DSM-IV but comprise styles and disorders emanating from Millon's theory.

Having developed a theory that posited the existence of certain personality disorders, Millon then developed instrumentation to assess these disorders. Although he primarily used a true-false methodology in scale development for the MCMI, he has also experimented with other assessment methodologies (e.g., diagnostic statements used for clinician ratings) as part of his instrument development, and Strack (1987, 1991) has used adjective checklist methodology to assess Millon's personality styles in nonclinical populations. The theory is not tied to an assessment methodology, and there may be multiple paths leading to the same assessment conclusion.

TEST ADMINISTRATION

The MCMI-III was developed for use with men and women (18 years of age and older) seeking mental health evaluation and/or treatment who read at minimally the eighth grade level. It was not meant to be used with nonclinical populations, and doing so will yield distorted test results. The inventory can be administered individually or in groups using a paper-and-pencil form, or via personal computer using a software program available from the test publisher. Administration time is typically 20 to 30 minutes.

The test does not require special instructions for administration. The directions printed on the answer sheet or presented via computer are sufficient for most people to accurately complete the questionnaire. However, it is good practice for examiners to develop rapport with testing clients prior

> # CAUTION
>
> ....
>
> Do not test patients with the MCMI-III if they are confused, overly sedated, or intoxicated as those states will interfere with the respondent's ability to appropriately answer the questions.

to introducing an assessment instrument. In this regard the examiner can explain how the test will be helpful to their issues and how it will be used on their behalf. Clients should be advised that they will be given feedback on their test results, so it is important for them to answer as honestly as possible.

Testing Individuals With Special Needs

MCMI-III administration versions are available in Spanish, on audiotape for the visually impaired, and via computer. Hearing-impaired patients should be able to take this test by reading the instructions on the test answer sheet or those provided via computer administration of the items. For patients who otherwise are unable to take this test, the examiner may read the statements aloud and have the person respond "true" or "false" or perhaps nod his or her head to indicate the same.

Examiners who administer the test verbally to a patient must understand that they are giving the test in a manner that deviates from the way the test was standardized. Also, there are interpersonal processes existing between examiner and client that are not immediately present when the client is tested without the presence of an examiner. For example, the client may be considering what the examiner will think if he or she answers the verbally presented question in a certain way. These processes may alter the way a client responds to the items and therefore alter their scores. If there is no way to give this test other than to read the questions to the examinee, then the examiner is obligated to report this deviation in the report and to make some evaluative statement as to how the validity of the test may or may not have been affected by this kind of testing procedure.

SCORING THE MCMI-III

CAUTION

The MCMI-III cannot be scored if (a) gender is not indicated, (b) the client is under age 18, or (c) more than 12 items have been left unanswered.

The test may be hand scored or computer scored using telescoring, mail-in answer sheets, or software for personal computers. Scoring stencils are available for hand scoring, which takes about 45 minutes. Because hand scoring can lead to errors owing to the many adjustments that are required for this test, Millon (1997a) recommends hand scoring each test twice to minimize errors.

If the test is administered with an answer sheet instead of via computer, upon the completion of the test the examiner should check the answer sheet for any double-marked items and make sure that no more than 12 items have been left unanswered. If any of these conditions exist, the answer sheet should be returned to the patient so that he or she can make the necessary corrections. The MCMI-III cannot be scored if (a) the sex of the client is unknown or unspecified, (b) the client is under age 18, or (c) there are 12 or more missing or double-marked items.

From Raw Scores to BR Scores

Raw scores for all scales except Disclosure (Scale X) are calculated by adding up the number of items endorsed for the scale, with care taken to assign the proper weight of 1 or 2 for each item. Disclosure is a composite score calculated from the raw scores of the basic 11 personality scales, as follows:

Disclosure = Schizoid + Avoidant + Depressive + Dependent + Histrionic + (Narcissistic × .67) + Antisocial + Aggressive + Compulsive + Passive-Aggressive + Self-Defeating

The raw scores for all scales except Validity are then transformed into initial BR scores, using the tables provided in Appendix C of the test manual. Millon provides separate tables for men and women because men and women differ in how they answer a personality inventory. Initial BR scores are then subjected to four possible corrections designed to compensate for distortions in test scores attributable to certain biases (see Rapid Reference 1.4).

≡*Rapid Reference 1.4*

Response Bias Corrections

As a means of improving diagnostic efficiency of the scales, Millon sought ways of mitigating the effects that response biases can have on the resulting profile. Following an elaborate four-step system, BR points are added or subtracted to various scale scores based on the respondent's status as inpatient or outpatient, duration of Axis I condition, level of self-disclosure, tendency to deny problems or complain excessively, and reported levels of anxiety and dysphoria. Below is a summary of corrections applied to MCMI-III BR scores.

Correction Factor	Effect on Scales
Level of Disclosure (Scale X)	If X > 123, BR points are subtracted from all scales. If X < 61, BR points are added to all scale scores.
Anxiety-Depression	If the Anxiety and/or Dysthymia scales are elevated ≥ BR 75, scores are lowered for Avoidant, Depressive, Self-Defeating, Schizotypal, and Borderline. The amount depends on inpatient/outpatient status and duration of Axis I condition.
Recent Inpatient Admission	When Axis I episode duration is 4 weeks or less, Thought Disorder, Major Depression, and Delusional Disorder scales are increased.
Denial-Complaint	When Histrionic, Narcissistic, or Compulsive come out as the highest personality scale, 8 BR points are added to that scale only.

Note. The corrections are applied in the above order after initial BR scores have been calculated. Because some of the corrections depend on inpatient/outpatient status and duration of Axis I episode, it is very important to properly indicate these on the test form prior to scoring.

The *disclosure adjustment* was designed to counterbalance the tendency of some clients to broadly underreport or overreport personal attributes and symptoms. When the raw Disclosure scale score is below 61, points are added to the initial BR scores of all personality and clinical syndrome scales. Points are subtracted from these scales if BR is above 123. The number of points added or subtracted is a function of how low or high the raw Disclosure scale is, and ranges from 0 to 20.

An *anxiety-depression adjustment* was developed to correct for the inclination of patients to overreport problematic features when feeling acutely anxious and/or depressed. A correction is made whenever Anxiety and/or Dysthymic Disorder are BR 75 or above, such that BR points are subtracted from scales Avoidant, Depressive, Self-Defeating, Schizotypal, and Borderline in proportion to (a) how elevated the scales are, (b) whether both scales are 75 or above or just one, (c) whether the client was an inpatient at the time of testing, and (d) how recently the client developed his or her presenting problem.

The *inpatient adjustment* was created to offset the tendency of some recently hospitalized clients to underreport the severity of their emotional problems. When a client is identified as an inpatient who developed a psychiatric condition (Axis I) within the past 4 weeks, 2 to 10 BR points are added to the Thought Disorder, Major Depression, and Delusional Disorder scales.

A *denial-complaint adjustment* is made to correct for the bias of some individuals to underreport the severity of their personality attributes. When the Histrionic, Narcissistic, or Compulsive scale is the most highly elevated among the 10 clinical personality patterns, the BR for that scale only is increased by 8 points.

Although the correction formulas are applied, in the order given, to all test protocols, it should be clear that some clients will not meet criteria for any of the corrections, whereas others will meet criteria for all of them. Because of this, the initial BR scores of some patients will not be altered, but the scores of others will be adjusted by a considerable amount.

Computer Scoring

There are two major computerized scoring programs available to interpret the MCMI-III. The test publisher has scoring and interpretive services and will provide a narrative report written by Millon. Psychological Assessment Resources, Inc., publishes an interpretive report developed by Robert J. Craig, Ph.D., ABPP, which requires that BR scores be available, either by hand scoring or by computer scoring, through the test publisher. The BR scores are then entered into the program and a narrative report is generated. Figure 1.3 (see page 43) illustrates a sample score profile.

HOW TO INTERPRET THE MCMI-III

Before interpreting the personality disorder and clinical syndrome scales, the examiner must (a) establish that the profile of scores is valid, and, if so, (b) interpret the

CAUTION

Look at and interpret the Validity scales before examining the personality and clinical symptom scales.

client's response style. The MCMI-III contains four scales for assessing response characteristics: Validity, Disclosure, Desirability, and Debasement. Only the Validity and Disclosure scales are used to determine whether a test is interpretable or not. All four give clues about the way the client approached the test.

Validity and Response-Style Scales

Validity

The Validity Index (Scale V) consists of three improbable statements. If two or more of these statements are answered in the endorsed direction (e.g., true), the test is not valid. Because the Validity Index does not appear on the profile sheet, the psychologist must inspect the answer sheet to score this index in the hand-scored form or refer to the printout in the mail-in scoring form. However, even if one of the items in Scale V is answered "true," caution should be exercised in interpreting the remainder of the test.

Disclosure

The Disclosure Index (Scale X) identifies patients who are unnecessarily secretive and defensive (low scores) or openly frank and self-revealing (high scores). There are no items in this scale, which is calculated from the degree of positive or negative deviation from the midrange of an adjusted composite raw score from Scales 1 through 8B. Raw scores below 34 and above 178 invalidate the profile.

DON'T FORGET

Scores <34 and >178 on Scale X invalidate the profile. If this occurs do not interpret the rest of the test.

Desirability

The Desirability scale (Scale Y) assesses the extent to which a respondent attempts to present himself or herself in an overly favorable, morally virtuous, or emotionally stable light. Clinical interpretation begins with BR scores above 74. The higher the BR score, the more the patient is denying psychological or personal problems. Scoring adjustments are made on scales known to be affected by high scores on Scale Y. Hence elevated scores on Scale Y do not invalidate the profile. Low scores on Scale Y are not interpreted. (See Rapid Reference 1.5.)

Debasement

The Debasement scale (Scale Z) detects exaggeration of psychological problems and symptoms and the tendency to report more problems than may be objectively present. Clinically elevated scores on Scale Z may suggest a cry for help, acute emotional turmoil, or symptom exaggeration for personal gain. As with scores on Scale Y, elevated scores on Scale Z do not invalidate the profile. The MCMI-III makes scoring adjustments on scales affected by high scores on Scale Z. (See Rapid Reference 1.6.)

Although it is common to interpret the Modifying Indices individually, one can also interpret their configuration or their elevations in relation to one another. For example, a low score on Scale X and a high score on Scale Y might reflect a "fake-good" response set. High scores on Scales

X and Z might reflect a "fake-bad" response set. Low scores on Scale X and high scores on Scales Y and Z suggest defensive responding (Scale X) and also the endorsement of antithetical symptoms and traits. The examiner would need to look at the personality and clinical symptom scales to make sense of such a Validity scale configuration (e.g., it might reflect manic and depressive traits and symptoms).

Clinical Personality Patterns Scales

Schizoid

The Schizoid scale (Scale 1) is a 16-item scale that represents the passive-detached component of Millon's typology. Nine items are given a weight of 1 and seven are weighted 2. Item content pertains to detachment, lack of sexual interest, behavioral withdrawal, avoidance of relationships, emotional suppression, introverted behaviors, and feelings of emptiness, irresponsibility, and a preference for being alone. (See Rapid Reference 1.7.)

Interpretation of High Scores High-scoring patients have severe relationship deficits. They appear aloof, introverted, emotionally bland and detached, with flat affect and an apparent low need for social contact. They have difficulties in forming and maintaining relationships and seem to prefer a solitary life. They also seem to require little affection and lack warmth and emotional expression. These patients are likely to drift through society in marginal social roles and are prone to develop anxiety reactions, Somatoform disorder, and brief reactive psychoses, particularly when social demands become inescapable. If married or in a committed relationship, their spouse or partner is likely to complain about a lack of emotional involvement or intimacy.

Clinical Notes Some patients in psychiatric programs achieve BR scores on Scale 1 in clinically elevated ranges, suggesting the presence of schizoid traits but not necessarily a diagnosis of Schizoid personality disorder. Although the presence of schizoid traits appears in some alcoholic subtypes and in some Post-Traumatic Stress Disorder patients, it is usually associated with elevations in Scale 8A (Passive-Aggressive). Also,

Rapid Reference 1.7

Interpreting Scale 1

The Schizoid scale measures severe relationship deficits and restricted emotional expression.

African American drug addicts often score in elevated ranges on MCMI-III Scale 1, reflecting a loner type of existence in which they do not want others to know their business. Although this reflects a lack of social outlets, it is probably not indicative of a Schizoid disorder.

Avoidant

The Avoidant scale (Scale 2A) is a 16-item scale that represents the active-detached component of Millon's typology. Eight items are weighted 1 and eight items are weighted 2. Item content pertains to feelings of rejection, avoidance of social situations, insecurities, sensitivities, and anxiety in social situations, feelings of worthlessness, anhedonia, self-blame, and expectations of criticism.

Interpretation of High Scores   Patients with significant elevation of Scale 2A are hypersensitive to rejection, both fearing and anticipating negative evaluations. Thus they manifest a wary detachment (avoidance). Because they are quite sensitive to signs of disapproval, they tend to withdraw from or reduce social contacts. Others are able to maintain a good social appearance despite their underlying fears. Their essential conflict is a strong desire to relate socially and an equally strong expectation of disapproval, depreciation, and rejection. They may use fantasy as their main defense. They are at risk for developing social phobias.

Clinical Notes   Studies have repeatedly found that many patients with major psychiatric disorders have elevated scores on Scale 2A along with Scale 8A (Passive-Aggressive). If you see this pattern of test scores, a psychiatric evaluation may be warranted. The 2A8A/8A2A code type appears to be a very reliable marker for psychological maladjustment. (See Rapid Reference 1.8.)

≈Rapid Reference 1.8

Interpreting Scale 2A

Clinical elevations on Scale 2A, combined with elevations on Scale 8A suggest psychological maladjustment.

Depressive

The Depressive scale (Scale 2B) is a 15-item scale that represents the passive-detached component of Millon's typology. Eight items are weighted 1 and seven are weighted 2. Item content pertains to self-blame, guilt, feelings of emptiness and worthlessness, pessimism, anhedonia, excessive worry over trivial matters, recurrent sadness, moodiness, feelings of failure, and admission of a previous suicide attempt.

Interpretation of High Scores   The high-scoring patient is generally gloomy, pessimistic, overly serious, quiet, passive, and preoccupied with negative events. These patients often feel quite inadequate and have low self-esteem. They tend to unnecessarily brood and worry and, though they are usually responsible and conscientious, they also are self-reproaching and self-critical regardless of their level of accomplishment. They seem to be "down" all the time and are quite hard to please. They tend to find fault in even the most joyous experience. They feel it is futile to try to make improvements in themselves, their relationships, or any other significant aspect of their life because their incessant pessimism leads them toward a defeatist outlook. Their depressive demeanor often makes others around them feel guilty, since these patients are overly dependent on others for support and acceptance. They have difficulty expressing anger and aggression and perhaps displace it onto themselves. Interestingly, while their mood is often one of dejection and their cognitions dominated by negative thoughts, they often do not consider themselves depressed.

Clinical Notes   This scale was designed to tap a depressive personality style, which is said to exist independent of a clinical depression. It is important to review elevations of Dysthymic Disorder (Scale D) and Major Depression (Scale CC) to ensure that elevations on Scale 2B are not associated with a clinical depression that might abate when the clinical disorder abates. In fact, there are no items in this scale that stipulate that these personality traits occur outside an episode of major depression, though that was the intent.

Dependent

The Dependent scale (Scale 3) is a 16-item scale that assesses the passive-dependent variant in Millon's typology. Eight items are weighted 1 and eight are weighted 2. Item content deals with traits of acquiescence; submissiveness; concerns about being abandoned;

CAUTION

Because Scale 2B is new to the MCMI, there is little independent research as to its validity. Be careful to check that elevations on this scale are not due to clinical depression.

fears of being rejected; self-blame; and feelings of inadequacy, worthlessness, and insecurity.

Interpretation of High Scores   These patients tend to lean on others for security, guidance, support, and direction, and they seek out relationships that provide them with such emotional protection. They are passive, submissive, conforming, dependent, self-conscious, obliging, and placating, and they lack initiative, confidence, and autonomy. Their temperament is pacifying and they try to avoid conflict. They have a strong need to be nurtured and they seek out relationships or institutions to take care of them. They fear abandonment, so they act in an overly compliant manner in order to ensure protection. When their security is threatened, they are prone to develop Anxiety and Depressive disorders or substance abuse disorders.

Clinical Notes   Scale 3 is often elevated in patients with major psychiatric disorders. Also, patients with clinical depression may obtain elevated scores on Scale 3. These scores often abate when the depression abates. The clinician is advised to ensure that scores on Scale 3 are not a symptomatic expression of a current affective disorder.

Scale 3 shows good congruence with other self-report measures of dependence but shows low correspondence to structured psychiatric interview schedules assessing dependence.

Histrionic

The Histrionic scale (Scale 4) is a 17-item scale that represents the active-dependent variant in Millon's typology. Ten items are weighted 1 and seven are weighted 2. Item content addresses gregarious behavior, ease of social engagement and social facility, easy display of feelings, extroverted traits, flirtatious behavior, and need of excitement.

Interpretation of High Scores   Clinical elevations describe individuals who are overly dramatic with strong needs to be the center of attention. They tend to be seductive in thought, speech, style, dress, or manner, and they seek constant stimulation, excitement, praise, and attention. They are emotionally labile, easily excited, and show frequent emotional outbursts. Outwardly they are very gregarious and outgoing, but they tend to manipulate people to receive attention and approval. They can be quite socially facile and seductively engaging. However, their relationships are often shallow and strained due to their repeated dramatic and emotional outbursts and their self-

CAUTION

Elevations on Scale 4 may indicate a histrionic personality style rather than a Histrionic personality disorder.

centeredness. When stressed they are at risk for developing Somatoform disorder and marital problems.

Clinical Notes   The character portrait just given fits well with descriptions of a Histrionic personality disorder. However caution is indicated when interpreting Scale 4 as a disorder as there is ample research to suggest that elevated scores may indicate a healthy histrionic *style* but not a disorder. The evidence is as follows: First, factor studies show that Scale 4 correlates positively with extroverted traits and behaviors and negatively with items pertaining to maladjustment. In addition, convergent validity studies indicate that Scale 4 correlates positively with measures of mental health and correlates negatively with measures of emotional maladjustment. A few studies also report that elevations on Scale 4 are associated with less distress, more positive life events, and fewer social problems. Third, manifestly normal people who have been given the MCMI have often attained their highest scores on Scale 4, including air force pilots in basic training and graduate students in psychology. Finally, except for substance abusers, Scale 4 elevations in psychiatric samples are infrequent (Craig, 1993a; 1997). Thus the major clinical decision is to determine whether an elevation on Scale 4 (a BR score above 84) represents a histrionic style or a Histrionic personality disorder.

In general Scale 4 is one of the strongest scales on the MCMI with excellent reliability, but prior versions of this scale have shown low correspondence with structured psychiatric interview schedules of the histrionic.

Narcissistic

The Narcissistic scale (Scale 5) is a 24-item scale, which measures the passive-independent component of Millon's typology. Sixteen items are weighted 1 and eight are weighted 2. Item content pertains to egocentricity, independence, grandiosity, and feelings of superiority and comfort in social situations.

CAUTION

....

The clinical task for Scale 5 is to determine if elevated scores suggest a Narcissistic personality disorder or a narcissistic personality style.

Interpretations of High Scores   These patients are extremely self-centered, expect others to recognize them for their special qualities, and require constant praise and admiration. They feel excessively entitled and demand social favors simply on the basis of who they are. They appear arrogant, haughty, conceited, boastful, snobbish, pretentious, and supercilious. They can be momentarily charming but show social imperturbability and exploit social relationships for self-gain. When they experience a narcissistic injury, they are prone to develop an affective disorder or even paranoia. Many substance-abusing patients demonstrate a Narcissistic personality disorder.

Clinical Notes   As with Scale 4, Scale 5 has a research base that suggests that elevated scores indicate either a clinical personality disorder or a healthy adaptational personality style associated with nonclinical people. In factor analysis studies, Scale 5 loads positively on items dealing with extroverted traits and behaviors and negatively on items pertaining to maladjustment. Scale 5 correlates moderately with indices of mental health and negatively with all MCMI-III clinical syndrome scales, and with the exception of a substance abuse disorder, elevations on Scale 5 are rare in psychiatric samples. Many nonclinical populations attain elevated scores on Scale 5 including air force pilots in basic training. On the other hand, research has also established that Scale 5 correlates positively with similar measures of pathological narcissism, especially with the Narcissistic scale of the MMPI and with the Narcissistic Personality Inventory (Craig, 1993a; 1997). Thus the clinical task is to determine whether clinically elevated scores represent a Narcissistic personality disorder or a narcissistic personality style. Prior versions of this scale have not correlated well with structured psychiatric interview schedules.

Antisocial

The Antisocial scale (Scale 6A) is a 17-item scale that measures the active-independent component of Millon's typology. Ten items are weighted 1 and seven items are weighted 2. His theory posits that the antisocial personality style is motivated to avoid control and domination; hence a substantial number of items in the scale pertain to the issue of independence. Other item content applies to traditional antisocial indicators, such as history of truancy and delinquency, and antisocial traits and attitudes.

Interpretation of High Scores   These patients are intimidating, dominating, narcissistic, aggressive, fearless, pugnacious, daring, blunt, competitive, argumentative, self-reliant, vengeful, and harbor resentments to perceived slights. They often have an angry and hostile demeanor. Warmth, gentleness, and intimacy are viewed as a sign of weakness. They try to provoke fear in others as a way of controlling them. They use acting out as their main defense. They are prone to substance abuse, relationship difficulties, and vocational and legal problems.

Clinical Notes   It is important to realize that a person can have an antisocial personality style in the absence of criminal behavior, though at the higher BR levels the absence of involvement with the criminal justice system is less likely (see Rapid Reference 1.9). Prior versions of this scale correlated moderately with similar measures of psychopathy, including both paper-and-pencil tests and structured psychiatric interview schedules.

Aggressive (Sadistic)

The Aggressive (Sadistic) scale (Scale 6B) is a 20-item scale measuring the active-discordant component of Millon's typology. Thirteen items are weighted 1 and seven are weighted 2. Item content includes aggressive and controlling traits.

Interpretation of High Scores   These patients tend to behave abusively toward others. They may exhibit traits that are dominating, hostile, intimidating, fearless, aggressive, hardheaded, antagonistic, arrogant, touchy, excitable, irritable, disagreeable, and angry. They use acting out as their main defense. They may react with brutal force when angered or provoked. Explosive outbursts are common. Some are able to sublimate these traits into socially approved occupations. Others may not engage in antisocial behavior but have an aggressive personality style. Patients with this personality style are prone to experience legal and marital problems.

≡Rapid Reference 1.9

Interpreting Scale 6A

If scores are elevated on Scale 6A, then look for evidence of criminal behavior.

<table>
<tr><td>

CAUTION

....

An Aggressive (Sadistic) diagnosis does not appear in DSM-IV. Patients with BR scores >84 on Scale 6B may be diagnosed as Personality Disorder NOS, with prominent aggressive traits.

</td></tr>
</table>

Clinical Notes   Look for evidence of spouse or child abuse among high-scoring patients. Also, high scores may suggest verbal rather than actual physical abuse. Prior versions of this scale showed modest correspondence with similar measures.

Compulsive

The Compulsive scale (Scale 7) is a 17-item scale that assesses the passive-ambivalent component of Millon's typology. Nine items are weighted 1 and eight items are weighted 2. Item content pertains to organized and perfectionistic behavior, impatience, good morals, obedient behavior, suppression of emotions, and rigidity.

Interpretation of High Scores   These patients are behaviorally rigid, constricted, meticulous, respectful, polite, conscientious, overly conforming, organized, and respectful. They are often perfectionistic, formal, cooperative, moralistic, efficient, and flexible. They are known to suppress their strong resentment and anger toward those (usually authority figures) whose approval they seek. They generally have a repetitive lifestyle with patterned behaviors. Fear of social disapproval results in their being a model of propriety, though they may treat subordinates autocratically. They have a strong sense of duty and strive to avoid criticism. They rely on achievement and accomplishment of personal goals to feel worthwhile. Obsessional thinking may or may not be present.

Clinical Notes   Although this scale was designed to measure a Compulsive personality disorder, there is substantial evidence to suggest that it may measure a compulsive personality style. First, Scale 7 is rarely elevated in samples of psychiatric patients. In fact, it correlates positively with items pertaining to control of behavior and emotions, which is often an indicator of emotional adjustment. Second, the scale shows persistent negative correlations with measures of psychiatric disturbance. Third, nonclinical populations, including 1st-year seminary students; air force pilots in training; family practice residents; and college students, particularly males, often score highest on Scale 7.

Fourth, the scale consistently correlates with measures of mental health and negatively with measures of emotional maladjustment. Fifth, higher Scale 7 scores often had better treatment outcomes re-

> ## CAUTION
>
> Scale 7 may be measuring a compulsive personality style, not a Compulsive personality disorder.

lated to improved mental health and improved self-esteem. Sixth, in the only published study featuring patients with a primary Obsessive-Compulsive disorder, the mean BR score on Scale 7 was 56 (e.g., normal). Finally, prior versions of this scale showed poor convergent validity with similar measures (Craig, 1993a; 1997). The evidence summates to suggest that elevated scores may be associated with a compulsive personality style but not a Compulsive disorder.

Passive-Aggressive (Negativistic)

The Passive-Aggressive (Negativistic) scale (Scale 8A) is a 16-item scale that assesses the active-ambivalent component of Millon's typology. Seven items are weighted 1 and nine are weighted 2. Item content deals with irritability, impulsivity, hostility, verbal attacks, loss of control over anger, and cruel behaviors.

Interpretation of High Scores   Traits that describe this character style include moody, irritable, negativistic, hostile, grumbling, pessimistic, querulous, anxious, complaining, and disgruntled. They seem to be constantly disillusioned. They often feel unappreciated and sulk over feelings that they have been treated unfairly. Their continued petulance results in problems with authority, coworkers, friends, and family. High-scoring patients can be passively compliant and obedient at one moment and negativistic and oppositional at the next.

Clinical Notes   Scale 8A elevation is an excellent predictor of loss of control over emotions. High scores usually suggest the presence of a serious psychiatric disorder. Prior versions of this scale showed poor correspondence with structured psychiatric interview schedules that also purportedly measured passive-aggressive behavior. One reason for this difference is the psychiatric definition of this disorder, which suggests that anger is expressed indirectly. Millon's concept of the term leans more toward a negativistic character style rather than acting in passive-aggressive ways.

≡Rapid Reference 1.10

Interpreting Scale 8B

DSM-IV does not have a diagnosis for a Self-Defeating personality disorder. To record this diagnosis, use Personality Disorder NOS, with prominent self-defeating traits.

Self-Defeating

The Self-Defeating scale (Scale 8B) is a 15-item scale designed to assess the passive-discordant component of Millon's typology. Eight items are weighted 1 and seven are weighted 2. The disorder is akin to the psychoanalytic concept of masochism. Item content pertains to patients' acting in a self-sacrificing manner, feeling they deserve to suffer, demonstrating submissive behavior, placing themselves in inferior relationships, exhibiting mild depression, allowing themselves to be taken advantage of, and displaying disparaging attitudes.

Interpreting High Scores   These patients often allow others to take advantage of them. They behave in a self-sacrificing and martyrlike manner and seem to seek out relationships in which they can acquire security and affection in return for allowing themselves to be dominated and even abused. Look for evidence of victimization among high-scoring patients.

Clinical Notes   Scale 8B seems to be moderately elevated in the profiles of many psychiatric patients. Instead of connoting the characteristics associated with a self-defeating personality, I believe that high scores in such cases reflect problematic behavior patterns, which are not in the best interest of the patient. Also, look for patterns of abuse and victimization among high-scoring patients. Finally, be mindful that there are very little research data with this scale on which to base definitive conclusions. (See Rapid Reference 1.10.)

Severe Personality Pathology Scales

The personality disorders in this section measure severe forms of the basic personality patterns. Millon believes that individuals with these characteristics are prone to develop psychotic disorders, including schizophrenia.

Schizotypal

The Schizotypal scale (Scale S) is a 16-item scale that assesses more severe structural pathology. Seven items are weighted 1 and nine are weighted 2.

Item content pertains to cognitive impairments, ideas of influence, interpersonal detachment and preference for social isolation, dependent behaviors, and feeling self-conscious.

Interpretation of High Scores   High-scoring patients present as emo-

CAUTION
....
Although Scale S should detect major psychiatric disorders, such as schizophrenia, research on earlier versions of this scale suggest poor concurrent validity.

tionally bland with flat affect or with an anxious wariness. Generally, they are socially detached and have a pervasive discomfort in social relationships. Accordingly, they remain on the periphery of society with few or no personal attachments. Thought processes may be tangential, irrelevant, or confused. They appear self-absorbed in their own thoughts. It is believed that they are prone to developed schizophrenia if sufficiently stressed.

Clinical Notes   Scale S should be one of the scales inspected when evaluating for psychosis and major psychiatric disorders such as schizophrenia. Unfortunately Scale S has not demonstrated consistent clinical utility and some pathology is missed by this scale. Prior versions of this scale have shown low to moderate convergence with other measures of Schizotypal personality disorder.

Borderline

The Borderline scale (Scale C) is a 16-item scale with seven items weighted 1 and nine items weighted 2. Item content pertains to unstable mood, anger, guilt, obstreperous behavior and reactions, dependency-seeking behavior, erratic moods, and unstable relationships.

Interpretation of High Scores   These patients show attachment disorders with patterns of intense but unstable relationships, labile emotions, a history of impulsive behaviors, and strong dependency needs with fears of abandonment. They are preoccupied with seeking emotional support and are particularly vulnerable to separation anxiety. They seem to lack a clear sense of their own identity, so they constantly seek approval, attention, and reaffirmation. They use splitting and devaluation as their main defenses. They are prone toward brief psychotic reactions and suicidal gestures. More severe cases may also self-mutilate.

Clinical Notes   Scale C has been shown to be elevated in patients with

===*Rapid Reference 1.11*

Interpreting Scale C

Elevations on Scale C may indicate a Borderline personality disorder or it may suggest erratic emotionality associated with other psychiatric disorders.

many other psychiatric disorders and probably reflects erratic emotionality associated with those disorders (Rapid Reference 1.11). There has been much research ($N = 22$ studies) on earlier versions of this scale. The volume of studies on this scale is sufficiently large to provide us with some tentative conclusions. In general, Scale C shows moderate to strong relationships with similar measures of the Borderline personality disorder.

Paranoid

The Paranoid scale (Scale P) is a 17-item scale with eight items weighted 1 and nine items weighted 2. Item content deals with ideas of control or influence, hypervigilant sensitivity, annoyance with others, delusional beliefs, grandiosity, and an edgy defensiveness.

Interpretation of High Scores   The patients are vigilantly mistrustful and often perceive that people are trying to control or influence them in malevolent ways. They are characteristically abrasive, irritable, hostile, and irascible and may also become belligerent if provoked. Their thinking is rigid and they can be argumentative. They may present with delusions of grandeur or persecution and/or ideas of reference. They use projection as their main defense.

Clinical Notes   Drug addicts often obtain mildly elevated scores on Scale P. They have issues related to concerns about law breaking and getting caught, and not wanting people to know their business, so they are usually secretive. They endorse items on the MCMI pertaining to these traits, which results in some elevations on Scale P, but they are usually not paranoid in the clinical sense. If the patient has elevations on Scale T (Drug Dependence) along with elevations on Scale P, then a clinical interview needs to determine whether there is or is not a clinical paranoia.

CAUTION

Earlier versions of Scale P suggested poor correspondence with other measures of paranoia.

Prior versions of this scale suggested that Scale P bore little relationship and had low correspondence to other measures of paranoia. This was true for both self-report inventories and structured psychiatric interview schedules.

Clinical Syndromes Scales

Anxiety Disorder

The Anxiety Disorder scale (Scale A) is a 14-item scale with eight items weighted 1 and six items weighted 2. It measures symptoms of generalized anxiety with item content pertaining to nervous tension, crying, indecisiveness, apprehension, and somatic complaints.

Interpretation of High Scores   The high-scoring patient has symptoms associated with physiological arousal. They would be described as anxious, apprehensive, restless, unable to relax, edgy, jittery, and indecisive. Symptoms can include complaints of insomnia, muscular tightness, headaches, nausea, cold sweats, undue perspiration, clammy hands, and palpitations. Phobias may or may not be present. High scores may meet the DSM criteria for Generalized Anxiety Disorder or other anxiety-related disorders.

Clinical Notes   Because of the variability of symptom expression, it is not possible to determine exactly which of the many symptoms of anxiety an individual patient has based on elevations of Scale A. However, Scale A is a strong scale and correlates well with other measures of anxiety. It is usually elevated in a number of clinical disorders, reflecting psychic distress and maladjustment. In conditions where anxiety would be expected, research has established that Scale A elevations are present. Thus one can have a great deal of confidence when interpreting this scale. One problem, however, is that Scale A is also highly correlated with Scale D (Dysthymic Disorder). Thus the scale may not be able to distinguish between anxiety and depression. If Scale D is also elevated, emphasize the depressive component of symptom expression. If absent, emphasize the anxiety component if Scale A is elevated. (See Rapid Reference 1.12.)

Rapid Reference 1.12

Interpreting Scale A

The validity of Scale A is quite good, but it does not distinguish among the many kinds of anxiety disorders found in DSM-IV.

Somatoform Disorder

The Somatoform Disorder scale (Scale H) is a 12-item scale with seven items weighted 1 and five items weighted 2. It measures elements of anxiety that may be displaced into associated physical symptoms. Item content pertains to vague bodily complaints, apprehension, crying, indecisiveness, and fatigue.

Interpretation of High Scores   High-scoring patients show the persistent pursuit of medical care, even in the face of evidence that there is little, if any, physical cause to their symptoms. Their physical complaints can be related to any organ system. A review of the MCMI-III Noteworthy Responses is necessary to determine which symptoms the patient has endorsed as present. They tend to be whiny, complaining, restless, and worried, and they antagonize those closest to them with their chronic complaints of pain. Yet they tend not to respond to interventions. Their symptoms and reactions to symptoms may be developed unconsciously to gain sympathy, attention, and reassurance.

Clinical Notes   High scores are usually seen among two kinds of patients: (a) those who displace their psychological problems and/or stress into somatic channels and (b) those with legitimate medical problems who are coping so poorly with their illness that their psychological reactions are compounding the manifestation of their symptoms. In either case, these patients show persistent preoccupation with feeling in poor health and overutilization of the health care system.

This is not a well-researched scale, and few, if any, studies have been directed at the kinds of patients for which this scale would be most useful (e.g., patients in medical settings). What is known about this scale comes from research using psychiatric patients.

Bipolar: Manic Disorder

The Bipolar: Manic Disorder scale (Scale N) is a 13-item scale with eight items weighted 1 and five items weighted 2. It measures hypomania and some more severe manic symptoms. The scale contains items dealing with flight of ideas, excessive energy, impulsivity, inflated self-esteem, grandiosity, and overactivity.

Interpretation of High Scores   Clinically elevated scores suggest a patient with labile emotions and frequent mood swings. During the manic phase, symptoms can include flight of ideas, pressured speech, overactivity, unrealistic and expansive goals, impulsive behavior, and a demanding quality in their interpersonal relationships. Extremely high scores may also suggest psychotic processes with delusions and hallucinations.

Clinical Notes   To determine if the bipolar mania is of psychotic proportions, the examiner should look for elevations in Scales SS (Thought Disorder), PP (Delusional Disorder), or CC (Major Depression). Also, the examiner should ensure that elevations from this scale are not drug induced (see Scale T). Prior versions of this scale had good correspondence to other measures of mania, including the MMPI Hypomania (Ma) scale.

Dysthymic Disorder

The Dysthymic Disorder scale (Scale D) is a 14-item scale with eight items weighted 1 and six items weighted 2. It measures depression of 2 or more years' duration. Dysthymic patients are able to carry on day-to-day functions despite their depressed mood. Item content addresses apathy, feeling discouraged, and lack of energy, crying spells, self-deprecatory cognitions, and guilt feelings.

Interpretation of High Scores   Patients scoring high on this scale are behaviorally apathetic, socially withdrawn, feel guilty, pessimistic, discouraged, and are preoccupied with feelings of personal inadequacy. They have low self-esteem and utter self-deprecatory statements, feel worthless, and are persistently sad. They have many self-doubts and show introverted behavior. If physical symptoms appear, they can include problems in concentration, poor appetite, and suicide ideation. Most do not meet the criteria for Major Depression.

Clinical Notes   There are many ways to feel depressed. Not all of the above characterization will fit every patient who scores high on Scale D. The above represents the prototypal Dysthymic Disorder patient. However, the individual clinician will have to do a more thorough assessment of the patient's individual symptoms of Dysthymic Disorder, which is not possible from the MCMI-III alone.

Research has indicated that Scale D was actually a better predictor of Major Depression than Scale CC (Major Depression). Scale CC had difficulty in diagnosing the disorder of Major Depression in versions MCMI-I and MCMI-II because it contained no vegetative/somatic symptoms, which are critical in distinguishing Major Depression from Dysthymic Disorder. This problem seems to have been corrected with the MCMI-III.

Previous versions of this scale showed generally moderate convergent valid-

≋ *Rapid Reference 1.13*
....

Interpreting Scale D

Scale D is a good measure of
chronic, mild depression.

ity with tests measuring similar constructs. Also, Scale D is highly correlated with Scale A. Thus, there is a
strong element of anxiety inherent
in both the construct and the scale.
(See Rapid Reference 1.13.)

Alcohol Dependence

The Alcohol Dependence scale (Scale B) is a 15-item scale with nine items
weighted 1 and six items weighted 2. Item content pertains to six items dealing directly with alcohol abuse and nine items dealing with traits often associated with problematic drinking. These include impulsivity, rationalizations,
and lack of adherence to societal standards, selfishness, and aggressiveness
toward family members.

Interpretation of High Scores   Clinically elevated scores on Scale B indicate that
the patient is reporting a history of current problematic drinking or personality traits frequently seen in alcoholics.

Clinical Notes   Studies show that Scale B correlates in the .70s with Scale T
(Drug Dependence). This is no accident since people who abuse alcohol commonly also abuse illicit drugs. Hence the scale has a built in associated to reflect
this reality.

This scale assesses alcohol dependence both directly, through items pertaining to alcohol abuse, and indirectly, through items reflecting behavior associated with problematic drinking. Thus it is theoretically possible that a patient can endorse the latter items and obtain a high score on Scale B yet not
be alcoholic. For example, if a patient endorsed all nonprototypical items, the
BR score would be 79.

A clinical interview is required to determine if the patient has been abusing alcohol and, if so, the specific areas (e.g., medical, psychological/psychi-
atric, social, legal, vocational, recreational, spiritual) that have been affected
by alcohol abuse/dependence. Earlier versions of this scale suggested it correlated with behaviors and traits associated with alcohol abuse, such as depression, dependence, anxiety, and extroversion.

Drug Dependence

The Drug Dependence scale (Scale T) is a 14-item scale with eight items weighted 1 and six weighted 2. Item content pertains to a history of and recurrent pattern of drug abuse, disruptions in interpersonal relationships, and impulse control problems. Six items (the prototype items) assess drug abuse directly and eight assess it by evaluating for legal problems, adherence to societal standards, antisocial practices, independence, nonempathic behavior, irresponsibility, and rationalizations. These items are also associated with Antisocial personality disorder traits.

Interpretation of High Scores   High scores suggest a person who has or had a problem with drug dependence and has personality and behavior traits associated with these problems. These include hedonism, self-indulgence, impulsivity, exploitiveness, and narcissistic personality traits. These patients are likely to be in considerable distress in social, occupational, familial, and legal areas. It is theoretically possible to endorse all nonprototype items on this scale and not abuse drugs. However, this is very unlikely.

Clinical Notes   Scale T correlates from .50 to .79 with Alcohol Dependence (B). This is no accident, since conceptually and clinically there is a strong relationship between people who abuse drugs and those who abuse alcohol. Hence the scale has a built in correlation to reflect this reality.

Research has found low concurrent validity in diagnosing drug dependence with prior versions of this scale. MCMI-I Scale T identified about one third to one half of known drug abusers. No research was available on the predictive accuracy of MCMI-II Scale T. Perhaps patients are able to deny their drug abuse and can conceal it from detection on the MCMI. One study did report that about 50% of drug-dependent patients, if motivated to do so, are able to obtain normal values on Scale T (Craig, 1997). All research has shown that Scale T's ability to rule out drug abuse is excellent.

Earlier versions of this scale showed moderate correspondence with MMPI MacAndrew Alcoholism Scale and other measures often associated with drug-abusing behaviors, such as extroversion, hostility, and dominance. It show little or no relationship to measures of behavior and traits that bear no conceptual relationship to drug abuse.

≋Rapid Reference 1.14

Interpreting Scale R

Scale R was designed to detect both military and civilian trauma.

Post-Traumatic Stress Disorder

The Post-Traumatic Stress Disorder scale (Scale R) is a new scale and was not in previous MCMI versions. It is a 16-item scale with eleven items weighted 1 and five items weighted 2. Item content deals with painful memories, nightmares, reports of a trauma, and flashbacks.

Interpretation of High Scores High-scoring patients report symptoms that might include distressing and intrusive thoughts; flashbacks; startle responses; emotional numbing; problems in anger management; difficulties with sleep or with concentration; and psychological distress upon exposure to people, places, or events that resemble some aspect of the traumatic event. A clinical evaluation is needed to determine which symptoms are present and the degree of functional impairment.

Clinical Notes If there is no trauma in the patient's history, the high scores could suggest emotional turmoil of a nontraumatic nature.

Most Post-Traumatic Stress Disorder scales were more specific to combat stress and may lack generalization to noncombat trauma. Scale R was constructed in such a way that it should pertain to both civilian and military trauma (Rapid Reference 1.14).

Thought Disorder

The Thought Disorder scale (Scale SS) is a 17-item scale with 11 items weighted 1 and 6 items weighted 2. It measures thought disorder of a psychotic nature. Item content pertains to ideas of influence, hallucinations, delusions, slights, and intrusive thoughts.

CAUTION

Prior versions of Scale SS showed poor concurrent validity. The scale detected thought disorders in patients who were willing to report psychotic symptoms, but missed thought disorders in patients who were trying to conceal them.

Interpretation of High Scores Patients with elevated scores on Scale SS are admitting to thinking that is disorganized, confused, fragmented, or bizarre. Hallucinations, and/or delusions may also be present. Their behavior is often withdrawn or seclusive. They often show inappropriate affect and appear confused and regressed.

Clinical Notes   Research has indicated problems with Scale SS in detecting major psychoses and schizophrenia. Prior versions of this scale indicated moderate correlations with similar measures such as the MMPI Paranoia and Schizophrenia scales.

Major Depression

Major Depression (Scale CC) is a 17-item scale with ten items weighted 1 and seven items weighted 2. Item content deals with suicidal ideation, cognitive and vegetative signs of depression, depressed affect, crying spells, and withdrawn behavior.

Interpretation of High Scores   High-scoring patients may be unable to manage their day-to-day activities. They are severely depressed, with feelings of worthlessness and vegetative symptoms of depression (e.g., loss of energy, appetite and weight, sleep disturbances, fatigue, and loss of sexual drive or desire). Suicidal ideation may be present. Their underlying personality style is likely to be of the emotionally detached type, especially dependent or depressed.

Clinical Notes   Research has clearly established that the MCMI-I and MCMI-II Scale CC was unreliable in diagnosing Major Depression. This was because the earlier versions of the scale did not contain vegetative symptoms that are the hallmark of the disorder. Often elevated scores on CC indicated Dysthymic Disorder or some other depression diagnosis. MCMI-III Scale CC has added a number of vegetative items to the scale, which should increase its diagnostic efficiency. Earlier versions of the scale did correlate well with similar measures, such as MMPI Scale D (Depression) and the Beck Depression Inventory.

Delusional Disorder

The item content of Delusional Disorder (Scale PP)—a 13-item scale with nine items weighted 1 and four items weighted 2—deals with delusions, grandiosity, and hypervigilance. The scale measures delusional thinking usually associated with a Paranoid disorder.

Interpretation of High Scores   Patients scoring in the clinically significant ranges on Scale PP are likely to be diagnosed with some type of Paranoid disorder. They have persecutory or grandiose delusions, and maintain a hostile, hypervigilant and suspicious wariness for anticipated or perceived threat.

They may also become belligerent and have irrational ideas of reference, thought influence, or thought control. The scale is thought to be a symptomatic expression of an underlying paranoid personality addressed in Scale P. *Clinical Notes* Earlier versions of this scale indicated that Scale PP was weakly related to similar measures. As with Scale SS, the scale detects Delusional Disorder in patients willing to admit their symptoms on the test. Some patients are able to avoid detection of Thought Disorder on the MCMI.

Demographic Variables

Most data concerning gender, race, and age come from MCMI-I studies. No information on these variables has been published for the MCMI-III. When a pattern of differences does emerge, this does not necessarily imply test bias, since an alternative explanation is that the test is tapping true differences in the populations.

Also, the *diagnosis* of patients in these samples may not have changed, even when the group obtained statistically higher scores on a given scale. These facts should be taken into account when digesting the data presented below, which came from six studies (Craig, 1993a).

Gender

Males score higher on Scale 6A; females score higher on Scales H and CC. No gender effects consistently appear on Scales 2 and 8A. No other conclusions are warranted from the data.

Race

Blacks consistently score higher on Scales 5, 6A, P, T, and PP. Whites consistently score higher on Scale D. Studies show no racial differences between Blacks and Whites on Scales 3, 7, 8A, and A. No data are available on differences between Whites and other ethnic groups on MCMI scales.

Age

No consistent patterns have been found for patient age.

Step-by-Step Procedures for Test Interpretation

Step 1: Examine the Validity Index and Response-Style Scales

1. The test is valid if Validity (Scale V) = 0. Results are of questionable validity if V = 1 and are invalid if V = 2 or 3.
2. The examiner must make sure Disclosure (Scale X) is in the valid range of 34 to 178.
3. The examiner must check Desirability (Scale Y) to see if the patient is understating psychopathology.
4. The examiner must check Debasement (Scale Z) to see if the patient is overstating psychopathology.

Then the examiner should write a paragraph describing the patient's response style using the interpretive notes presented earlier.

Step 2: Examine the Severe Personality Pathology Scales

When there are multiple scales elevated in both the clinical personality patterns and severe personality pathology scales, a general rule of thumb is to interpret scales suggesting more severe personality pathology first. Thus if Schizotypal (Scale S), Borderline (Scale C), and/or Paranoid (Scale P) are clinically elevated, place the interpretive emphasis on these scales. Use the other elevated scales to provide associated features of the personality.

Step 3: Examine the Clinical Personality Patterns

Look for elevations in Scales 1 through 8B and interpret those scales that are clinically elevated. If more than three scales are scored at BR 75 or above, examiners should frame their interpretations using the highest two or three scales. Also, if there are multiple elevations, the examiner should think about what factor or factors are driving the elevations in those scales. For example, if Antisocial (Scale 6A), Aggressive (Sadistic) (Scale 6B), and Passive-Aggressive (Negativistic) (Scale 8A) are all elevated, anger is the emotion that permeates all these scales. If Schizoid (Scale 1), Avoidant (Scale 2A), and Dependent (Scale 3) are all elevated, emotional detachment and passivity account for these combined elevations.

Step 4: Examine the Clinical Syndrome Scales

The examiner should first interpret the severe clinical syndrome scales—Thought Disorder (Scale SS), Major Depression (Scale CC), and Delusional Disorder (Scale PP)—if the BR scores are 75 or above. Then the remaining clinical syndrome scales should be interpreted, from highest to lowest: When BR scores are 75 or above, the examiner can diagnose the syndrome as present; when BR scores are 85 or above, the syndrome may be the primary diagnosis (i.e., the main reason the client came for help). When there is more than one scale with a BR score of 85, the highest score is the primary Axis I diagnosis.

Step 5: Interpret the Meaning of Symptoms Within the Context of the Client's Personality Style or Disorder

If a patient has a mixed Narcissistic (Scale 5) and Antisocial (Scale 6A) personality, and elevated scores on Drug Dependence (Scale T), perhaps drug abuse is part of narcissistic indulgence. Or perhaps the patient has experienced a narcissistic injury and uses drugs to quell the hurt from this perceived injury. Or perhaps the patient is generally deviant and drug abuse is part of that overall deviance, characterized by acting out. Or perhaps there is a deep resentment of perceived attempts to control the patient and episodes of drug abuse function as a continuing sign of "independence" and a statement that the patient will not be controlled. Whatever the reason, the examiner must try to understand the meaning of the symptom in the person's life.

Step 6: Integrate Test Findings With Other Sources of Data

The examiner must never base clinical decisions on a single source of data, but instead use multiple sources of data and integrate test findings with ancillary information (e.g., history, clinical interview, collateral information, and medical records).

STRENGTHS AND WEAKNESSES OF THE MCMI-III

A clinician should know or suspect in advance of administering the test whether the client may have a personality disorder. Other inventories often can be used with normal and nonclinical populations, whereas the MCMI-III can only be used with clinical patients. Several characteristics of the MCMI-

III, which highlight its major strengths and weaknesses relative to similar self-report inventories, follow.

Strengths

1. *Developed from a Comprehensive Clinical Theory.* The test is an instrument derived from Millon's (1997a) comprehensive clinical theory of psychopathology.

2. *Reflects Diagnostic Criteria Used in DSM-IV.* The test is coordinated with the multiaxial format provided in DSM-IV and is linked to its conceptual terminology and diagnostic criteria.

3. *Provides Diagnostic Accuracy.* The MCMI-III takes into account the base rates, or prevalence, of personality disorders and clinical syndromes, thereby affording the opportunity for increased diagnostic accuracy.

4. *Utilizes Validation Process.* It was developed according to Loevinger's (1957) three-step validation process that allowed for refinement of the test from item selection to scale development to external validation using Millon's theory as the criterion.

5. *Easy to Administer.* It is relatively quick to administer (20 to 30 minutes) and measures a wide range of personality traits and symptoms.

6. *Compact Design.* There is no need for a separate test booklet since items and space for the respondent's answers are on the same form.

Weaknesses

1. *Imbalance Between True and False Items.* With the vast majority of items keyed in the "true" direction, the test is susceptible to patients with an acquiescent response set (e.g., the tendency to report "true" when faced with an item that is equally true and equally false for the respondent).

2. *Pathology and Disorder Assessments.* The test is relatively weak in assessing patients with minor personality pathology and those with psychotic disorders.

3. *Assessment of Styles Versus Disorders.* The Histrionic, Narcissistic, and Compulsive scales appear to have difficulty in assessing those pathologies and seems more able to detect a histrionic, narcissistic, or compulsive personality style rather than a personality disorder.

4. *Validity Problems.* The test shows poor convergent validity with standard psychiatric rating schedules across most of its scales.

5. *Personality Subtypes Not Accounted For.* There may be subtypes of a given personality disorder that the MCMI-III does not tap. Millon has theorized about some of these subtypes, but they are not incorporated into the test construction.

6. *Sample Population.* The normative sample is modest in size and underrepresents minority groups.

7. *Few Validation Studies.* Although Millon's theory provides a rich context for interpreting test results and making predictions about patient behavior, few validation studies have been conducted to verify the accuracy of the theoretical deductions.

CLINICAL APPLICATIONS OF THE MCMI-III

Assessment of Personality Disorders

The MCMI-III provides a very good means for rapidly assessing the presence or absence of personality disorders. It is well known that Axis II disorders can affect the course and direction of Axis I disorders (e.g., clinical syndromes). Knowledge of a personality disorder within an individual patient can therefore influence treatment decisions and has relevance for predicting the patient's response to treatment. Also, personality disorders can be the focus of treatment in their own right and this diagnostic information is therefore useful in treatment planning. Of course, it is also of value to learn that the patient does not have a personality disorder.

In forensic settings the MCMI-III can be useful in cases where personality disorders may be instrumentally related to a crime and also relevant at the penalty phase where personality disorders may be a mitigating factor in assigning the sentence.

Assessing Personality Style

In addition to assessing for personality manifestations at the diagnostic level, the MCMI-III can provide us with value information concerning the presence of personality traits, which are important in understanding and treating all patients. Having this information can help us understand a patient's reaction to interventions and help to explain daily behavior patterns that may be dysfunctional.

Assessing Clinical Syndromes

The MCMI-III is able to assess most of the major (e.g., more severe) clinical syndromes in DSM-IV. Although it cannot provide specificity of those syndromes (e.g., Generalized Anxiety Disorder vs. Social Phobias), it does give us their categorical diagnosis (e.g., Anxiety). Research has also shown that objective diagnostic tests usually suggest the presence of clinical disorders that are occasionally missed in a clinical interview.

Assessing Severity of Disorders

Not only does the MCMI-III assess personality disorders and clinical syndromes, it is also able to reflect their severity. This knowledge is useful in a number of settings including mental health clinics, marital therapy, criminal evaluations, and routine screening.

Assessing Treatment Outcomes

By giving the MCMI-III prior to interventions and again after treatment the effectiveness of both pharmacological and psychosocial interventions can be assessed. The clinician can come to some conclusion as to which syndromes have improved by looking at pretest and posttest scores. When doing so, keep in mind that personality disorders are relatively ingrained and should not respond to short-term intervention approaches. Note too that some change in scale scores will occur by chance and as a function of the psychometrics of the test (e.g., internal consistency and test-retest reliability of the scales).

INTEGRATING MCMI-III AND MMPI-2 DATA: ILLUSTRATIVE CASE REPORT

The patient is a 37-year-old divorced, non-Hispanic White woman, who was self-referred for outpatient psychotherapy. She holds a B.A. in business management and is currently employed full-time in a management capacity. She presented with complaints of unresolved anger toward her father, whom she reported as having physically abused her during her childhood and adolescence. She was unable to recall incidents of sexual abuse, but she offered that on one occasion her father entered her bedroom while she was undressing and would sometimes enter the bathroom unannounced while she was using it. Since becoming an adult and leaving home, she reported that her father would ridicule her in front of family members. Because of this she broke off all contact with him and has not seen him or spoken to him in 7 years.

In spite of having no contact with her father, the patient finds that she "cannot get him out of my head." She often dwells on memories of abusive experiences and can become obsessed with reliving painful memories. On a few occasions while thinking about past abuse, she scratched her arms with a pair of scissors. She reported being very grouchy at work and has, on occasion, "thrown things around the house." Her roommate is now threatening to leave because of her volatile emotions. She attempted suicide twice in the past by taking overdoses of household medications, but apparently she never received psychiatric treatment following these episodes. She admitted that she is "an alcoholic" but has stated that she does not want to address this problem since "it will get better on its own," once she gets control of her anger. She reported being "depressed a lot" but works daily and receives excellent performance reviews. The MCMI-III and MMPI-2 (Butcher et al., 1989) were given to rule out a Borderline personality disorder and a Post-Traumatic Stress Disorder. Figures 1.3 and 1.4 present the test findings.

MCMI-III Results

As can be seen in Figure 1.2, the Modifying Indices show no unusual response patterns, indicating that she cooperated with the testing. With regard to the personality scales, clinically significant elevations are noted on Depressive (Scale 2B), Compulsive (Scale 7), and Borderline (Scale C). With 2B the highest personality scale, and a BR score of 76 on Scale C, she probably does not have a Borderline personality disorder. The Scale C elevation is

Millon Clinical Multiaxial Inventory-III

Confidential Information for Professional.Use Only

ID Number: 12877
Valid Profile

Personality Code: -**2B 7 * 1 6B + 2A 5 3 6A " 8A 8B 4 ' ' // - ** C * //

Syndrome Code: A ** R * // CC ** - * //

Demographic: 12877/ON/F/37/W/D/--/--/--/-----/--/-----/

Category		Score Raw	Score BR	Profile of BR Scores 0	60	75	85	115	Diagnostic Scales
Modifying Indices	X	85	54						Disclosure
	Y	10	47						Desirability
	Z	17	72						Debasement
Clinical Personality Patterns	I	11	73						Schizoid
	2A	7	58						Avoidant
	2B	16	84						Depressive
	3	6	40						Dependent
	4	3	14						Histrionic
	5	9	49						Narcissistic
	6A	3	36						Antisocial
	6B	6	61						Aggressive (Sadistic)
	7	21	76						Compulsive
	8A	4	27						Passive-Aggressive (Negativistic)
	8B	2	21						Self-Defeating
Severe Personality Pathology	S	8	63						Schizotypal
	C	13	76						Borderline
	P	10	70						Paranoid
Clinical Syndromes	A	14	92						Anxiety Disorder
	H	4	34						Somatoform Disorder
	N	3	36						Bipolar: Manic Disorder
	D	7	47						Dysthymic Disorder
	B	7	68						Alcohol Dependence
	T	3	62						Drug Dependence
	R	17	80						Post-Traumatic Stress
Severe Syndromes	SS	14	70						Thought Disorder
	CC	14	85						Major Depression
	PP	4	68						Delusional Disorder

Figure 1.2 MCMI-III Profile for a 37-Year-Old Divorced, Non-Hispanic White Woman Who Was Self-Referred for Psychotherapy

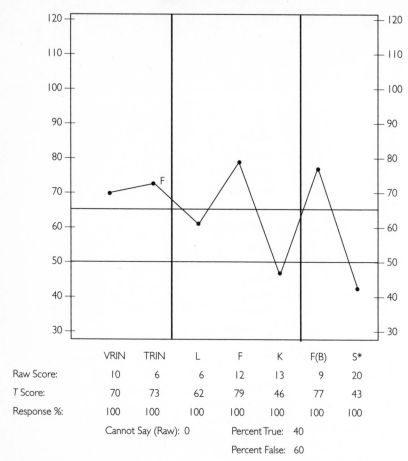

MMPI-2 Validity Pattern

	VRIN	TRIN	L	F	K	F(B)	S*
Raw Score:	10	6	6	12	13	9	20
T Score:	70	73	62	79	46	77	43
Response %:	100	100	100	100	100	100	100

Cannot Say (Raw): 0   Percent True: 40

Percent False: 60

*Experimental

Figure 1.3 MMPI-2 Results for Figure 1.2 Patient

best understood as reflecting turbulent emotionality. She is more likely to exhibit a mixed depressive/compulsive personality style with borderline and schizoid features. A diagnosis of Personality Disorder NOS on Axis II would be appropriate if evidence from the clinical interview verified that she met diagnostic criteria.

Her personality pattern is replete with anxious apprehensiveness (Scales A, R) and depressive thoughts (Scales 2B, CC) that probably dominate her

MMPI-2 Basic and Supplementary Scales Profile

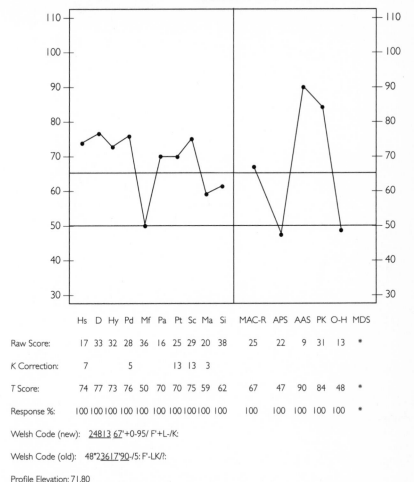

	Hs	D	Hy	Pd	Mf	Pa	Pt	Sc	Ma	Si	MAC-R	APS	AAS	PK	O-H	MDS
Raw Score:	17	33	32	28	36	16	25	29	20	38	25	22	9	31	13	*
K Correction:	7		5				13	13	3							
T Score:	74	77	73	76	50	70	70	75	59	62	67	47	90	84	48	*
Response %:	100	100	100	100	100	100	100	100	100	100	100	100	100	100	100	*

Welsh Code (new):   24813 67'+0-95/ F'+L-/K:

Welsh Code (old):   48"23617'90-/5: F'-LK/?:

Profile Elevation: 71.80

*MDS scores are reported only for clients who indicate that they are married or separated.

Figure 1.3 (continued)

life. She is quite troubled and becomes easily dejected, perhaps in the belief that others will reject her. She is prone to erupt in temper tantrums against those whom she feels are uncaring, unsupportive, overly critical, and disapproving. Her Scale C elevation suggests that she is unpredictable and will

MMPI-2 Content Scales Profile

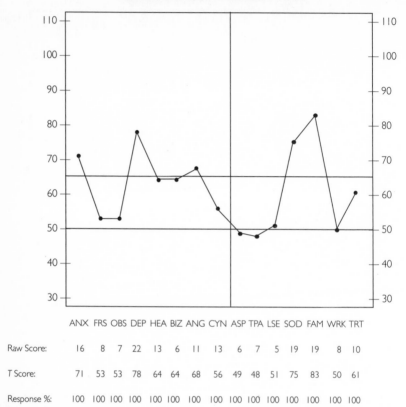

	ANX	FRS	OBS	DEP	HEA	BIZ	ANG	CYN	ASP	TPA	LSE	SOD	FAM	WRK	TRT
Raw Score:	16	8	7	22	13	6	11	13	6	7	5	19	19	8	10
T Score:	71	53	53	78	64	64	68	56	49	48	51	75	83	50	61
Response %:	100	100	100	100	100	100	100	100	100	100	100	100	100	100	100

Figure 1.3 (continued)

vacillate between depression, explosive anger, and perhaps self-destructive activities. She may have learned to expect ridicule and hence sees the slightest bit of disapproval from others as yet another example that people cannot be trusted. Her compulsive (Scale 7) traits probably help her contain her emotions when she needs to (e.g., at work) and to keep focused on tasks when significantly distressed. Nevertheless, it appears that these features of her personality have been overwhelmed by the more disorganizing depressive and borderline forces. She has reported distressing recollections of traumatic experiences (Scale R), which were identified in her "true" responses to the statements: "I'm ashamed of some of the abuses I suffered as a child" and "I hate to think about some of the ways I was abused as a child." The

Supplementary Score Report

	Raw Score	T Score	Response (%)
Anxiety (A)	16	56	100
Repression (R)	21	62	100
Ego Strength (Es)	24	30	100
Dominance (Do)	12	35	100
Social Responsibility (Re)	17	38	100
Post-Traumatic Stress Disorder–Schlenger (Schlenger & Kulka, 1987) (PS)	35	76	100
Depression Subscales (Harris-Lingoes, 1955)			
Subjective Depression (D1)	17	72	100
Psychomotor Retardation (D2)	9	68	100
Physical Malfunctioning (D3)	6	70	100
Mental Dullness (D4)	5	61	100
Brooding (D5)	6	68	100
Hysteria Subscales (Harris-Lingoes, 1955)			
Denial of Social Anxiety (Hy1)	3	45	100
Need for Affection (Hy2)	6	46	100
Lassitude-Malaise (Hy3)	10	79	100
Somatic Complaints (Hy4)	7	65	100
Inhibition of Aggression (Hy5)	5	62	100
Psychopathic Deviate Subscales (Harris-Lingoes, 1955)			
Familial Discord (Pd1)	6	74	100
Authority Problems (Pd2)	5	69	100
Social Imperturbability (Pd3)	3	47	100
Social Alienation (Pd4)	6	60	100
Self-Alienation (Pd5)	8	73	100
Paranoia Subscales (Harris-Lingoes, 1955)			
Persecutory Ideas (Pa1)	3	57	100
Poignancy (Pa2)	5	65	100
Naivete (Pa3)	5	50	100

Figure 1.3 (continued)

	Raw Score	T Score	Response (%)
Schizophrenia Subscales (Harris-Lingoes, 1955)			
Social Alienation (Sc1)	10	77	100
Emotional Alienation (Sc2)	5	86	100
Lack of Ego Mastery, Cognitive (Sc3)	3	61	100
Lack of Ego Mastery, Conative (Sc4)	5	65	100
Lack of Ego Mastery, Defective Inhibition (Sc5)	3	59	100
Bizarre Sensory Experiences (Sc6)	7	72	100
Hypomania Subscales (Harris-Lingoes, 1955)			
Amorality (Ma1)	1	45	100
Psychomotor Acceleration (Ma2)	7	60	100
Imperturbability (Ma3)	4	56	100
Ego Inflation (Ma4)	3	49	100
Social Introversion Subscales (Ben-Porath, Hostetler, Butcher, & Graham, 1989)			
Shyness / Self-Consciousness (Si1)	10	63	100
Social Avoidance (Si2)	8	74	100
Alienation—Self and Others (Si3)	4	47	100

Uniform T scores are used for Hs, D, Hy, Pd, Pa, Pt, Sc, Ma, and the Content Scales; all other MMPI-2 scales use linear T scores.

Figure 1.3 (continued)

Axis I diagnoses suggested by the MCMI-III include Generalized Anxiety Disorder, Major Depression, and Post-Traumatic Stress Disorder. The test did not detect alcohol abuse, which was reported during the initial interview. It is likely that she answered "false" to most of the items asking whether alcohol is a problem in her life.

MMPI-2 Results

Figure 1.3 gives summary scores for the MMPI-2 (Butcher et al., 1989). The patient endorsed a number of psychological problems, suggesting that she is in much emotional distress (F). Her defensive structure has been weakened (K, Es), and she is unable to cope effectively with the stresses in her life. Elevations on 7 of 10 basic clinical scales indicate T greater than 70, suggesting that she is chronically maladjusted. She is moody, angry, distrustful, resentful, and in much distress. Her depression contains both physical and cognitive symptoms (DEP and Depression subscales). She reports many family problems (FAM, Pd1) and feelings of alienation (2, Pd5). She is also quite angry (F, 4, 8, ANG) and has a high potential for explosive behavior. Her interpersonal relationships are likely to be filled with disturbances. She is somewhat inhibited in social situations (SOD, Si1, Si2) and sees her social relationships as problematic. She also admits to problems with substance abuse (AAS) and her MacAndrew Alcoholism Scale–Revised (MAC-R) score confirms this. She may have suffered traumatic experiences (PS) such that substances may be used to cope with the symptoms. Her need for affection is quite strong (Hy2), but her feelings of alienation (Pd5, Sc1, Sc2) prevent her from satisfying these needs. Her tendency to withdraw, her extensive distress and maladjustment, poor coping skills, and significant depression suggest that she is a suicidal risk. Diagnoses associated with the MMPI-2 results are an affective disorder and/or personality disorder.

Integration of Test Findings

The patient cooperated with the entire interview and testing process. Both self-report measures noted significant anxiety and depression and viewed her as psychologically maladjusted. She appears to have difficulty managing her emotions, especially anger, as noted on both tests. Traumatic experiences and symptoms figured prominently on both measures. Her alcoholism was more accurately identified by the MMPI-2. Both tests suggested a preoccupation with negative, particularly depressive, thoughts, that may dominate her life, and both suggested that she may be a suicide risk. A Borderline personality disorder was not identified by either test, but results of both instruments point to a prominent affective disorder and Post-Traumatic Stress Disorder on Axis I, and possibly a mixed personality disorder on Axis II.

Treatment goals suggested by the testing include (a) alleviating the patient's intense anxiety and depression, (b) carefully monitoring and eliminating her suicidal thoughts and self-mutilating behavior, (c) helping her cope more effectively with the symptoms of her traumatic past, (d) discontinuing the use of alcohol, (e) improving her relationship skills, and (f) teaching her ways to modulate and control her feelings, especially anger.

🖋 TEST YOURSELF 🖋

1. The MCMI-III should only be used with

(a) normal (nonclinical) clients.

(b) patients being evaluated or treated in a mental health setting.

(c) patients in a medical setting.

(d) clients being evaluated for vocational preferences.

2. The MCMI-III uses a base rate score transformation because

(a) these scores have better psychometric properties than other standardized scores.

(b) personality disorders are normally distributed in the general population.

(c) a *T*-score distribution results in too high a mean to be interpreted meaningfully.

(d) psychiatric disorders are not normally distributed.

3. Base rate scores

(a) are normally distributed.

(b) take advantage of prevalence rates of existing disorders.

(c) are a transformed score with no evidence of utility.

(d) cannot be used since base rates change from setting to setting.

4. Intercorrelations for MCMI-III scales are typically

(a) lower than ± .25.

(b) in the range of −.50 to +.50.

(c) nonsignificant.

(d) greater than ± .75.

5. **The Validity Index consists of**

    (a) a combination of all the validity scales on the MCMI-III.

    (b) all items marked "false."

    (c) three items of an implausible nature.

    (d) items reflecting inconsistent responding.

6. **A BR score of 202 on Scale X indicates**

    (a) random responding.

    (b) faking good.

    (c) faking bad.

    (d) an invalid profile.

7. **A BR score of 105 on Scale Z**

    (a) suggests random responding.

    (b) suggests faking good.

    (c) suggests faking bad.

    (d) invalidates the profile.

8. **The DSM-IV diagnosis most frequently associated with BR scores above 84 on Scale 8B is**

    (a) Antisocial personality disorder.

    (b) Aggressive personality disorder.

    (c) Personality Disorder NOS, prominent aggressive traits.

    (d) none of the above.

9. **If you suspect the patient may be psychotic, which MCMI-III scales would be most relevant for this assessment?**

10. **The patient is highly organized, rather meticulous and efficient, strongly motivated to meet deadlines to avoid the disapproval of superiors, and tends to suppress angry feelings. The MCMI-III personality scale most likely to be elevated is _____.**

Answers: 1. b; 2. d; 3. b; 4. b; 5. c; 6. d; 7. c; 8. c; 9. the Severe Syndromes Scales: Thought Disorder (Scale SS), Major Depression (Scale CC), and Delusional Disorder (Scale PP); 10. Compulsive

Two

ESSENTIALS OF MBMD ASSESSMENT

Carrie Millon and Sarah E. Meagher

INTRODUCTION

During the past 30 years, clinicians and researchers have produced a vast amount of evidence demonstrating the relationship between psychosocial factors and health outcomes as well as healthcare costs. As eloquently argued and expounded upon by Antoni, Millon, and Millon (1997) with evidence based on a report by Reiger (1994), clinical behavioral medicine interventions may in fact reduce the frequency of utilization of medical services such as ambulatory care visits, cesarean sections, and major surgery by an estimated 17% to 56%. Specifically, psychosocial interventions are associated with an average reduction of 1.5 hospital days for surgical patients, and increasing a person's sense of control and optimism can improve health outcomes and decrease healthcare costs. Exciting new lines of research have been exploring the role of personality factors and health outcomes for specific diseases. In a recent paper, Harper, Chacko, Kotik-Harper, Young, and Gotto (1998) found that a combination of personality factors and other psychosocial risk factors (as measured by the Millon Behavioral Health Inventory, MBHI; Millon, Green, & Meagher, 1982) can even predict survival time and post-transplant care required by heart transplant patients.

When the MBHI was made widely available in 1982, the field of health psychology was still in its infancy. The MBHI had been developed using what existing evidence there was and relying heavily on theoretical models yet to be tested. The explosion of interest in health-related issues since then, combined with a vast amount of information and lessons learned from the MBHI, inspired Theodore Millon and his colleagues to embark on a major reconceptualization and expansion of the original test.

The MBHI was normed on a mixture of both clinical and nonclinical populations, which led to a loss of diagnostic behavioral precision when dealing with a variety of diverse medical patients engaged in clinical appraisals. The decision to develop a purely medical normative group with appropriate reference norms served as a major impetus for constructing the Millon Behavioral Medicine Diagnostic (MBMD; Millon, Antoni, Millon, Meagher, & Grossman, 2001). Beyond the need for clinically relevant norms, it was evident that the MBHI, useful as it was for general psychological assessment, was not sufficiently sensitive and broad enough to encompass the wide range of medically-based populations. Users of the MBHI over the past 20 years have been recommending ways to enhance the instrument; for example, by adding scales for psychiatric syndromes and for making management and treatment recommendations. Although minor adjustments to the MBHI were introduced regularly during this period, there was clearly a need to substantially revise and ultimately to replace it with a tool that would strengthen its psychometric features, broaden its disease-based populations and its management utility, and to make it consonant with recent developments in the fields of health psychology and behavioral medicine.

HISTORY AND DEVELOPMENT

Advances Since the MBHI

Since its introduction, the MBHI went on to become the most frequently utilized health inventory in the United States. (See Rapid Reference 2.1 for a quick historical overview.) Over the past two decades the developers of the MBHI received considerable feedback from clinicians and researchers on how the test performed in a wide variety of settings and with every conceivable type of medical patient. This feedback suggested the wisdom of modifying the instrument in certain realms. For example, several of the scales that were created entirely on empirical grounds (e.g., gastrointestinal susceptibility) were not as useful as was initially desired. As a consequence, several of these domain areas were not included when conceptualizing the scale composition of the MBMD. Other MBHI scales with minor difficulties were reformulated, some with slightly different areas of focus. When the focus of measurement was changed significantly, the scale name was also changed (e.g., MBHI Future Despair became Future Pessimism for the MBMD). Most importantly, scales relating to psychiatric status (for example, Depression), as well as scales appraising stress moderators (Social Isolation) and treatment prognostics (Problematic Compliance) were added.

Well over 150 psychologists, physicians, nurses, and other healthcare personnel were consulted to guide the reconstruction of the MBMD. Many of these individuals were current or former users of the MBHI, but a significant number were not acquainted with the test. Including the latter group proved to be instrumental in helping developers of the MBMD view the test from a fresh perspective by pointing to issues and directions that were not envisioned in the original instrument. Themes that repeatedly emerged were: (a) the necessity of broadening the instrument's focus on pathology to one that also encompassed each patient's assets or behavioral strengths; (b) the value of identifying patients who were clinically depressed, who would abuse medication, who were not likely to comply with prescribed regimens, who evinced unusual pain sensitivities, felt unsupported by family and friends, were potentially heavy utilizers of medical services, or were otherwise management risks; and (c) the need to detect patients who were engaged in problematic health behaviors such as excessive drinking or physical inactivity.

The range of patient populations and clinical settings envisioned for the new instrument expanded appreciably beyond those encompassed by the MBHI. Special attention was given to the inclusion of HIV/AIDS groups, organ transplant patients, long-term diabetes cases, persons with neurological disorders, as well as those seen in comprehensive rehabilitation programs, oncology centers, gastroenterology clinics, other speciality clinics, and routine HMO and VA programs.

A wider range of external correlates for scales was gathered for the MBMD, as compared with the MBHI, in an effort to strength test validity. Similarly, evidence in the form of staff ratings was obtained from clinical judges who were well acquainted with their patients. These data served as a means of corroborating the accuracy of patient self-reports on a number of MBMD scales.

Indices were added to identify and correct distorting response patterns that might diminish accuracy of the scales, that is, a tendency to over complain about one's medical state or to deny and cover up symptoms, fears, and concerns. Correcting for these kinds of response tendencies have proven useful in strengthening the accuracy of other self-report inventories, such as the MCMI and MMPI, and should enhance the accuracy of the MBMD.

As with all Millon instruments, the MBMD was developed according to a

≋ *Rapid Reference 2.1*

Millon Behavioral Medicine Diagnostic (MBMD)

Authors: T. Millon, Ph. D., M. Antoni, Ph. D., C. Millon, Ph. D., S. Meagher, M.S., S. Grossman, M.A.

Publication Date: 2001

What the test measures: The domains captured in this test include response patterns and coping styles as well as psychiatric concerns, stress moderators, treatment and management issues, and problematic health habits.

Age Range: 18–85

Administration Time: Approximately 20–25 minutes

Qualifications of examiners: A specialized degree in the health care field and accompanying licensure or certification

Publishers: National Computer Systems
    P.O. Box 1416
    Minneapolis, MN 55440
    Phone 800–672–7271

Consult the National Computer Systems product catalog for latest pricing.

three-stage process outlined by Loevinger (1957). In this method, test construction and validation occur simultaneously. In the first stage of development, called theoretical-substantive, over 800 test items were written to ensure full coverage of characteristics to be assessed by each of the major sections of the test, with a range of 22 to 46 items per scale. The item pool was reduced on rational grounds such as item complexity, readability, and probable extreme endorsement frequency. After this initial reduction of items, eight health-oriented psychologists were asked to match each item to the scale they considered most appropriate. Items that were consistently categorized correctly were retained, resulting in 350 prototypal items. Several small pilot studies helped narrow this number down to 299 items, which constituted the Research Form of the test.

The second stage of development, the internal-structural phase, was conducted with over 200 patients who were administered the Research Form of the test. During this phase further item reductions were achieved by several means. Items with particularly high or low endorsement frequency, those with low partial correlations to the scales they were intended to represent, and items with weak theoretical or substantive relations to the construct measured by the scale were eliminated. Final scale composition was achieved through an iterative process where additional items were removed, based on these criteria, until the developers were satisfied with the psychometric properties of the item sets. Like all Millon inventories, there is considerable overlap, intercorrelation, and cluster among the MBMD scales. However, they do so in ways that are in close accord with Theodore Millon's (1969, 1990; Millon & Davis, 1996) model of personality, as well as health psychology research and theory (Antoni, Millon, & Millon, 1997; Harper et al., 1998; Millon et al., 2001).

In the final stage of test development, the external-criterion phase, the relationships between MBMD scales and other diagnostic instruments that have been used in medical settings were examined. These external correlates included the Beck Depression Inventory, Brief Symptom Inventory, the Perceived Stress Inventory, the State-Trait Anxiety Inventory, the Spiritual Belief Inventory, the Social Provisions Scale, the Life Orientation Test, and the Cognitive Difficulties Scale. Correlations with these measures helped establish that the test scales accurately assess the constructs they were intended to measure.

Scale Reliability

Addressing the question of reliability with a test that is designed to measure complex psychological and medical behavior is difficult. (See Rapid Reference 2.2 for a summary of MBMD scales.) This is especially so when the test is appraising factors that are transient and situational. Change over time is inevitable in these states and low test-retest reliabilities may be a logical function of the nature of the construct rather than an intrinsic measurement error. Internal consistency estimates (coefficient alpha) for MBMD scales ranged from .47 to .89 with a median of .79 (Millon et al., 2001; p. 29). Test-retest coefficients over a 7- to 30-day interval ranged from .71 to .92 with a median value of .83 (Millon et al., 2001; p. 29).

Normative Sample

As described above, norms for the MBMD were based solely on medical patients from a heterogeneous sample of medical settings. Subjects included patients just being diagnosed, to those with long-term illnesses who were being seen for follow-up visits. Although it was not feasible to obtain a random sample, significant efforts were made to obtain a representative sample of all medical patients. Over 750 medical patients with a variety of medical conditions from cancer, diabetes, organ transplantation, HIV, chronic pain, to neurological disorders were used to norm the MBMD. These patients ranged in age from 18 to over 80 years old and included a broad sampling of racial and ethnic groups (61% White, 16% African American, 19% Hispanic).

Prevalence Scores

As with all Millon clinical inventories, the MBMD relies on a statistic that reflects the prevalence of a particular disorder among the population rather than the traditional T-score that assumes a normal distribution of scores. The MBMD uses the term Prevalence Score (PS) to denote this construct rather than many other Millon inventories that use the term Base-Rate (BR) score. They are, however, identical in every other respect. To determine prevalence rates of these constructs, a group of physicians, nurses, and psychologists were asked to rate the prevalence of problematic levels of the constructs represented in the MBMD. More specifically, they were asked to differentiate between the percentages of patients for whom the characteristics were moderately serious (*present*) and those for whom it was clinically serious (*prominent*). From these estimates two arbitrary numbers were chosen as diagnostic cutoff points: PS scores of 75 to 84 indicate the presence of a disorder, coping style, stress moderator, or treatment prognostic, while PS scores of 85 and above indicate a characteristic that is most prominent for the individual. For the Stress Moderator and Treatment Prognostic scales, another group of physicians, nurses, and psychologists were asked to estimate the percentage of patients who exhibited behaviors or attitudes tapped in these domains which could be considered *assets* to their treatment course. The arbitrary cutoff of a PS score below 35 was chosen to denote the presence of an asset in one of these scales.

DON'T FORGET

Prevalence Scores (PS) and Base Rate (BR) scores mean the same thing. They rely on the prevalence or real distribution of a construct within a population rather than the T-score assumption of a normal distribution.

≡ Rapid Reference 2.2

Summary of MBMD Scales

Validity:
Two implausible items detect random or confused responding. When one is endorsed, results are considered of questionable validity, when two are endorsed, the test is considered invalid.

Response Patterns: *These scales gauge distorting response tendencies in the patient's self-report.*

X. Disclosure. Inclination of patient to hesitate in sharing information about oneself

Y. Desirability. Inclination of patient to present a favorable image of oneself

Z. Debasement. Inclination of patient to present a problematic image of oneself

Negative Health Habits: *Gauges recent or current problematic behaviors affecting health.*

N. Alcohol. Assesses presence and extent of alcohol consumption

O. Drug. Assesses presence and extent of illicit drug use

P. Eating. Assesses presence and extent of abnormalities in eating

Q. Caffeine. Assesses presence and extent of caffeine consumption

R. Inactivity. Assesses deficit of regular physical exercise

S. Smoking. Assesses presence and extent of smoking behaviors

Psychiatric Indications: *Identifies psychiatric co-morbidities that may affect health management.*

AA. Anxiety–Tension. Assesses presence and extent of anxiety symptoms

BB. Depression. Assesses presence and extent of depressive symptoms

CC. Cognitive Dysfunction. Assesses presence and extent of confused or distorted thinking

DD. Emotional Lability. Assesses presence and extent of inconsistent emotional factors

EE. Guardedness. Assesses presence and extent of pathological suspiciousness

Coping Styles: *"Normal" DSM personality styles which reflect ways of dealing with life stress and illness*

1. Introversive. A nonclinical Schizoid personality style

2A. Inhibited. A nonclinical Avoidant personality style

2B. Dejected. A nonclinical Depressive personality style

3.   **Cooperative.** A nonclinical Dependent personality style

4.   **Sociable.** A nonclinical Histrionic personality style

5.   **Confident.** A nonclinical Narcissistic personality style

6A. **Nonconforming.** A nonclinical Antisocial personality style

6B. **Forceful.** A nonclinical Sadistic personality style

7.   **Respectful.** A nonclinical Compulsive personality style

8A. **Oppositional.** A nonclinical Negativistic personality style

8B. **Denigrated.** A nonclinical Masochistic personality style.

Stress Moderators: *Scales identify attitudes and relationships that may affect health care*

A. **Illness Apprehension.** Assesses excessive focus on potential bodily dysfunctions

B. **Functional Deficits.** Assesses ability to conduct activities of daily living

C. **Pain Sensitivity.** Assesses the presence and intensity of physical pain

D. **Social Isolation.** Assesses familial and non-familial sources of emotional support

E. **Future Pessimism.** Assesses outlook toward future, especially health recovery

F. **Spiritual Absence.** Assesses spiritual support for dealing with life stressors

Treatment Prognostics: *Scales identify patient characteristics that may influence treatment outcome*

G. **Interventional Fragility.** Anticipates likelihood of decompensatory reaction to treatment

H. **Medication Abuse.** Anticipates risk for rejection or addiction to prescribed regimens

I. **Information Discomfort.** Anticipates willingness to share and to be receptive to personal health data

J. **Utilization Excess.** Anticipates excessive desire for medical resources (beyond those warranted)

K. **Problematic Compliance.** Anticipates likelihood of adherence to medical regimen

Management Guide: *Scales identify problems that may call for behavioral interventions*

L. **Adjustment Difficulties.** Anticipates the presence of psychological complications

M. **Psych Referral.** Anticipates likelihood of needing pharmacologic or psychosocial therapy for emotional problems

THEORETICAL FOUNDATION

The theoretical parentage of the MBMD may be found in Theodore Millon's (1969) original biosocial-learning theory of personality and psychopathology, his more recent evolutionary model (1990; Millon & Davis, 1996), and the vast clinical literature on health psychology that has been published in the past 20 years. As with all Millon clinical tests, Millon's theories serve as the foundation for the coping styles scales. The MBMD includes nonclinical personality style variants of the schizoid, avoidant, depressive, dependent, histrionic, narcissistic, antisocial, sadistic, compulsive, negativistic, and masochistic styles. (Refer to Chapter One, *Essentials of MCMI-III Assessment,* for more information on how Millon's polarities are used to develop these constructs.) Millon believes that personality coping styles are influential in the genesis of pathology and the course of illness, and indeed, recent research has begun to provide empirical support for this relationship.

The additional scales on the MBMD were created with the guidance of the clinical literature on the importance of (a) assessing psychiatric factors such as depression, anxiety, and emotional lability in medical patients, (b) assessing factors that moderate stress from social support to spiritual faith, (c) assessing factors that affect the treatment prognostics for a patient such as a tendency to abuse medications or overuse medical services, and (d) noting lifestyle or behavioral habits that can have detrimental consequences on health such as smoking or a sedentary lifestyle. As previously mentioned, the addition of many of these scales were the direct result of input from the many researchers and clinicians who had used the MBHI and the burgeoning health psychology literature that has been published in the past two decades.

TEST ADMINISTRATION

The MBMD is an appropriate measure to administer in small group settings (i.e., waiting rooms, small clinics) or individually. As is always good clinical practice, it is advisable to develop a rapport with the examinee, but most people find the MBMD a non-threatening test and have little trouble complying with instructions. It is acceptable for properly trained nurses, secretaries, and receptionists to administer the MBMD under supervision, as well as psychologists and physicians. Administration is sufficiently simple and straightforward that patients can complete the test even when time, space, and privacy are limited. It is generally not advisable to allow patients to take the MBMD home to complete.

Patient Characteristics

The MBMD was designed for use with medical patients ages 18 and older. The items were written at or below the sixth grade reading level. Test forms are available in both English and Spanish. Although respondents are expected to demonstrate a variety of symptoms as a result of their medical problems, the MBMD should not be administered to patients who are especially fatigued, anxious, debilitated, or who are under heavy sedation.

Directions for Administration

A common way to introduce the measure to patients is to explain that they will be completing a questionnaire that will help their medical care providers understand their special problems and concerns, and ultimately design better, individualized treatment plans for them. It is also important to inform the patient that adequate measures will be taken to ensure the confidentiality of their responses and results. Explaining the potential benefits for the patient should ensure that they will answer the questions seriously and straightforwardly, but it may be necessary to stress the importance of their answering as honestly and thoughtfully as possible. Directions for taking the MBMD are printed on the test form and are easy for the patient to read and understand.

Following the cover page, there are 165 true-false statements that typically take the patient 20 to 25 minutes to answer. Patients indicate whether a statement is true or false as applied to them by filling in one of the circles printed next to each item or on the accompanying answer sheet. Answers must be recorded using a soft-lead No. 2 pencil, and the circles must be completely filled in to be correctly read by optical scanners. If the test is going to be scored by entering the data by hand into a computer, it is not necessary to use a pencil or completely fill in the circles, as long as the answer is clearly distinguishable. If a patient has skipped items or double marked answers, the examiner should urge the patient to complete the test or to choose the single best response for an item. More than 11 missing or double marked items will render the test invalid.

Testing Individuals with Special Needs

Administration procedures can be altered to accommodate those who are hard of hearing, have poor vision, or poor motor control. It is advisable to learn as much as possible about the respondent's impairment prior to testing so that proper accommodations can be made. Visually impaired persons and those with motor control problems can be assisted by administering the test by audiocassette (available from the publisher in both English and Spanish). Additionally, a large print version of the MBMD is available from the publisher when working with older patients or patients with poor vision.

SCORING THE MBMD

The MBMD can be scored in one of three ways: It may be scored by hand, answer sheets can be mailed to the publisher for processing, or tests can be handled via onsite computer scoring. On-site computer scoring is the most preferred mode for processing the test, as it is virtually instantaneous and leaves little margin for error. Mail-in and onsite scoring allow the practitioner a choice of receiving a full narrative MBMD interpretive report which includes a profile report and a one page, tear-off Healthcare Provider Summary, or the profile report by itself. Scoring the MBMD by hand generates only a profile sheet. MBMD testing materials differ depending on the scoring method chosen. Two paper-and-pencil formats, one for hand scoring and one for mail-in computer scoring, are available from the publisher. For the computer scoring method, there is a combination test booklet and answer sheet, as well as an online computer format.

Hand scoring, although possible, proves to be a very complex procedure; scoring errors are common, and it is recommended that each test be scored twice to increase accuracy. To carry out scoring of the MBMD by hand, the following materials will be required.

- The MBMD Hand-Scorer's User Guide
- A completed MBMD Hand-Scoring Answer Sheet
- A complete set of plastic overlay scoring templates ("keys")
- A blank MBMD Hand-Scoring Worksheet
- A blank Hand-Scoring Profile
- The MBMD Manual
- A calculator

The major steps to be performed in hand scoring the MBMD include: performing validity checks, using the templates to determine raw scores, determining the initial prevalence scores, and calculating adjustments to the initial scores in order to determine the final prevalence scores to plot on the profile sheet.

It should be noted that making corrections and adjustments to the MBMD's predecessor, the MBHI, was a relatively simple procedure. That is not the case with the MBMD. Many corrections are built in when the MBMD is scored either via mail-in or by onsite computer. When scoring by hand, many complex algorithms must be employed. Adjustments may be made on the basis of the respondent's Response Pattern (Scales X, Y and Z) and are designed to correct for patterns that may distort the patient's scores. Corrections for response pattern can increase or decrease the prevalence score for Scales AA–EE and A–M. Additional corrections may be made based on the number of prevalence scores for Scales 1–8B that are greater than or equal to 60. This is a designed to correct for over- or underreporting on the Coping Style scales. In general, those patients with fewer numbers of Scales 1–8B elevations will have adjustments ranging from +5 to +15 points added to the prevalence scores of these scales. Conversely, those patients who generate greater numbers of high scores within the Coping Style scales will have their prevalence scores reduced by –5 to –15 points. Similarly, an additional prevalence score transformation is made to correct for over- or underreporting on the Psychiatric Indications, Stress Moderators, Treatment Prognostics, and Management Guides scales (Scales AA–EE, A–K, and L–M). All of these adjustments are in place to correct for the traditionally known "fake-good" and "fake-bad" response style sets. For the specific

DON'T FORGET

Computer scoring is the most reliable and efficient way to process the MBMD.

> # DON'T FORGET
> ....
> When hand-scoring the MBMD, repeat all steps twice to ensure accuracy.

transformations required, refer to either the hand-scoring templates or Appendix E of the test manual (Millon, 2001, pp. 129–133).

Regardless of the scoring methodology employed, all completed MBMD answer sheets must be checked to ensure their validity. Several conditions can render the test invalid. If the patient's gender is not recorded, it is not possible to select the correct prevalence (PS) transformation table for scoring the test. Similarly the patient's age must be recorded. The MBMD is based on normative data for people 18 to 85 years of age. Without age data, or with an age outside of this range, it is not possible to use the normative prevalence data accurately. An MBMD will also be considered invalid if there are 11 or more omitted or double marked responses, as this will impact the integrity of the test's scales in that an adequate number of items may not have been completed for every scale. Finally, the validity items built into the test (items 106 and 124) should be reviewed by the examiner. Endorsement of these items indicates that a patient may have paid insufficient attention to the content of the item, or may have had trouble reading and comprehending these items. If one of these items is endorsed (i.e., answered true) the test should be considered of questionable validity and the clinician should take this information into consideration when interpreting the results of the test. If both of these items are endorsed, the test is to be considered invalid.

When the patient returns the test to the examiner, he or she should scan the form for completeness of required information and look for double-marked (both T and F) responses or an excessive number of omitted items (11 or more). If errors are found, the form should be returned and the patient should be encouraged to complete deficiencies or correct errors. Moreover, to avoid any processing delays for scoring, it is important to check whether all answers were filled in with a soft lead pencil (pen markings cannot be read by optical scanners), to erase any marks outside the circles, and to see that the form is free of tears and perforations.

HOW TO INTERPRET THE MBMD

The interpretation of any self-report measure must take into account information about the test itself, its advantages as well as its limitations, in addition to information about the test respondent. Data gathered from the MBMD, as with all self-report instruments, must be viewed within the context of a much wider breadth of knowledge regarding the individual taking the test. The clinician must synthesize MBMD test results with his or her knowledge of that patient's demographic background, salient medical and personal information, and any relevant behavioral observations.

The MBMD is a multilayered, interwoven instrument. To realize the maximum potential of the instrument, the test user must be somewhat sophisticated in synthesizing multiple sources of information. The computerized interpretive narrative report does much of this automatically, but a thoughtful clinician can generate similarly integrated and synthesized results by using the results of the Psychiatric Indications and Coping Style scales to "color" the interpretation of the other scales.

Profile Assessment

While single scale elevations are informative as to specific traits and areas of potential concern, it is the profile, or constellation of scale scores, that provides the most information to the clinician. Prior to configural analysis, it is important to be familiar with the features and characteristics that exemplify each of the individual scales. Driven by the underlying theory and subsequent statistical clustering of characteristics in the construction population, the narratives provided in the computer-generated report synthesize and integrate the characteristics tapped by each of the high point scales. The MBMD's underlying theory allows for extensive individual differences and the narrative reports generated effectively reflect this distinctiveness. It is the interplay between a patient's coping style, his or her perception of differing stressors, and the individual experience of assuming the patient role that is highlighted in the MBMD report. The meaning of single scale elevations will be examined in the following sections. At this point however, it may be helpful to illustrate how slightly different high point profiles can have very different interpretations and implications for treatment.

Two women with similar medical diagnoses (invasive breast cancer) are evaluated by the MBMD. Both patients score highest on Scale 3 (Cooperative Style) of the coping style scales. This scale, when interpreted individually, describes individuals who are generally unassertive and in need of strong supportive figures in their life. They tend to exhibit poor self-esteem and deny or minimize their difficulties, not wanting to make "trouble" for others. The interpretation of these profiles is significantly altered by the addition of differing subsidiary scale elevations. The second highest Coping Style score for the first patient is on Scale 2A (Inhibited Style), whereas the next highest scale for the second woman is Scale 4 (Sociable Style). Consequently, the first woman is likely to be fearful of others and ill at ease. She sees life through a shroud of sadness and will be difficult for healthcare personnel to engage. Conversely, the second woman, albeit dependent in style, presents in a dramatic and engaging manner. It is important that she be seen as a "good" patient who actively seeks approval via an eagerness to comply with healthcare directives. Her enthusiasm however is unlikely to be long lived and will need to be bolstered with renewed attentiveness from the healthcare team. As can be seen from this example, these individuals, more alike than dissimilar, are quite different in both the manner in which they are likely to report symptomatology and to respond to the disease process. Consequently, different strategies for each are indicated for optimal case management.

Step-by-Step Procedures for Test Interpretation

The eight steps involved in interpreting the MBMD follow.

Step 1: Assess Test Validity

Validity of the test results is largely dependent on how well the individual taking the MBMD matches normative groups used to establish the prevalence-rate scores. The normative sample used in establishing the base rate norms was sufficiently large and diverse enough to minimize the potential for respondent divergence. Nonetheless, caution should be taken when interpreting results if the person taking the MBMD is of an uncommonly found ethnic or racial group, from a remote geographic region, or presents with extreme educational or age levels.

The first step in interpreting the MBMD inventory is assuring that the report generated is indeed valid. The MBMD has a validity scale built into the instrument to identify persons who may be "randomly responding" to test items or who may be too disoriented to focus on the task of test completion. This indicator is composed of two highly unlikely items (item 106: "I flew across the Atlantic more than 30 times last year" and item 124: "I was on the cover of sev-

eral magazines recently"). When both items are endorsed as true, the protocol is considered invalid. However, clinicians are advised to be cautious in interpreting questionable protocols (any score greater than 0) as it is usually indicative of inadequate reading abilities, confusion, or random responses.

Step 2: Evaluate Response Patterns

The MBMD includes a series of gauges to assess potentially problematic styles or distortions on the part of patients that may complicate the reliability or validity of the test results. Three such indices are employed. The results the patient receives on each of the several clinical scales may be adjusted upward or downward, depending on the scores obtained on these gauges.

Disclosure (Scale X)   The Disclosure scale assesses whether a patient is inclined to be candid and self-revealing or remote and reserved. It is calculated by the degree of positive or negative deviation from the midrange of scores respondents give to the items comprising the scale. Sample items for this scale include "It makes me very uncomfortable when other people know about my problems" and "No one needs to know my business."

Desirability (Scale Y)   The Desirability scale ascertains the degree to which the results may have been affected by the patient's desire to appear socially attractive, morally virtuous, or emotionally well-composed. The higher the score, the greater care that must be given in determining whether the patient may be concealing important psychological stressors or behavioral difficulties in his or her life. Typical items on this scale include, "I like to follow instructions and do what others expect of me" and "I seem to fit in right away with any group o people I meet."

Debasement (Scale Z)   The Debasement scale reflects tendencies opposi those detected by Scale Y. However, it is possible for both indices to be hig This typically occurs among patients who are unusually self-disclosing. In ge eral, those scoring in the upper 15% on Scale Z exhibit an inclination to preciate or devalue themselves by reporting more troublesome emotion medical difficulties than are likely to be uncovered in an objective review especially high score may signify "a cry for help" from a patient who is, in experiencing an unusual amount of behavioral or medical turmoil. Item this scale include "I have a habit of making my problems sound worse they really are" and "A lot of my answers on this test have been affected current bad mood."

Step 3: Note Negative Health Habits

There are numerous lifestyle behaviors that patients exhibit that may exacerbate their medical difficulties and undermine efforts to effectively treat their illness or, conversely, help promote their health and well-being (i.e., exercise). The following indicators identify six such possible behaviors that have been shown to contribute to a variety of health outcomes: alcohol consumption, drug use, problematic eating, caffeine intake, inactivity, and smoking. Items on these indicators are fairly obvious in content to the patient and should not be used as a screening measure. Instead they are intended as a quick method to alert the healthcare team of areas that are likely to impact treatment and recovery.

Alcohol (Indicator N)   The Alcohol indicator notes the presence of a problem with alcohol consumption. This problematic habit is identified among patients who endorse one or both of the following items: "It is difficult for me to get through the day without a few drinks" or "Members of my family have complained recently about my drinking."

Drug (Indicator O)   The Drug indicator identifies patients who admit to using non-prescription drugs and may have developed a dependency on them. These patients may endorse the following items: "I have told lies to my family to conceal my use of drugs" or "Taking drugs has been a regular part of my social life."

Eating (Indicator P)   The Eating indicator alerts professionals to the possibility of a chronic pattern of over-eating in the patient. The following items may be endorsed by patients with difficulties in this area: "I'm a yo-yo dieter, going up and down," "I always overeat when I'm depressed or under stress," and "I've been overweight ever since I was a child." It should be noted that all of these items refer to excessive consumption of food and being overweight rather than malnourishment and being underweight.

Caffeine (Indicator O)   The Caffeine indicator indicates the presence of an excessive consumption of caffeine. These exacerbations are identified when patients endorse the items "I get very irritable if I haven't had a cup of coffee for a few hours" or "I need plenty of caffeine to get me through the day."

Inactivity (Indicator R)   The Inactivity indicator remarks on whether regular physical exercise is a part of the patient's life. Problems in this area are indicated when patients endorse the items: "I rarely find the time to exercise," "I know I should exercise but I just can't get started," or "I've tried exercise programs, but I just can't seem to stick with them."

Smoking (Indicator S)   The Smoking indicator reflects whether a patient admits to smoking tobacco products. This behavior is known to exacerbate extant illnesses, especially those associated with heart disease and cancer. Patients with difficulties in this area endorse the items: "I smoke about a pack of cigarettes a day," "I get irritable if I go too long without a cigarette," and "I've tried to quit smoking many times, but I always start again."

Step 4: Assess Psychiatric Indications

Perhaps the most commonly asked referral question of clinical psychologists in medical settings is the psychiatric status of patients. Several *Diagnostic and Statistical Manual of Mental Disorders-IV* (DSM-IV; American Psychiatric Association, 1994) Axis I phenomenon are particularly prevalent in medical populations and are likely to complicate medically-oriented treatment efforts. These include Anxiety-Tension, Depression, Cognitive Dysfunction, Emotional Lability, and Guardedness. While elevated scores on these scales should not be used as the sole means of diagnosing a patient with an Axis I disorder, they can serve as supportive evidence for such a diagnosis.

Anxiety-Tension (Scale AA)   Many medical patients experience greater stress as a result of their illness and treatment than they do normally in their everyday lives. High levels of anxiety or tension, particularly chronic stressors such as job stress, are found to relate to the increased incidence and severity of numerous disorders and diseases. Patients who score high on this scale may be disposed to suffer numerous somatic disorders, especially those associated with the cardiovascular and digestive systems. Persistent high levels of anxiety and tension are thought to pose a troublesome presence in approximately 20% of medical patients. Items that tap the problematic side of this anxiety-tension scale include: "I feel very tense when I think about the day's events" and "For some unknown reason, I suddenly get very panicky."

Depression (Scale BB)   Patients' awareness of the limitations their disease has placed on their lives, and being faced with their own mortality, commonly lead to symptoms of depression. These depressive symptoms are implicated in the exacerbation of a variety of diseases. This scale differs from other "depression" indices on the MBMD (the Dejected and Future Pessimism scales) in that it focuses on the patient's vegetative or mood state, such as a poor appetite, social withdrawal, discouragement, guilt, behavioral apathy, self-deprecating comments, and a loss of interest in pleasurable activities. Approximately 35% of medical patients suffer from various degrees of depression. MBMD scale items that signify the depressive end of the mood state include: "I often feel sad and unloved" and "I rarely feel a sense of joy these days."

Cognitive Dysfunction (Scale CC)   Although only 3 to 6% of a heterogeneous group of medical patients have significant difficulty in this area, it is extremely important to identify them for many reasons including difficulty with adherence to medical protocols and an inability to function independently. This scale evaluates patients' perceptions of their own capacity to accurately recall aspects of past experience or to think abstractly by transcending the immediate and concrete. Among items aiding in this self-report diagnostic gauge are: "I seem to be losing my ability to concentrate" and "Loss of memory has been a big problem for me."

Emotional Lability (Scale DD)   Although relatively uncommon in a heterogeneous group of primary physical disorders—around 6%—patients scoring high on the emotional lability scale are an especially troublesome population psychiatrically, approaching clinical features akin to the symptoms of what has been called the *borderline personality*. These patients experience intense endogenous moods and exhibit recurring periods of dejection and apathy which are often interspersed with episodes of anger, anxiety, or euphoria. They are typified by a dysregulation in affect which is often accompanied by repetitive suicidal thoughts or self-mutilating behaviors. These tendencies may be seen in endorsed responses to items such as: " I am a very emotional person" and "My feelings toward my relatives often swing back and forth from love to hate."

Guardedness (Scale EE)   Another realm of management difficulty is found in medical patients who display mistrust and an edgy defensiveness against those they see as hostile and deceptive. Some exhibit irritability and suspiciousness, and often provoke annoyance, if not exasperation, on the part of healthcare providers. This is a problem for 10 to 15% of physically ill patients who may be identified by endorsed responses to items such as: "I watch out for people trying to cheat me" and "No one needs to know my business."

Step 5: Understand the Patient's Characteristic Coping Style

This group of scales is significant in that it provides a "context for understanding" many of the more transient features and behaviors that typify patients. These scales seek to identify the ever-present and pervasive ways in which patients habitually approach and deal with their life experiences. Styles

are patients' automatic ways of handling everyday hassles, as well as
how they approach major life stressors, such as unanticipated illnesses,
physical trauma, or significant surgical events. These characteristics
rarely stand alone as a single scale

> # DON'T FORGET
>
> The majority of patients scoring high
> on the coping style scales, 1–8B, are
> more likely to manifest a *normal* cop-
> ing style than a *personality disorder*.

but blend with other salient features, and the MBMD interpretive narrative is
fashioned from a configural profile of several scales. Generally, the highest two
or three scales form a configuration which then synthesizes the various coping
dimensions exhibited by the patient. As many of the characteristics measured
by these scales reflect normal interpersonal functioning, the majority of patients scoring high on the coping style scales are likely to manifest a *normal* coping style as opposed to a *personality disorder*.

Introversive (Scale 1)   High scorers on the Introversive scale (Scale 1) are rather
colorless and emotionally flat, tending to be quiet and restrained in speech.
They are often unconcerned about their problems. Typically, they are lacking
in energy and just plod along through life in a dull way. They usually are vague
and difficult to pin down concerning symptoms and may be passive with regard to taking care of their physical state. Physicians should give clear directions and not expect these patients to take the initiative in following a
treatment plan. Simple concrete steps delivered via a structured treatment plan
will be most helpful in patients scoring highest on this Coping scale. Typically
endorsed items on this scale include: "I have found very few things in life to be
pleasurable" and "I really don't understand human feelings like others do."

Inhibited (Scale 2A)   High scorers on the Inhibited scale (Scale 2A) tend to be
fearful of others and are often shy and ill at ease. The physician must be careful how he or she phrases comments as these patients are highly anxious and
easily hurt. Because they are distrustful of what others may do to them, the
physician will have to devote extra effort to establishing rapport. These patients have low opinions of themselves and fear others will take advantage of
them. Thus, they may keep their problems to themselves yet want understanding and attention. With a sympathetic attitude, physicians should be able
to gain their cooperation. Employing patience and a sympathetic approach is
likely to work best in gaining this type of patient's trust and subsequent adherence to required treatment regimens. Items frequently endorsed by those scor-

ing high on this scale are: "I wish other people were more accepting of me" and "I've always felt that most people think poorly of me."

Dejected (Scale 2B)   High scorers on the Dejected scale (Scale 2B) are inclined to be persistently and characteristically disheartened persons, who are unable to experience the pleasures or joys of life. Notably glum and pessimistic, they are easily disposed to "give up" trying to work through their emotional or physical problems. Their disconsolate and somewhat hopeless orientation will call for greater effort than usual by healthcare staff in helping these patients to care for themselves in a constructive manner. Typical items endorsed by high scorers include: "I feel guilty most of the time" and "My life has always gone from bad to worse."

Cooperative (Scale 3)   High scorers on the Cooperative scale (Scale 3) tend to be good-natured, gentle and generous with others. They are likely to be eager to attach themselves to a supportive physician and will tend to follow advice closely. These patients rarely take the initiative in treatment, but will expect to be told exactly what to do. They tend to deny their own needs and are inclined to deny the existence of real problems. Thus, the physician will have to probe carefully and ask questions explicitly. A sense of security is derived for these patients from specific and clear-cut directives. These patients often become very dependent and may resist when suggestions are made for referral to other doctors or clinics. Providing them with too many treatment alternatives may be contraindicated in that it will increase their anxiety. They may prefer to be told the "best" alternate for their specific circumstance. Among their most frequently endorsed responses are: "I almost always put other people's needs above my own" and "I worry a lot that the people I depend on will leave me."

Sociable (Scale 4)   High scorers on the Sociable scale (Scale 4) tend to be outgoing, talkative, and charming. However, these patients are rather changeable in their likes and dislikes. They may appear to be very cooperative with the physician in following the treatment plan, but this alliance and cooperation is often short-lived. These patients are often more concerned with a superficial appearance of being pleasant and attractive than with solving their presenting problems. They tend to be more vocal than other patients in reporting symptoms, and will usually acquiesce to whatever their medical team recommends while they are in the office or hospital. However, they are frequently inconsistent in following a treatment plan and will not be conscientious in keeping follow-up appointments. Responses endorsed by these patients include: "I am a dramatic kind of person" and "I think I'm a very sociable and outgoing person."

Confident (Scale 5)   High scorers on the Confident scale (Scale 5) act in a self-assured and confident manner. However, they have a great fear of bodily injury and will thus be motivated to follow any treatment plan that will ensure their well-being. They expect to be given special treatment and will tend to take advantage of everybody on staff. Although the physician may find this abrasive, it is important that he or she manage these patients fairly and explain the course of treatment fully. If these patients are impressed with the critical importance of following the medical regimen, they will do so carefully. Although these patients are typically demanding, the extra time and energy demanded of healthcare personnel is likely to result in increased compliance on the part of the patient. Typical item responses for this group include: "I have always had a talent for being successful" and "Many people respect and envy me."

Nonconforming (Scale 6A)   High scorers on the Nonconforming scale (Scale 6A) tend to be somewhat unconventional, if not arbitrary and occasionally inconsiderate in their manner. They are skeptical of the motives of others and have a tendency at times to act insensitively and impulsively. Owing to these less than attractive inclinations, these persons should be dealt with firmly and directly, assuring them that healthcare staff is there to assist them in solving their physical problems in a professional manner. Estimates are that only about 5% of medical patients are characterized by this nonconforming style of coping. Typical items responded to affirmatively by these patients include: "I usually do what I want without worrying about how it affects others" and "It's okay to take advantage of the gray areas in the law."

Forceful (Scale 6B)   High scorers on the Forceful scale (Scale 6B) tend to be domineering, tough-minded and are often hostile and angry. The healthcare team should be careful not to show feelings of intimidation, or allow themselves to be provoked by these patients. A straightforward approach in which the physician "pulls no punches" and makes no apologies is best in increasing chances for patient adherence. Given their tendency to distrust others, these patients may not follow the planned treatment program, instead doing whatever they want. These patients react to frightening situations with anger and hostility. When feeling uncertain of their bearings, high scorers instinctively respond with challenge. In dealing with these patients, the physician needs to maintain a fine balance between being either overly authoritative or overly indecisive. Items endorsed frequently by these persons include: "I'll stop anyone who tries to boss me around" and "In this world you either push or get shoved."

Respectful (Scale 7)   High scorers on the Respectful scale (Scale 7) are likely to be responsible, conforming, and cooperative. They hold their feelings inside and will try to impress members of the healthcare team as being well controlled, serious-minded, and responsible. These patients usually take medications carefully and follow therapeutic recommendations closely. There is a strong tendency, however, to cover up symptoms; and many may have resisted sharing their problems. Most do not like to be seen in the patient role since it signifies a weakness and inefficiency on their part. Nevertheless, they usually will be compliant and behave like an "ideal patient." Typical responses endorsed on the MBMD include: "It's good to have a routine for doing things in order to avoid mistakes" and "I like to follow instructions and do what others expect of me."

Oppositional (Scale 8A)   High scorers on the Oppositional scale (Scale 8A) contrast with those high on scale 7; they are often unpredictable and difficult. Many may be erratic in following a treatment plan—overmedicating or undermedicating without advising the attending physician or nurse. These patients often seem displeased and dissatisfied with their physical and psychological state. At times, they will complain about their treatment, but this may quickly switch to expressions of regret and contrition. Mood changes often occur for no obvious reason. Rapport may be easy on some days but difficult on others. Typical responses endorsed include: "When people are bossy, I usually do the opposite of what they want" and "I get very annoyed when others put pressure on me."

Denigrated (Scale 8B)   High scorers on the Denigrated scale (Scale 8B) are persons who habitually focus on the most troublesome aspects of their lives, behaving as if they deserve to suffer the "slings and arrows" of their misfortunes. They may assert that they deserve the infirmities and ailments they experience, actively and repetitively recalling troubles and afflictions of the past. Among responses typifying these patients are: "I am my own worst enemy" and "I often set myself up to fail."

Step 6: Evaluate Stress Moderators

The vastly expanding research and clinical literature in health psychology and behavioral medicine of the past two or three decades has provided the profession with a growing body of evidence and insight into factors which may either exacerbate or weaken the biologic status and course of various medical disorders. It is these psychosocial modulators of disease condition and progression that are identified through the scales that comprise this section.

Scores lower than BR 35 are indicative of lower than average levels of concern regarding the construct measured by that scale, and constitute an asset in that realm, indicating a projected better than average management of an illness should one exist or occur. Scores falling between a BR of 35–74 are considered average and have neither positive nor negative consequences. Scale elevations in the "presence" range of BR 75–84 indicate marked difficulties for both the patient's health status and his or her capacity to manage disease. Score elevations over BR 85 signify that this is a major area of concern for the patient and will likely negatively impact health significantly.

Illness Apprehension versus Illness Acceptance (Scale A)   Concern about one's medical condition is an issue creating great anxiety for many patients. To be worried, perhaps excessively, about the presence of a medical illness is often a source of psychic aggravation in and of itself, an intensification of the stress generated when one becomes aware of the serious nature of a clinical disorder. Patients who score high on the Illness Apprehension scale (Scale A) suggest a degree of the "liability" called illness apprehension; on the other hand, patients who score low (below PS 35) display an unusual level of what is termed illness acceptance, that is, they possess a behavioral "asset" in that they appear self-possessed and rather imperturbable. Among the items indicative of excessive apprehension are: "My health seems to be failing faster than that of most people my age" and "I am afraid that I may suddenly die from an illness."

Functional Deficits versus Functional Competence (Scale B)   Restrictions upon earlier capabilities or limitations in the ability to carry out "activities of living" are identified in this scale. Anatomic adversities (injuries, surgery), the setbacks of disease (muscle or joint deterioration), and

DON'T FORGET

In Stress Moderators, Treatment Prognostics, and Management Guide scales, PS scores below 35 indicate an "asset" in that realm and are interpretable.

aging infirmities are common afflictions that may increasingly limit the functional capacity of patients. High scorers on the Functional Deficits scale (Scale B) exhibit significant reductions in their capacity to carry out life functions as well as they once could. Conversely, patients who score below PS 35 display sturdy levels of physical competence and functional ability. Those who exhibit problematic deficits are likely to endorse items such as: "I can't take care of myself as well as I used to" and "The quality of my life has gotten much worse because of my illness."

Pain Sensitivity versus Pain Tolerance (Scale C)   The experience of pain is undoubtedly among the most distressing of symptoms for a significant number of medical patients and is a primary clinical component among those with chronic or repetitive backaches, headaches, cancer, or joint and arthritic diseases. That pain colors a patient's overall outlook and increases the difficulty of management is well-known and evidenced by the growing number of pain clinics and rehabilitation programs in the nation. High scorers on the Pain Sensitivity scale (Scale C) are judged as possessing an appreciable degree of pain that may be related to their medical condition. Patients scoring below PS 35 do not evidence any sign of pain-related discomfort associated with their illnesses. Items utilized to identify pain sensitive patients include: "I would do anything to stop the pain I feel" and "Pain makes it very difficult for me to work now."

Social Isolation versus Social Support (Scale D)   Levels of familial and friendship support, both real and perceived, appear to be a significant moderator of the impact of life stressors. High scorers on the Social Isolation Scale (Scale D) are more prone to suffer physical and psychological ailments than those who score low, are more likely to have a poor adjustment to hospitalization, and may not seek medical assistance until their illness becomes extremely discomforting. On the other hand, such patients may seek hospitalization as a way to gain attention and emotional support. Patients scoring below a PS 35 perceive high levels of familial support or support from friends and neighbors. Healthcare professionals should take advantage of this asset by helping the patient mobilize this resource for increasing the likelihood of adherence and follow-through. Those feeling isolated will be likely to respond true to the following items: "Most people won't care much if I were sick" and "There's little emotional support within my family."

Future Pessimism versus Future Optimism (Scale E)   This scale focuses on the patient's willingness to look forward to and plan for the future. This may tap the patient's response to his or her current medical difficulties rather than represent a lifelong tendency to view things pessimistically, such as gauged in the "Depression" and "Dejected" scales. High scorers on the Future Pessimism scale (Scale E) do not anticipate a productive life before them, often viewing their medical state as serious and potentially life-threatening. They may require considerable support from healthcare personnel. Patients who score below PS 35 are likely to view their life circumstances optimistically, an "asset" for long-term treatment efficacy. Those scoring at the pessimistic pole are prone to endorse items such as the following: "I think things will get much worse in the coming months" and "My future looks like it will be full of problems and pain."

Spiritual Absence versus Spiritual Faith (Scale F)   Belief in spiritual nourishment as a source of protection and care, usually associated with a strong religious faith, appears to be associated with enhanced survivability when faced with serious medical illnesses; whether or not this association is coincidental (i.e., a function of better health habits, or the benefits of marital stability) cannot yet be determined. Nevertheless, the association, causal or not, appears indisputable, albeit modest in magnitude. Patients who score low on this scale are more devout believers in a spiritual or religious support system and healthcare providers should make use of this asset in their treatment planning. Those lacking in spiritual support are likely to endorse items such as: "I am not a very spiritual person" and "I have no deep religious beliefs."

Step 7: Assess Treatment Prognostics

This section is designed to identify behavioral and attitudinal aspects of a patient's life that may complicate or enhance treatment efficacy, that is, things that patients are likely to do or think that will affect medical progress. Again, both low scores and high scores are interpretable.

Interventional Fragility versus Interventional Resilience (Scale G)   High scorers on the Interventional Fragility scale (Scale G) experience considerable fears at the thought, and especially the presence and sight, of medical implements or instruments that they associate with pain and illness. They have an intense negative anticipation and reaction to medical procedures and appear vigilant and hyperanxious about these procedures. Patients who score below PS 35 handle the prospects of medical/surgical interventions remarkably well, appearing to be especially stoic and imperturbable. Items useful in identifying a problematic or potentially fragile response include: "I get extremely anxious when I don't know what the doctors are going to do to me" and "If I have to go through another medical procedure, I think I'll just go crazy."

Medication Abuse versus Medication Conscientiousness (Scale H)   Most patients adhere to whatever treatment regimen or prescriptive medication has been recommended. Patients who score high on the Medication Abuse scale (Scale H) give evidence of ineffective or abusive inclinations, that is, failure to comply to the prescribed regimen, or misuse of prescriptive drugs. On the other hand, patients who score below PS 35 are extremely diligent, if not rigid, about adhering to physician recommendations. Items helpful in identifying problematic inclinations include: "Sometimes I take medications that were prescribed for others in the chance that they'll help me" and "If I don't get relief from medicine, I may increase the dosage on my own."

Information Discomfort versus Information Receptivity (Scale I)   Some patients desire to know as much as they can in regard to their medical condition, wanting as many details as possible about their current state and their future prospects. Others wish to avoid this knowledge, even to the point of not wanting to know the name of their disorder, much less its character and prognosis. Patients who score high on the Information Discomfort Scale (Scale I) exhibit "information discomfort" and do not desire to hear news about their ailment, its progression, and potential treatment options. Patients who score below PS 35 on this scale are informationally receptive and wish to learn as much as they can about their condition. The "deniers" may be identified by their true response to an item such as "I'd rather not know the details of an illness I might have" and a negative response to an item such as, "I want my doctor to review with me the results of all my medical tests."

Utilization Excess versus Appropriate Utilization (Scale J)   In this day of managed care there is an increasing sensitivity to the problem of patients who may demand more services than are called for, in light of their legitimate medical needs. Although special medical services are often appropriate and fully justified, a circumstance that healthcare personnel must rigorously attend to in providing medical care, there are some patients who are unnecessarily intrusive and demanding of clinical staff, who insist on repeated attention from specialists, or who annoy or use up staff time unjustifiably. Patients who score high on the Utilization Excess scale (Scale J) exhibit this problematic habit. This scale has been empirically supported by the results of the staff rating gauge used in validation of the test (see the MBMD manual for a more thorough explanation). Those patients who score below PS 35 display a tendency toward underutilization, that is, requesting somewhat fewer services than may be justified. Items employed to assist in determining potential overutilizers include: "I feel particularly resentful when I am refused medical benefits I know I am entitled to" and "Very few people appreciate just how hard my life really is."

Problematic Compliance (Scale K)   A major issue for healthcare programs are patients who either inadvertently or intentionally resist following medical recommendations. In this scale we are looking beyond "medication abuse" as noted on Scale H. Included are disinclinations to follow home-care advice or nutritional instruction, to be reluctant to keep appointments or, alternately, to be on time for them, as well as exhibiting an apparent contempt for healthcare personnel. It is estimated that some 25–30% of all medical patients cannot be counted on to comply fully with the counsel and recommendations of their health providers. Conversely, about 30% of patients are judged appropriately compliant, and 20% appear to be unusually compliant. The noncompliant group is likely to respond *false* to items such as: "I make sure that I'm on time for all my doctor's appointments" and "I would change my lifestyle on my doctor's advice."

Step 8: Integrate with the Management Guide Scales

This final pair of gauges draws upon previously noted items and scales as a means of integrating and summarizing the major problematic areas of a patient. It should serve to highlight *adjustment issues*, that is, potential difficulties that may call for the services of attentive physicians, nurses, health psychologists, and other counseling and behavior medicine specialists. Approximately 30% of a diverse group of medical patients possess psychosocial handicaps that may benefit from special attention by these health professionals. Certain patient groups, such as heart transplant recipients, may be more needy in this regard than others, diabetics, for example.

There are certain types of patients, such as those tending to score high on the psychiatric indication scales, who are likely to benefit from the therapeutic intervention of clinically-oriented psychologists or psychiatrists; this latter group of about 25% of medical patients tend to achieve high scores on the Psych Referral scale.

STRENGTHS AND WEAKNESSES OF THE MBMD

In the early 1990s, Millon and his colleagues began to give thought to a possible revision of the MBHI. Other Millon inventories (MACI and MCMI-III) had recently undergone revision in an effort to more closely reflect changes in the DSM-IV. When the Millon group initially began their work on the revision of the MBHI, their objective was to enhance the instrument by adding scales to identify psychiatric syndromes, and to rework the test sections on management and treatment recommendations by drawing upon more recent developments in the fields of health psychology and behavioral medicine. It soon became clear, due to both the limited breadth of the MBHI normative population and the absence of assessment sections on psychiatric illness, lifestyle behaviors, and moderator variables in physical illness, that a simple revision of the MBHI would not be possible. The MBMD is considered a replacement inventory for the MBHI in that it is based on a reconceptualization of those factors that impact a patient's progression through the course of illness. In designing the MBMD, much consideration was given to addressing the known weaknesses of the MBHI. Furthermore, a series of formal surveys and discussions with a wide ranging field of healthcare professionals were undertaken at several points during the development of the MBMD, which were useful in pointing to issues and guiding the Millon group in directions not encompassed by the MBHI.

Referring back to Chapter 2 in the first edition of this text, which covers the MBHI (Millon & Meagher, 1999), the following weaknesses of the instrument were noted:

1. Information on Moderator Variables Lacking
2. Psychiatric Diagnoses and Processes
3. Recently Derived Personality/Coping Styles Not Represented
4. Lifestyle Behaviors Not Addressed
5. Insufficient Data on Treatment Prognostics

In constructing the MBMD, specific efforts were made to resolve these long standing deficit areas of the MBHI. These specific areas will be reviewed first in evaluating the strengths and weaknesses of the MBMD.

1. *Inclusion of Moderator Variables.* There has been a vast increase in the literature and in professional knowledge on the importance of modera-

tor variables (i.e., those factors that can impact both directly and indirectly on the course and treatment of an illness). Two of the MBMD scale domains, Negative Health Habits and Stress Moderators, reflect the ways in which problematic behaviors and specific attitudes and belief systems can affect an illness process. The Negative Health Habits Domain assesses lifestyle behaviors that can exacerbate a medical condition or undermine treatment efforts. Included are those behaviors that have been shown to have the strongest contribution to the widest variety of health outcomes. The MBMD Stress Moderator scales are designed to identify patients' intrapersonal and extrapersonal characteristics that can directly affect both psychiatric and personality features on a number of medical outcomes. It should be noted that, unlike the MBHI, which focuses primarily on pathological features, the MBMD scales allow for the evaluation of each patient's assets and behavioral strengths as well.

2. *Inclusion of Psychiatric Assessment Scales.* Many psychologists who have used the MBHI over the last two decades have found that their referral sources (often physicians) were primarily interested in whether psychiatric conditions might complicate the course and treatment of a patient's physical illness. Surgical or medical treatment efforts can be seriously undermined by even moderate psychiatric difficulties. After a thorough review of the literature, the Millon group selected five areas of psychiatric disturbance widely believed to have the most potential impact on medical treatment. Included in the Psychiatric Indications section of the MBMD are the following scales: Anxiety-Tension, Depression, Cognitive Dysfunction, Emotional Lability, and Guardedness. Each scale proves to be highly correlated with other single-focus instruments as well as independent clinical staff ratings. These scales are not intended to provide precise DSM-IV Axis I diagnoses but rather provide supportive evidence for such a diagnosis.

3. *Coping/Personality Style Scales Expanded and Renamed.* Since the publication of the MBHI in the late 1970s, an enormous amount of scholarly research and literature has been generated in the field of personality/coping style. The eight coping styles found in the MBHI derive from Millon's (1969) original model of personality. Since the publication of the MBHI, Millon's theory has expanded to more fully elaborate the means by which people transact with their environment. The MBMD incorpo-

rates these changes with the inclusion of three additional coping style domains (Dejected-2B, Forceful-6B and Denigrated-8B). These coping styles correspond to more recent revisions made in the personality disorders section of the DSM-IV (Depressive, Sadistic, and Masochistic). Furthermore, as the MBMD was normed on and is designed for use with medical populations, the coping style narratives are specifically focused on how patients interact with healthcare personnel and behave throughout the diagnostic and treatment process. The names given to the MBMD Coping Style scales are designed to reflect how a patient is likely to come across to healthcare personnel, thereby stressing the interpersonal quality of each personality construct. It should be noted that the majority of patients scoring high on the coping style scales are more likely to manifest a normal coping style rather than that of an overt personality disorder.

4. *Lifestyle Behaviors Addressed in the MBMD.* Many patient lifestyle factors are known to significantly impact facets of illness and the treatment of such illness. Many of these behaviors can compromise health whereas others can provide health-promoting effects. They are important to the overall prognosis in that they provide healthcare personnel with a more comprehensive picture in treatment planning. These lifestyle factors may also be predictive of the amount of time required for convalescence, rehabilitation, and recovery. The Negative Health habits section of the MBMD includes those lifestyle behaviors shown to have the strongest contribution to the widest variety of health outcomes (Alcohol, Drug, Eating, Caffeine, Inactivity, and Smoking). Scores in this section of the instrument are categorized as follows: *unlikely problem area, possible problem area,* and *likely problem area.* These indicators, although brief, correspond very highly with the judgment of knowledgeable clinicians.

5. *Validated Treatment Prognostics Scales.* The MBHI utilized several empirically derived scales that were designed to evaluate the probability that a disease process may be impacted upon by somatic factors. Underlying the construction of these scales was the assumption that some patients are more likely to experience unusual problems in their illness as a result of emotional difficulties. Although this assumption proved to be sound, the empirically-derived MBHI scales designed to measure these areas were not, and they were not carried over to the MBMD. Since the MBHI

was published, many changes have taken place in the medical field and in health care delivery. The era of managed care demands increased account-ability, and places an emphasis on lowered healthcare costs and risk reduc-tion. In order for the healthcare field to better accomplish this, information is needed that can address a patient's probable compliance, potential med-ication abuse, and overall management risk. Toward this objective, the MBMD group developed a Staff Rating Scale which was filled out by healthcare personnel (PhDs, RNs and MDs) who were well acquainted with the patients they rated. The same patients were also given the Research Form of the MBMD. Analysis of these data resulted in the construction of five validated scales to identify behavioral and attitudinal features of a pa-tient's life that can complicate (or enhance) treatment efficacy.

While attempting to shore up areas in which the MBHI was deficient, developers of the MBMD successfully maintained and transferred many of the positive features found in the MBHI. (See Rapid Reference 2.3 for the strengths of the MBMD.)

Strengths

1. *Developed from a Comprehensive Clinical Theory.* The MBMD as a whole, and the basic Coping Styles scales in particular, are anchored to Theodore Millon's theory of personality (e.g., Millon, 1969, 1990; Millon & Davis, 1996). Assessment instruments are both more understandable and useful if linked to a comprehensive behavioral theory or tied to empirical validation data in their construction. However, most assess-ment devices were developed independently of any health-oriented theory and have not relied on systematic develop-mental research. Both of these im-portant elements have driven construction of the MBMD. The Coping Style section of the MBMD can be considered the heart of the instrument. It can be seen as the first filter through

> **DON'T FORGET**
>
> The MBMD is a multidomain instru-ment. The Coping Styles scales, 1–8B, serve as a backdrop or filter for the other scale domains. Much infor-mation can be gleaned about a pa-tient from the individual scales, but the richness of this test is in its syn-thesis of coping patterns.

which the interpretative report passes and in turn, colorizes and blends with the other sections of the report. Increased knowledge about a patient's particular coping style allows the healthcare team to better monitor and plan treatment, thereby influencing a wide range of medical outcomes.

2. *Constructed for Medical Populations.* At present, few psychological instruments currently in use with medical populations are distinctively suitable for assessment and management of the physically ill. The MBMD was developed specifically for physically ill patients and the medical decision-making issues that healthcare personnel must make in the treatment of these patients. In meeting this objective, the normative range of both MBMD patient populations and clinical settings expanded appreciably beyond those encompassed in the MBHI. Patients with HIV/AIDS, organ transplants, cardiological problems, diabetes, neurological disorders, rehabilitative issues, cancer, and gastrointestinal disorders were included in the normative population of the MBMD. Only medically ill persons were used in the normative group, as "normals" are not an appropriate comparison group. Item selection for the MBMD was made on the basis of data that compared groups of general medical populations thereby optimizing the discrimination efficiency of the scales. Many other instruments currently in use with medical populations (e.g., MMPI-2, CPI, PRE, POI, EPPS) were designed with either psychiatric or normal adult populations in mind. If medical norms are available, in most cases they were developed as a secondary feature of these instruments.

3. *Clinically Relevant for Medical Populations.* When the MBHI was first published the field of health psychology was in its early stages. The concept of a mind-body connection was just gathering momentum in the Western world. Very few psychologists worked in primarily medical settings. The boundaries between psychologist, psychiatrists, and other physicians were firm. Bridges began to be built between the staunch towers of psychology and medicine—forged by the work of health psychologists in the early 1980s. Today, psychologists and physicians work in tandem to better care for their patients by optimizing treatment plans and identifying potential problem areas while keeping the costs of health care down. The underlying principal of the MBMD recognizes that psy-

chological or behavioral issues play a part in the course and treatment of almost every medical condition. In the development of the instrument, extensive thought was given to optimizing its clinical utility for psychologists and physicians alike. The MBMD's lofty objective was to cover every factor or element supported by current research which has been proven to impact medical outcomes. Furthermore, the Millon group set out to package the results of this assessment in such a way so as to be easily accessible to both physicians and psychologists. Specific statements are made in the interpretive report regarding many facets of a patient's adjustment to an illness, such as compliance with a specific regimen, likelihood of medication abuse, perceived support from family or friends, problematic health behaviors, and many others. This is in sharp contrast to many other instruments that utilize broad abstractions of people in general, or relate broad psychiatric dimensions that are difficult to extrapolate to physically ill populations.

4. *Brevity, Yet a Wide Scope of Coverage.* Given the nature of the respondents taking the MBMD, it was essential that the test be brief and easy to administer. The number of items was kept small enough to encourage the use of the instrument in all types of diagnostic and treatment settings. Although the number of items in the final form of the instrument was kept low, the breadth of the test allows for the assessment of a wide variety of behaviors and attitudes considered relevant to medical patients. This broad scope of both medically and psychologically significant scales included in a single form enables it to economically tap almost every area of potential concern to mental and healthcare personnel. The final form, with 165 items, is much shorter than combinations of other instruments designed to assess the many facets tapped by the MBMD. The MBMD is geared to a sixth grade reading level and takes between 20–25 minutes to complete, thereby lessening the potential of patient resistance or fatigue.

5. *Focus on Areas of Patient Concern and Strengths.* As noted earlier, a consistent criticism of the MBHI has been the apparent overrepresentation of pathological features. This has been addressed by the developers of the MBMD in several ways. As noted earlier, the scale names of the Coping Styles section of the MBMD were chosen to reflect the interpersonal qualities a patient exhibits as they transact through a medical system, rather than a pathological style as was the case with the MBHI. All of the

chosen scale names are designed to be more user-friendly and less clinical in nature. Furthermore, all scales allow for the expression of strengths and speak to how these can be utilized by both the healthcare team and the patient to assist in treatment. This focus on the patient's assets as well as liabilities help healthcare personnel build on a patient's strengths when considering treatment avenues. Lastly, because the MBMD was normed on, and is intended for use with medical populations, the interpretation of the elevation in the Coping Style scale scores has changed. Higher elevations in these scales do not necessarily indicate the presence of a personality disorder, but instead recognize the predominance of a "normal" coping style.

6. *Allows for Cross-Domain Synthesis.* The MBMD interpretive report is somewhat shorter than the MBHI report, but addresses more areas of clinical importance. The major advance of the MBMD report is the use of cross-domain synthesis. The MBMD synthesizes the characteristics tapped by each domain's scales. Although the Coping Styles section is not the first domain group listed on the profile sheet, this section provides the context for interpreting the meaning and character of the other

≡Rapid Reference 2.3

Strengths of the MBMD

- Inclusion of Moderator Variables
- Inclusion of Psychiatric Assessment Scales
- Coping/Personality Style Scales Expanded and Renamed
- Lifestyle Behaviors Addressed
- Validated Treatment Prognostic Scales
- Developed from a Comprehensive Clinical Theory
- Constructed for Medical Populations
- Clinically Relevant for Medical Populations
- Brevity, Yet a Wide Scope of Coverage
- Focus on Areas of Patient Concern and Strengths
- Allows for Cross-Domain Synthesis
- Computer-Generated Printout Provides Either Profile or Narrative Report

domain groups. The Coping Style scales serve as the backdrop to the other domains; they are best viewed through the filter of an individual's coping style. The interpretive sequence of the MBMD should begin with the basic Coping Styles, followed by the Psychiatric Indications, then Stress Moderators, and the Management Guides domain. For instance, elevations in the Scale BB (Depression) in the Psychiatric Indications scales will take very different forms, in both experience and expression, dependent on a patient's given coping style. Depression can differ on the basis of who the patient is and what makes him/her depressed. The cross-synthesis approach allows for these differences. Similarly, Coping Style scale elevations provides the framework for colorizing the Stress Moderator scales, allowing the examiner to assign differential psychological meanings to the scales of this domain. In the same way, information about psychiatric status is used to color the interpretation of a patient's high point scales in the Treatment Prognostics domain which, in turn, impacts interpretation of the Management Guides scales. Highlighting the interrelationships that exist between coping style, psychiatric status, psychological stressors and treatment issues allows the healthcare professional to view a patient in such a way as to lend depth, relatedness, and individuality to their assessment.

7. *Computer-Generated Printout Provides Either Profile or Narrative Report.* As was the case with the MBHI, two computer-generated MBMD reports are available: a profile report and an interpretive report. Both reports address the patient's psychiatric status, coping style, stress moderators, treatment prognostics, management guide, and response patterns as well as negative health habits. Reports are organized in a format familiar to health psychologists and draw on information from scale score elevations and profile configurations. Included in the Interpretive Report is a one-page Healthcare Provider Summary that contains essential assessment findings and treatment recommendations. It is a tear-off sheet (which can be inserted into a patient's chart) that can be read quickly by referring physicians, nurses, and other adjunct medical personnel who may not have a clinical background or do not have the time to read the more comprehensive report designed for use by health and clinical psychologists. These narrative reports serve to synthesize all the information from the individual scale elevations as well as from each

domain area. Consequently, they greatly reduce the amount of time required to formulate highly individualized reports and analyses, but they insure a level of uniformity among interpretations inasmuch as they have been based on both established theory and empirical research.

Often the weaknesses of a psychological instrument do not become apparent until it has been in use for some time. As the MBMD was published in the Spring of 2001, little time has passed to allow for sufficient feedback from users of the Inventory. At present, known weaknesses in the MBMD—the MBHI replacement instrument—are limited.

Weaknesses

1. *Research Data is Lacking.* Again, due to the very recent publication of the MBMD, very little research has been completed that utilizes this instrument. Extensive studies using the MBMD were employed in the initial validation of the instrument. Confirmatory studies are being carried out currently but have not yet reached the stage of data analysis. It will likely be several years before sufficient data has been collected that gauge the veracity of the Treatment Prognostic scales.

2. *Prevalence Scores May Need to Be Adjusted.* At present, gender is the only parameter for which normative distinctions have been made. Over time, a number of moderator variables may justify normative prevalence rate changes (ethnicity, age, socioeconomic class). However, evidential data will need to show whether these changes will improve the current prevalence score transformations and interpretive inferences now in use. Pertinent research will require repeated subsets of patient samples chosen along very specific criteria. These patient groups will need to be assessed by disease entity as well as geographic locale. If variations become apparent, prevalent scores based on local Base Rates (BRs) should be developed.

3. *Not Appropriate for All Respondents.* There are several circumstances where it would not be appropriate to administer the MBMD to a patient. As previously mentioned, it is inappropriate for use with children, adolescents, those of advanced gerontological age, or those unable to read at a sixth grade level. Recall that several medically related conditions, not

uncommonly found in the presence of illness, can alter and perhaps invalidate the results of the test. These would include severe anxiety, confused state, drug intoxication, severe discomfort, and sedation. Lastly, patients who differ greatly in some capacity from the normative population may deviate sufficiently as to render the test results invalid. These might include patients suffering from a rare disease entity

> # CAUTION
> ....
> The MBMD is inappropriate for use with patients:
> - Younger than 18 and older than 85
> - Who can not read at a sixth grade level
> - Who exhibit medical conditions that can alter test results
> - Who significantly deviate from the normative population in disease entity or cultural similarity

not tapped by the normative population or who may be suffering with multiple illnesses. Other patients to whom this may pertain would be those individuals living in other countries with cultures dissimilar to that of the United States, or patients who have recently immigrated to this country.

CLINICAL APPLICATIONS OF THE TEST

There are well known factors associated with both the maintenance and deterioration of health. Similarly, there are numerous factors that influence the patient/clinician relationship that can impact the quality of health care provided. The identification and subsequent application of these factors to medical practice via routine screening and assessment could greatly contain the accelerating cost of health care in this country.

Routine psychological screening and assessment is a low-cost strategy that has a remarkably high payoff potential. The relative cost of mental health assessment as compared with the amount of effort and resources spent on technologically advanced biomedical examinations is glaringly disproportionate. It could be used in helping to understand the factors that influence patients' decisions to utilize early health screening devices. Improved evaluative techniques could assist in the identification of underserved populations who could benefit from augmented services, or determining if one medical procedure or another is best suited to a patient. This type of screening could also provide data for predicting and monitoring the outcome of differing medical procedures. Similarly, recovery and rehabilitative rates could be tracked as well as the quality of life for patients.

The MBMD was developed to help clinicians enhance their understanding of their patients as individuals, and facilitate the specific steps required to develop effective treatment and management plans tailored to these individuals. Detailed information about a patient's psychiatric status, coping style, pertinent stress moderators, negative health habits, and treatment considerations is critically important in maintaining health, optimizing the effects of, and recovery from, treatment, and reducing the overall healthcare costs for that patient. Scores and interpretive printouts associated with the MBMD are not intended for direct use by patients themselves; however, such information can be discreetly shared with patients by appropriate healthcare personnel who may interpret the findings within a broader context of professional advice and treatment.

The potential settings where the MBMD may be employed are numerous and will be addressed shortly. Because it is easy to administer, score, and interpret, the MBMD can be easily integrated into the routine evaluative procedures of outpatient clinics, hospitals, rehabilitation programs, and general medical practices. Regardless of specific site, however, the MBMD may have its greatest utility as a standard screening tool. In primary care settings, it can be used to screen patients who are at heightened risk for certain medical diseases as well as for triaging patients for psychosocial services and medical intervention.

When used as a screening instrument, the MBMD can either be administered just prior to a first visit or be incorporated as part of the initial visit. The MBMD can also be used as a means of collecting ongoing patient information, thereby providing data for treatment evaluation or for managed care-review purposes. Data gathering on a routine basis can provide objective evidence of treatment efficacy and patient improvement—two areas often essential in research studies, and

CAUTION

Neither the profile sheet nor the narrative generated by the computer-scored MBMD should be shared directly with the patient. Results of the test should be shared within a broader context of advice and treatment.

serves to demonstrate the financial benefits of various behavioral and cognitive interventions.

Furthermore, the MBMD can save time and increase treatment effectiveness by:

- flagging patients with significant psychiatric problems and recommending specific interventions.
- identifying patients who may not comply with medication regimens so that more explicit information can be given to them.
- helping to structure post-treatment plans and self-care responsibilities in the context of the patient's social network.
- detailing personal and external assets that can be used during treatment or recovery to facilitate adjustment to physical limitations or lifestyle changes.

At the institutional level, the MBMD is helpful for developing treatment plans, especially in managed care setting, in that it includes details concerning specific issues that can affect treatment choices, medical use patterns, and related costs of care. It may help decrease costs by reducing assessment and interpretation time, expediting triage, and decreasing complications after major procedures. In addition, the clear link between the interpretive report's narrative explanations and scores makes it easier for clinicians to justify using the DSM-IV code, *psychological factor(s) affecting medical condition(s),* for treatment and improving consequent financial reimbursement. Lastly, the MBMD may help to increase the effectiveness of lifestyle change programs by identifying patients who are most likely to benefit and identifying support persons who are likely to enhance patients' adherence to such programs.

There are several clinical and institutional settings where the MBMD may be usefully employed. Because the relative costs of the MBMD are nominal when compared to those of routine laboratory expenditure, there are numerous medical sites where it could be consistently administered. In the following paragraphs, several of these medical and affiliated settings will be noted.

GENERAL PRACTICE OF INTERNAL MEDICINE

The MBMD, unlike its predecessor the MBHI, was designed for use by health psychologists as well as physicians (see Rapid Reference 2.4). As such, the format of the report is designed for use by both. In recent decades, the wall between mind and body has crumbled with the recognition of the many subtle influences each holds over the other. Physicians, once resistant to the perceived infringement of psychology into so-called medical territory, now welcome input on psychosocial factors that can benefit patient treatment while reducing costs. It is now recognized that over 30% and perhaps as much as 50% of patient clientele evidence distinct, somatic, emotional or behavioral origins to their complaints. In using the MBMD, physicians have available a quick, thorough, and easily understandable assessment of key factors that can affect treatment course, as well as suggestions on how to manage problematic areas.

MAJOR DIAGNOSTIC CENTERS

As is the practice at several notable centers (e.g., The Mayo Clinic), instruments such as the MBMD are often routinely administered to all patients as a means of screening for psychiatric or somatic complications. However, in contrast to an instrument such as the MMPI-2, the MBMD is specifically designed to assess a broad range of illness moderators including those with psychiatric elements. Given that these centers do not typically deal with routine illness but rather diseases that have life-altering consequences, the MBMD can help guide the healthcare team in identifying emotionally vulnerable patients, relaying difficult news, and optimizing treatment plans for each patient's individual circumstances.

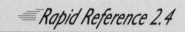

Rapid Reference 2.4

Utilizing the MBMD

The MBMD can be appropriately utilized in the following settings:

- General Practice of Internal Medicine
- Specialty Medical Clinics
- Major Diagnostic Centers
- Rehabilitation Centers
- Managed Care Facilities
- Hospital Surgical Units
- Public Health and Prevention Centers
- Research Facilities

Specialty Medical Clinics

Because somatic, emotional, and behavioral factors very often play a special role in the disease entities under systematic study, the MBMD may be especially useful as a routinely administered instrument in settings such as pain clinics, diabetes units, HIV clinics, asthma and allergy clinics, burn units, sexual dysfunction clinics, obesity programs, and any of a number of additional special programs in which emotional components contribute to the syndrome under treatment. Information about a patient's coping style can be important for predicting several salient medical issues in these settings. These issues include: psychological adjustment to the burdens of chronic illness; the ability to make lifestyle changes required by certain diseases; appointment keeping and other indices of medical adherence, and responses to rehabilitation efforts.

Hospital Surgical Units

The psychological status, personality, and emotional resilience of patients are increasingly recognized as playing an important role in survival during major forms of surgery (e.g., recovery from coronary bypass surgery). Moreover, there is increasing recognition of the close relationship between the pre-surgical psychological adjustment of the patient and his or her psychiatric state during recovery. The Treatment Prognostic summative index scale, Adjustment Difficulties, taps dimensions related to management risk. These domain areas cover issues of compliance, experiential pain, symptom fabrication, medical complications, and overutilization associated with excess expenditure. Consequently, the MBMD can be extremely helpful in the evaluation of patients who are candidates for major surgery so as to assess their coping capacities for dealing with the stress of surgery itself and the adaptive recovery process that follows.

Rehabilitation Centers

The MBMD is especially well suited for appraising a variety of patient responses that may influence the course of an established disease or impede the effectiveness of medical or surgical treatment programs. Among the special settings within which such assessments may be of value are hemodialysis centers as well as transplant services, programs of chemotherapy designed to maximize cancer recovery or stabilize HIV progression, post-myocardial infarction coronary retraining programs, spinal rehabilitation, and so on.

Managed Care Facilities

Although touched upon in an earlier section, the potential use of the MBMD in managed care settings should be emphasized. In recent years the managed care system has been the target of sharp criticism. The underlying philosophy that ignited the managed care movement was sound but the practices were soon seen to be flawed. This system hoped to reduce the spiraling costs of health care, cap unnecessary tests and procedures, focus on healthy checkups, educate clients in preventive care, and ultimately monitor and manage the care given to patients. Since the inception of managed care organizations in the early 1990s, premiums have steadily risen, needed treatments are often denied, and neither physicians nor patients are content with the level of service given and received. The treatment a patient receives today is dependent on his or her insurance status and plan, physician incentives, and the variable reimbursement of differing procedures. As a consequence to the many changes in today's world of medicine, healthcare providers need to be better informed regarding a patient's problematic compliance, potential medication abuse, and overall management risk.

The MBMD addresses these concerns and many others pertinent to issues that often arise in managed care. The MBMD looks at matters that affect treatment choice, medical use patterns, and related costs of care. It can save time and money in the managed care setting by limiting the evaluative phase and concomitant costs, identifying patients with significant psychiatric or compliance issues, guiding the healthcare team in the most efficacious treatment routes, and distinguishing those patients most likely to benefit from specific interventions. Furthermore, the narratives of the MBMD interpretive report (particularly the physician-geared tear-off sheet) are accessible to all healthcare personnel because they are formatted in a user-friendly fashion.

Public Health and Preventive Programs

Among the major new programs that have developed in recent years for the purpose of reducing such highly prevalent diseases as hypertension and diabetes, there is a growing concern that noncompliance to medical regimens is creating a significant loss of effectiveness. Predicting which patients are likely to adhere to specific pharmacological regimens or comply with systematic programs designed to extinguish the smoking habit or change nutritional and eating behaviors has become a major concern in the field of preventive medicine. The MBMD is a tool that can be helpful in assessing these resistant-type behaviors.

Research Facilities

As stated previously, to date research with the MBMD has been limited, due to its recent publication. Yet the research that has been done—mostly for the sake of scale validation—has been impressive, and suggests that the instrument has future utility as a research tool in many varied settings. Studies completed at this writing include the instrument's utility in predicting health related behavior such as adherence to complex antiviral regimens in HIV-infected individuals, as well as the validity of the Treatment Prognostic scales as related to clinician observations in a variety of patients with various diseases. The MBHI, predecessor to the MBMD, has proven efficacious in many research settings. It has been shown that the MBHI provided salient information about a patient's coping style and attitudes toward health that were important for predicting:

- help-seeking behavior after the onset of myocardial infarction symptoms.
- the promotion of early neoplastic changes in women at risk for cervical cancer.
- initial psychological reactions to news of a life-threatening illness.
- psychological adjustments to the burdens of a chronic disease.
- the ability to make the lifestyle changes required by certain disease entities.
- adherence to appointments and other commitments of health care.
- responses to rehabilitative efforts.
- decision making concerning treatment choices.
- the progression of physical disease and related immunological declines.
- recovery and survival after major procedures such as heart transplant.

Impressive as the MBHI has been as a research instrument, the MBMD requires much research, in a variety of settings, to test its mettle. Future work with a variety of patient populations and hypotheses will be useful in ascertaining that the MBMD is equal to, and hopefully better than, the MBHI. The MBMD authors feel that future research should employ prospective designs to test the viability of the MBMD for predicting:

- psychological responses to major medical interventions.
- the incidence of success and complications following medical procedures.
- costs of different medical treatments in focused randomized trials.
- the likelihood of medication abuse in various populations.
- the self-care abilities of patients with newly diagnosed chronic disease.
- use and expenditures in large healthcare systems.

Given the brevity, comprehensiveness, and ease of administration, the MBMD should lend itself well to research with many different patient populations, clinical settings, and investigative hypotheses.

ILLUSTRATIVE CASE REPORT

A. L. is a married, 53-year-old, African-American man, who was diagnosed with diabetes eight years ago. He holds an Associate degree in accounting and has been employed for the last twelve years as an accounts payable clerk for his local municipal government. A. L. reports that he is "the most reliable and competent" employee in his department and he expresses great dissatisfaction with the way his bosses manage the other employees. He is very proud of his efficiency on the job and has few other interests in his life. He has been married to his wife for 30 years and their two children are grown and living in the area, although he reports that they have "never really been close."

When A. L. was diagnosed with diabetes, he immediately made the prescribed lifestyle changes. He quit his pack-a-day smoking habit, lost twenty-five pounds, and has been carefully following the food plan his dietician designed. He keeps a meticulous food log that he e-mails to the dietician weekly. Despite his efforts and his daily injections of insulin, his glucose levels are not well controlled, and A. L. has begun developing neuropathy of the lower extremeties. Both of his parents died from complications of diabetes when they were in their early 60s and his older brother has developed retinopathy as well as cardiac complications as a result of diabetes. A. L. is very anxious about his future and fears that he will end up in a wheelchair. He has already noticed certain difficulties at work in that he is not able to stand for hours a day and run back and forth between offices as he used to do. This greatly distresses A. L. as he defines his life by his work performance. He reports spending a great deal of time worrying that he will be reprimanded at work or even fired because of his diminishing capabilities.

A. L. was administered the MBMD by his diabetologist who was concerned that he was anxious and losing hope of ever gaining control over his disease. Both the Profile Sheet and Narrative Report are presented in Figure 2.1.

MBMD™

Millon™ Behavioral Medicine Diagnostic

Interpretive Report

with Healthcare Provider Summary

Theodore Millon, PhD, DSc,

Michael Antoni, PhD, & Carrie Millon, PhD

ID Number 164

Male

Age 53

African-American

Married

Associate Degree

11/20/2001

Figure 2.1

Medical Problem(s): Diabetes   **Valid Profile**
Code: AA // - ** 7 * // - ** E̲ B * - + // - ** I * H̲ K̲ + //

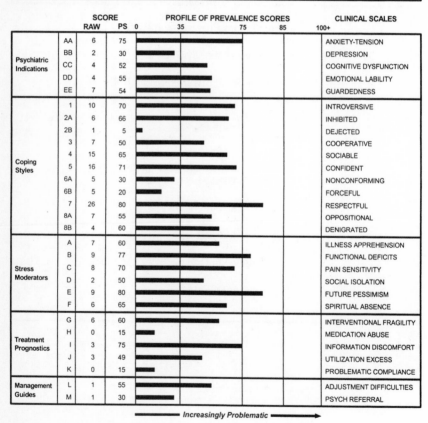

Figure 2.1 (continued)

This report is based on the assumption that the MBMD assessment was completed by a person who is undergoing professional medical evaluation or treatment. MBMD data and analyses do not provide physical diagnoses. Rather, the instrument supplements such diagnoses by identifying and appraising the potential role of psychiatric and psychosomatic factors in a patient's disease and treatment. The statements in this report are derived from cumulative research data and theory. As such, they must be considered probabilistic inferences rather than definitive judgments and should be evaluated in that light by clinicians. The statements contained in the report are of a personal nature and are for confidential professional use only. They should be handled with great discretion and should not be shown to patients or their relatives.

> **Interpretive Considerations** - This section identifies noteworthy response patterns and indicates negative health habits that may be affecting the patient's medical condition.

Unless this patient is a well-functioning adult with modest life stressors, his responses suggest either a need for social approval or naivete about psychological matters. Although scoring adjustments that correct for these tendencies were probably successful in retaining the validity of the interpretation, this interpretive report should be read with these characteristics in mind.

> **Psychiatric Indications** - This section identifies current psychiatric symptoms or disorders that should be a focus of clinical attention. These symptoms or disorders may affect the patient's response to healthcare treatment and his ability to adjust to or recover from his medical condition.

This man is currently reporting relatively high levels of anxiety. This elevation may be due to a recent medical diagnosis or an upcoming medical procedure and is likely to be temporary. Characteristically, this patient is agreeable, confident, and adaptive to changing circumstances, but he is reluctant to focus on serious personal problems. With help from the healthcare team, he is likely to take adaptive measures to reduce his anxiety.

> **Coping Styles** - This section characterizes the patient's coping style and/or defenses. These include "normal" parallels of DSM-IV, Axis II personality styles that may influence the patient's response to healthcare treatment and his ability to adjust to or recover from his condition.

This patient is likely to exhibit a sociable and self-assured manner, behaving in most situations in a confident and calm fashion. Although he is inclined to be self-centered, he is capable of expressing and dealing well with a variety of emotions. His self-confidence, however, may result in a tendency to reject the knowledge and opinions of peers and authorities. Similarly, he may be inclined to deny his shortcomings and be indifferent to the role they play in creating difficulties with others. His unruffled composure and nonchalant air of calm equanimity may quickly give way under conditions of social rebuff, the press of excess demands, or the discovery of a severe illness. He may become morose and irritable. He will be disinclined to admit his deficiencies or to follow advice and medical recommendations unless he considers them worthwhile.

Figure 2.1 (continued)

This patient may not take a potential major illness seriously. His unassailable attitude ("It can't happen to me") will lead him to take troubling news at first with calmness, if not with disdain or incredulity. At a deeper level, however, he may be quite anxious or fearful. Once the potential consequences of indifference to his health become apparent, he is likely to start taking his illness seriously. Although he will be motivated at that point to follow a prescribed regimen, he will look for ways to relieve discomfort quickly so he can regain his illusion of invulnerability.

With healthcare personnel, this patient is generally friendly and cooperative, even though he is prone to act at times in a self-assured or high-handed manner. He may try to reverse roles with doctors, acting like a know-it-all who is able to diagnose and recommend treatment. This behavior allows him to feel that he is the master of his fate and has some measure of control. Issues of cooperation may arise with him because of his tendency to resist facing reality. He does not take well to following the rules and expectations of others. He may think that following a prescribed regimen is beneath him. As a consequence, he may abandon his commitment to a medication program when his symptoms begin to abate. Despite acting superior and overly self-confident, he is not usually difficult to deal with in the short term. However, a firm stance should be taken if he seems indifferent about a serious illness. Giving him a role in his care will draw on his desire for self-mastery and thereby enhance the likelihood of compliance.

Stress Moderators - This section notes the patient's personal and social assets and liabilities and how they may affect his ability to manage the stressors and burdens of his medical condition and treatment.

Liabilities: Functional Deficits, Future Pessimism
Assets: None Reported

This individual reports some difficulty handling daily routines and responsibilities since the onset of his illness. It is unlikely that he has been sensitized to the role of being sick, and he is likely to feel more healthy and alert than other patients dealing with similar conditions. His energy can be used to engage him in maximal self-care responsibilities and a greater involvement in activities of daily living.

This patient may become pessimistic about his future if his medical condition worsens or if he experiences unanticipated physical limitations. If he displays any such emotional difficulties following these changes, they will take the form of impatience about returning to his independent lifestyle. Encouraging him to gather information about the latest technological breakthroughs and treatment options for his condition (using the hospital library or Internet resources) may help him preserve his sense of independence and control over his current situation.

Treatment Prognostics - This section, which is based on the patient's psychological profile, forecasts his response to medical procedures and medication.

Liabilities: Information Discomfort
Assets: Medication Conscientiousness, Optimal Compliance

Figure 2.1 (continued)

This patient's ability to receive or communicate detailed medical information may be affected by his psychological profile. His tendency to be anxious and worried in anticipation of or just after receiving important medical information (e.g., test results) may unduly elevate his arousal levels. This could result in extreme tension and concern or possibly a panic attack. Healthcare providers should be prepared to respond to these signs of anxiety if they occur. Anticipatory anxiety symptoms may be treatable by relaxation-based interventions. Mild post-treatment anxiety reactions may respond to similar techniques. More extreme and persistent reactions may require pharmacologic intervention. Given his risk for being overwhelmed by serious medical information, the physician should advise him to bring a supportive friend or family member with him at these times and should present medical information in a manageable and less detailed form.

There is little likelihood that this patient will use prescribed medication in an inappropriate or dangerous manner. He is likely to be cooperative and responsive to healthcare recommendations. This may help facilitate his adjustment to treatment and may be used by the healthcare team to improve health outcomes.

Management Guide - This section provides recommendations for the general management of this patient based on his psychological profile.

This patient's profile does not suggest extreme difficulty with regard to recovery or elevated expenditures. However, the following issues may be important to monitor or consider when developing a treatment regimen:

- This patient's ability to withstand stressful medical procedures (e.g., major surgery) may be compromised by his tendency to display anxiety and excessive worry. This may affect him to such a degree before or after the procedure that he may have trouble normalizing his arousal level.

- This patient's ability to receive or communicate detailed medical information may be affected by his psychological profile. His tendency to be anxious and worried in anticipation of or just after receiving important medical information (e.g., test results) may unduly elevate his arousal level. This could result in extreme tension and concern or possibly a panic attack.

This patient's tendency to become very tense and anxious before or after medical procedures may cause him to have trouble managing his arousal level. He may be a good candidate for supportive psychosocial group intervention or individual counseling to ameliorate these mental health problems. Such intervention may be a cost-effective way to optimize his quality of life and minimize the post-treatment adjustment and recovery period.

Noteworthy Responses - The patient's endorsement of the following item(s) is particularly worthy of follow-up by the healthcare team.

Figure 2.1 (continued)

Panic Susceptibility
Item # 1   I feel very tense when I think about the day's events.
Item # 28   I get very anxious when I think about my medical problems.

Disorientation
Item # 157   I now need to follow routines so that I don't get confused.

Medical Anxiety
Item # 3   I get extremely anxious when I don't know what the doctors are going to do to me.

ITEM RESPONSES

1: 1	2: 1	3: 1	4: 2	5: 2	6: 2	7: 1	8: 2	9: 2	10: 2
11: 2	12: 2	13: 1	14: 2	15: 1	16: 2	17: 1	18: 1	19: 2	20: 2
21: 1	22: 1	23: 1	24: 2	25: 2	26: 1	27: 2	28: 1	29: 2	30: 2
31: 2	32: 1	33: 1	34: 1	35: 1	36: 2	37: 1	38: 1	39: 2	40: 2
41: 2	42: 2	43: 1	44: 1	45: 2	46: 2	47: 1	48: 2	49: 2	50: 2
51: 2	52: 1	53: 2	54: 2	55: 2	56: 1	57: 1	58: 2	59: 2	60: 2
61: 2	62: 2	63: 2	64: 2	65: 2	66: 2	67: 1	68: 2	69: 2	70: 2
71: 1	72: 1	73: 1	74: 2	75: 2	76: 1	77: 1	78: 2	79: 2	80: 1
81: 1	82: 2	83: 2	84: 1	85: 2	86: 2	87: 1	88: 1	89: 1	90: 1
91: 2	92: 2	93: 2	94: 2	95: 2	96: 2	97: 1	98: 2	99: 1	100: 1
101: 1	102: 2	103: 2	104: 2	105: 2	106: 2	107: 2	108: 1	109: 2	110: 2
111: 2	112: 2	113: 2	114: 2	115: 2	116: 2	117: 2	118: 2	119: 2	120: 1
121: 2	122: 2	123: 2	124: 2	125: 2	126: 2	127: 2	128: 1	129: 2	130: 2
131: 2	132: 2	133: 2	134: 1	135: 2	136: 2	137: 2	138: 2	139: 2	140: 2
141: 2	142: 2	143: 1	144: 1	145: 2	146: 2	147: 2	148: 2	149: 2	150: 2
151: 2	152: 2	153: 2	154: 1	155: 2	156: 2	157: 1	158: 1	159: 2	160: 2
161: 2	162: 2	163: 1	164: 2	165: 2					

Figure 2.1 (continued)

Millon™ Behavioral Medicine Diagnostic—Healthcare Provider Summary

This patient is a 53-year-old African-American male who is married and has an associate degree. He reports that diabetes is the major problem for which he is seeking medical help.

Psychiatric Indications
This patient is currently reporting anxiety that may be due to a recent medical diagnosis or an upcoming medical procedure. His anxiety is likely to be time-limited in nature. With encouragement, this patient is likely to take adaptive measures to reduce his current anxiety level.

Coping Styles
This patient is generally confident and self-assured, typically behaving in a manner that elicits favorable attention and approval, especially from those with medical status or authority. It is important to him to conform to healthcare standards and to be judged well by healthcare personnel. To that end, he will go out of his way to exhibit responsible and efficient behavior.

Case Management Issues

Stress Moderators
● This patient may become pessimistic if his medical condition worsens. Encouraging him to gather information about the latest treatment options for his condition (from the hospital library or the Internet) will help to preserve his sense of independence.

● He reports some difficulty carrying on daily routines and responsibilities since the onset of his illness, but he probably feels more healthy and alert than other medical patients.

Treatment Prognostics
● This patient's ability to communicate regarding medical information may be affected by anxiety and worry. Medical discussions or test results may elevate his arousal level, resulting in extreme tension or possibly a panic attack.

● There is little likelihood that this patient will use prescribed medications in an inappropriate or dangerous manner.

● His scores indicate that he has other assets in this area. For further information, consult with the attending mental health professional.

Management Guide
Psychological factors are not likely to contribute to excessive medical complications and/or expenditures for this patient.

End of Report

Figure 2.1 (continued)

TEST YOURSELF

1. **When hand-scoring the MBMD, all steps should be repeated twice.** True or false?

2. **The MBMD**

    (a) is appropriate for use with either psychiatric or medical patients.

    (b) was first designed for psychiatric patients and later adapted for physically ill persons.

    (c) was developed for use with a physically ill population.

    (d) is appropriate for use with physically ill children.

3. **The MBMD provides medical diagnoses as well as psychosocial assessment of patients.** True or false?

4. **PS scores below 35 on the Coping Styles scales mean that a patient possesses an "asset" with regard to that type of coping?** True or false?

5. **Patients who score high on the Cooperative Scale are**

    (a) often erratic in following a treatment plan.

    (b) easily upset by physical ailments and expect to be given special treatment by healthcare providers.

    (c) overly sensitive to criticism by healthcare providers.

    (d) likely to attach themselves to healthcare professionals.

6. **It is valid to administer the MBMD in either group or individual settings.** True or false?

7. **Which of the following conditions will render the MBHI invalid?**

    (a) Seven or more items left blank

    (b) If the patient is 21 years of age or younger

    (c) Endorsement of one of the test's "validity" items

    (d) None of the above

8. **The MBMD is a revision of the MBHI.** True or false?

9. **Which of the following is a strength of the MBMD?**

    (a) It was developed from a comprehensive theory.

    (b) It can be scored either by computer or by hand.

    (c) It focuses on areas of patient concern and strengths.

    (d) a and c

10. Use of the MBMD is appropriate in which settings?

    (a) Managed care facilities, mental health clinics, and specialty clinics

    (b) Rehabilitative centers, hospital surgical units, and Internal Medicine practices

    (c) Research facilities and public health and prevention programs

    (d) All of the above

11. The MBMD uses which of the following in scale score presentation?

    (a) T-scores

    (b) Base Rate scores

    (c) Prevalence scores

    (d) Raw score

12. Low scores on the Stress Moderator scales indicate:

    (a) low levels of that moderator.

    (b) the presence of assets in areas tapped by these scales.

    (c) high levels of stress in areas tapped by these scales.

    (d) a and c

Answers: 1. True; 2. c; 3. False; 4. False; 5. d; 6. True; 7. d; 8. False; 9. d; 10. d; 11. c; 12. b

Three

ESSENTIALS OF MACI ASSESSMENT

Robert Tringone

INTRODUCTION

The Millon Adolescent Clinical Inventory (MACI; Millon, 1993) is a 160-item, self-report inventory that was developed as a major revision of the Millon Adolescent Personality Inventory (MAPI; Millon, Green, & Meagher, 1982). It has 31 scales that are divided into four sections: (a) one Validity Scale and three Modifying Indices, (b) 12 Personality Patterns Scales, (c) eight Expressed Concerns Scales, and (d) seven Clinical Syndromes Scales. As with the other Millon inventories, the MACI has a distinct advantage over other objective personality inventories since its personality patterns constructs are theoretically derived from Millon's personality theory (1969, 1981, 1990). Additionally, the MACI has a unique configuration where separate scales assess more acute and transient clinical syndromes associated with Axis I disorders and more stable personality patterns associated with Axis II disorders (McCann, 1997, 1999; Millon & Davis, 1993). The MACI has been totally normed with an adolescent clinical population from diverse clinical settings where its appropriate uses include developing diagnostic impressions and formulating treatment plans (Millon, 1993). Rapid Reference 3.1 provides basic information on the MACI and its publisher; Rapid Reference 3.2 illustrates how the MACI scales evolved from the MAPI scales.

> ### DON'T FORGET
> ....
> **Purposes and Uses of the MACI**
>
> - Provides adolescent clinical assessment in mental health settings with clients who are 13 to 19 years old
> - Assesses Expressed Concerns and Clinical Syndromes in the context of Personality Patterns
> - Assists in reaching diagnostic impressions and formulating treatment plans

≡ *Rapid Reference 3.1*

Millon Adolescent Clinical Inventory (MACI)

Author: Theodore Millon, Ph.D.

Publication date: 1993

What the test measures: 12 basic personality styles, 8 common adolescent expressed concerns, and 7 clinical syndromes

Age range: 13–19 years

Administration time: 20–30 minutes

Qualifications of examiners: The manual recommends that "all individuals using the MACI should have at least a master's degree in a relevant field of mental health and should meet membership qualifications for their appropriate professional organization."

Publisher: National Computer Systems

P. O. Box 1416

Minneapolis, MN 55440

Phone: 800-627-7271

Fax: 800-632-9011

MICROTEST Q Assessment System Software Preview Package (MACI manual and answer sheets with test items to conduct three assessments and receive three Interpretive Reports using the MICROTEST Q assessment system software), $90 (2002 price).

Mail-In Scoring Service Preview Package (MACI manual and answer sheets with test items to conduct three assessments and receive three Interpretive Reports using the Mail-In Scoring Service), $90.

Prices vary according to test format (MICROTEST Q vs. Mail-In Scoring) and report format (Interpretive Report vs. Profile Report) with increasing discounts per test administration for larger orders.

Hand Scoring Starter Kit (MACI manual, hand-scoring user's guide, 10 test booklets, 50 answer sheets, 50 worksheets, 50 profile forms, and answer keys), $299.

≡Rapid Reference 3.2

A Comparison of MAPI and MACI Scales

MAPI Scales

Personality Scales

1. Introversive
2. Inhibited

3. Cooperative
4. Sociable
5. Confident
6. Forceful

7. Respectful
8. Sensitive

Expressed Concerns

A. Self-Concept
B. Personal Esteem
C. Body Comfort
D. Sexual Acceptance
E. Peer Security
F. Social Tolerance
G. Family Rapport
H. Academic Confidence

Behavioral Correlates

TT. Societal Conformity
SS. Impulse Control

UU. Scholastic Achievement
WW. Attendance Consistency

MACI Scales

Personality Patterns

1. Introversive
2A. Inhibited
2B. Doleful
3. Submissive
4. Dramatizing
5. Egotistic
6A. Unruly
6B. Forceful
7. Conforming
8A. Oppositional
8B. Self-Demeaning
9. Borderline Tendency

Expressed Concerns

A. Identity Diffusion
B. Self-Devaluation
C. Body Disapproval
D. Sexual Discomfort
E. Peer Insecurity
F. Social Insensitivity
G. Family Discord
H. Childhood Abuse

Clinical Syndromes

AA. Eating Dysfunctions
BB. Substance-Abuse Proneness
CC. Delinquent Predisposition
DD. Impulsive Propensity
EE. Anxious Feelings
FF. Depressive Affect
GG. Suicidal Tendency

HISTORY AND DEVELOPMENT

The origins of the MACI date back to 1974 when the Millon Adolescent Inventory (MAI) was developed. The MAI was the fore-runner to the MAPI, the more recognizable of the two inventories, since the latter was published and distributed by National Computer Systems (NCS) in 1982. The MAI and the MAPI shared the same item pool but differed in their normative samples. The MAPI had two forms, MAPI-C (Clinical) and MAPI-G (Guidance), which were designed for use in their respective mental health and school settings. Clinical precision and utility, however, were compromised to a degree in its clinical application. Over the years, clinicians struggled with this issue. As a result, the MACI was developed with a pure clinical reference group, and new scales were constructed to reflect changes in the clinical population. Furthermore, major developments had taken place within Millon's personality theory, which guided the introduction of the "new" Personality Patterns Scales.

> ### DON'T FORGET
>
> **Reasons for Developing the MACI**
>
> - Clinicians requested more clinically oriented scales.
> - Major revisions had been made within Millon's personality theory.
> - The test needed to be more consistent with developments in the DSM-IV.
> - The normative sample needed to be more representative of a clinical population.

Test Construction and Validation

All Millon theory-based instruments follow the same three-step construction and validation sequence proposed by Loevinger (1957). In the first stage, the theoretical-substantive stage, a large item pool was generated according to a specific theory that delineated a set of constructs. In the development of the MACI, 181 new items were generated that would target new MACI Clinical Syndromes Scales and revise the existing MAPI Personality Patterns and Expressed Concerns Scales. These new items were appended to the original 150 MAPI items. The result was the MACI Research Form, a 331-item form that would allow clinicians to receive Profile and Interpretive Reports from the original MAPI and provide the test developers with the data to create the MACI as well as compare the two instruments to each other.

In the second stage, the internal-structural stage, analyses were conducted to examine the relationships between the test's items and scales, as well as to determine how well the scales measured the constructs they were designed to represent. At this level the MACI went through two data collection phases. In the first phase, more than 700 adolescents provided self-reports on the MACI and other measures, while their clinicians provided diagnostic information and behavioral ratings. Item selections for the preliminary scales were made with these data. In the second phase, test responses were obtained from two cross validation samples, and through an iterative process the MACI scales were refined into their current form. Internal consistency reliability (alpha) coefficients computed for all MACI scales with the developmental sample ranged from .73 (Desirability and Body Disapproval scales) to .91 (Self-Devaluation scale). The alpha coefficients for the Personality Patterns Scales for this same group ranged from .74 (Submissive scale) to .90 (Self-Demeaning scale). Test-retest reliability coefficients (two MACI administrations 3 to 7 days apart) ranged from .57 (Peer Insecurity scale) to .92 (Borderline Tendency scale) with a median stability coefficient of .82. Although item-to-scale correlations are not available, scale-to-scale correlations are provided in the MACI manual (Millon, 1993). An analysis of these values revealed that interscale correlations follow theoretically driven hypotheses. The Unruly and Forceful scales, for example, have strong positive correlations with each other as well as with the Oppositional, Social Insensitivity, Family Discord, Substance-Abuse Proneness, Delinquent Predisposition, and Impulsive Propensity scales, while the Doleful and Self-Demeaning scales have strong positive correlations with each other as well as with the Identity Diffusion, Self-Devaluation, Depressive Affect, and Suicidal Tendency scales.

During the third validation stage, labeled the external-criterion stage, comparisons were made between the new instrument and existing instruments that purported to measure similar or related constructs. In this spirit, the MACI results were compared with the collateral test results. Strong correlations were found between many of the MACI scales and the Beck Depression Inventory (BDI) as well as the Beck Hopelessness Scale (BHS), which were consistent with current theory and research. The MACI Doleful, Oppositional, Self-Demeaning, Borderline Tendency, Identity Diffusion, Self-

Devaluation, Body Disapproval, Depressive Affect, and Suicidal Tendency scales all had correlations above .40 with the BDI and the BHS. The MACI Identity Diffusion, Self-Devaluation, Eating Dysfunctions, Depressive Affect, and Suicidal Tendency scales all had correlations above .40 with the Beck Anxiety Inventory (BAI); however, the Anxious Feelings scale did not have a significant correlation with the BAI. The MACI Eating Dysfunctions scale had strong correlations (> .40) with 8 of 11 Eating Disorder Inventory–2 (EDI-2) scales, while the MACI Substance-Abuse Proneness scale had a very strong correlation (.64) with the POSIT Substance Use or Abuse scale.

Base Rate Scores

Base rate (BR) scores are the preferred reporting statistic since they reflect the fact that clinical disorders have different prevalence rates in the population. This premise holds true with the MACI's adolescent normative sample. The prevalence rates for the MACI Personality Patterns, Expressed Concerns, and Clinical Syndromes were initially set according to the clinicians' judgments when they were asked to provide ratings regarding the two primary or most salient characteristics that best fit their clients. The percentage of times that a Personality Patterns, Expressed Concerns, and Clinical Syndromes Scale was judged to be the "most prominent" determined the prevalence rate for each scale, which is referred to as the *prominence* rate. In turn, the percentage of times that a scale was judged to be the "second most prominent" determined what is referred to as the *presence* rate for each scale. These prominence and presence rates have been set for each scale across four separate norm groups: (a) 13- to 15-year-old females, (b) 16- to 19-year-old females, (c) 13- to 15-year-old males, and (d) 16- to 19-year-old males. Minor adjustments were made to these empirically derived rates for two reasons: in order to incorporate results from epidemiological studies that provided more data regarding the prevalence rate of the characteristics and syndromes addressed by the MACI, and because clinicians weren't asked to make judgments about the Doleful personality pattern during the first phase of the MACI development project.

Base Rate Transformations and Anchor Points
BR scores extend from 0 to 115. For each scale, the frequency distribution of the raw scores, a cumulative score of weighted MACI items on each scale,

was generated. BR anchor points of 75 and 85 were assigned to each scale's cumulative raw score value that matched each scale's prominence and presence rates. For example, if the Inhibited personality pattern was determined to be the most prominent characteristic of 10% of a specific normative group (e.g., 13- to 15-year-old males), the raw score value that corresponded to the 90th percentile (100−10) would be converted into a BR score of 85. At the same time, if the presence rate was 5% for the Inhibited scale in the same normative group, then the raw score value that corresponded to the 85th percentile rank (100−10−5) would be converted into a BR score of 75. Linear transformations are then made across the entire BR score range. The only MACI BR points that are anchored at specific raw score values are 1, 75, 85, and 115.

Refinements in Base Rate Transformations

For the Borderline Tendency scale, the Expressed Concerns Scales, and the Clinical Syndromes Scales, the raw score to BR score transformations were assigned in the manner described above. Prior research, in particular with the MCMI-II, found that certain response styles, acute states, and personality styles have different effects on the overall profile (Millon, 1987). On the MACI, four BR score adjustments are made on selected scales to "correct" for these factors. Adjusted BR scores for the Borderline Tendency Scale, Expressed Concerns Scales, and Clinical Syndromes Scales were then recalculated and compared with the targeted prominence and presence rates for each scale. Multiple passes were made until these rates were as close as possible to the targeted rates on each scale for each norm group.

For Personality Patterns Scales 1 through 8B, another restriction was placed on the BR score transformations. Rank ordering of these scales was added so that the proportion of times that a particular scale attained the highest BR score in a profile match that scale's target prominence rate. Furthermore, the proportion of times that a particular scale attained the second highest BR score in a profile matched that scale's target presence rate. From our previous example, the Inhibited scale should be the highest Personality Patterns Scale in 10% of the 13- to 15-year-old male profiles and it should be the second highest Personality Patterns Scale in another 5% of the profiles.

Finally, BR scores have also been set for the three Modifying Indices. Again, borrowing from prior research with the MCMI-II (Millon, 1987), it was determined that a BR score of 85 or above would signify that the adolescent scored within the highest 10% of the normative sample on these scales, a BR score of 75 to 84 would signify scoring within the next 15% of the sample, a BR score of 35 to 74 would represent those who scored within the next 60%, and BR scores below 35 would represent those who scored within the lowest 15% of the sample on these scales.

Available Test Forms

The MACI is available in several formats. The most advanced and sophisticated administration and scoring method is through NCS Assessments' MICROTEST Q Assessment System Software. This software package allows the user access to the Millon inventories and more than 20 other NCS-supported instruments. With the MICROTEST Q system, adolescents can either take the MACI online or they can complete it in its booklet form. In the latter instance, the clinician can enter the adolescent's responses with the keyboard or it can be scanned. Full Interpretive Reports and Profile Reports can be generated within minutes. A second method is through mail-in scoring. The adolescent completes the MACI, the form is sent to NCS Assessments to be scored, and a report (clinicians must prepurchase full Interpretive or Profile Reports) is mailed back to the clinician. While this method is less expensive than the MICROTEST Q system, it usually takes 1 to 2 weeks to get the test results back. Hand scoring is also an available option. A Hand-Scoring User's Guide and hand-scoring templates help the clinician tally raw score points for all scales, make BR score transformations and adjustments, and plot the subsequent profile on a profile form. Although this is the least expensive method, it is time consuming and susceptible to scoring mistakes. The MACI forms and reports are available in English and Spanish versions. Additionally, English and Spanish audiocassettes are available for those adolescents whose reading is below a sixth grade level.

THEORETICAL FOUNDATION

Millon's personality theory is the underlying theory for the MACI. Initially proposed as a biosocial-learning theory (Millon, 1969, 1981), the theory itself has evolved and is now formulated as an evolutionary model (Millon,

1990; Millon & Davis, 1996). Both "levels," however, are grounded in the same three primary polarities—self-other, active-passive, and pleasure-pain. The biosocial-learning model describes these polarities and the personality constructs that are derived from their combinations and vicissitudes at clinical levels while the evolutionary model addresses similar processes at more abstract levels. For present purposes, the focus will be at the clinical level.

When personality patterns are perceived as learned strategies to secure positive reinforcement and minimize punishment, the self-other polarity represents the *source,* whether turning to one's self or the outside world, in order for people to enhance their lives and gain satisfaction or to avoid psychic pain and discomfort. The active-passive polarity represents the *behavior* employed to maximize rewards and minimize pain. Active personality types typically take the initiative and interact with their environment to achieve gratification and avoid distress, whereas passive types are often much more reserved and maintain a more accommodating stance vis-à-vis their environment. In this model, the pleasure-pain polarity represents the *nature* of the response elicited from others, which can be positive or negative (Millon, 1981).

The self-other and active-passive polarities can be combined in a five-by-two matrix to derive basic personality patterns. Persons with a dependent orientation have learned to seek reinforcement (e.g., attention and affection) from others. In contrast, those with an Independent orientation have learned to rely on themselves for primary reinforcement (e.g., self-esteem and security). Ambivalent styles are in conflict over whether to depend on themselves or others as well as whether to comply with or defy others' wishes or requests. Detached persons are unable to experience praise and rewards from either source and have deficiencies or imbalances with the third polarity, the pleasure-pain polarity. There is also a fifth orientation, the discordant orientation, where the experience of pleasure and pain is reversed. Figure 3.1 illustrates the personality patterns that are derived according to the theory. These names represent the personality patterns that the MACI assesses. These constructs have correspondences to many of the personality disorders recognized by the fourth edition of the *Diagnostic and Statistical Manual of Mental Disorders* (DSM-IV; American Psychiatric Association, 1994). Figure 3.2 illus-

Sources of Reinforcement					
Behavior Pattern	Independent (Self)	Dependent (Others)	Ambivalent (Conflicted)	Discordant (Reversal)	Detached (Neither Self nor Others)	Detached (Pain)
Active	Unruly	Dramatizing	Oppositional	Forceful	Inhibited	
Passive	Egotistic	Submissive	Conforming	Self-Demeaning	Introversive	Doleful

Figure 3.1 Derivation of Personality Patterns from Active-Passive and Self-Other Polarities

Sources of Reinforcement					
Behavior Pattern	Independent (Self)	Dependent (Others)	Ambivalent (Conflicted)	Discordant (Reversal)	Detached (Neither Self nor Others)	Detached (Pain)
Active	Unruly | Antisocial	Dramatizing | Histrionic	Oppositional | Negativistic	Forceful | Aggressive-Sadistic	Inhibited | Avoidant	
Passive	Egotistic | Narcissistic	Submissive | Dependent	Conforming | Obsessive-Compulsive	Self-Demeaning | Masochistic	Introversive | Schizoid	Doleful | Depressive

Figure 3.2 Continuum of Personality Patterns to Personality Disorders

trates these relationships. The MACI Personality Patterns Scales have less severe names and do not represent personality "disorders" per se since adolescent personality disturbances may be more attributable to their attempts to adjust to and negotiate the numerous internal and external influences, changes, and challenges they face. Adolescent personalities may still be developing and may be more malleable than adult personalities, which consist of more enduring traits. Rapid Reference 3.3 summarizes the personality patterns assessed by the MACI.

≡Rapid Reference 3.3

Summary of MACI Scales

Personality Patterns

1. Introversive (passive-detached pattern). These adolescents remain socially and emotionally distant from others. Typically quiet and listless, they live on the periphery and have few friends. They seem to lack the capacity to experience their emotions in any depth.

2A. Inhibited (active-detached pattern). These adolescents are shy and uncomfortable in social situations. They fear rejection and humiliation and will often "test" whether others can be trusted. They are prone to anxiety and depression and often have poor self-esteem.

2B. Doleful (passive-pain pattern). These adolescents exhibit persistent dejection, cheerlessness, and gloominess. Their moods are depressed, dysphoric, and morose. Their pessimistic outlook translates into low self-esteem and guilt regarding their perceived inadequacies.

3. Submissive (passive-dependent pattern). These adolescents are cooperative and noncompetitive and have strong needs for support and guidance. They avoid taking the initiative and often underestimate their abilities. Although they are very responsible, they are very unsure of themselves and prefers others to make decisions for them.

4. Dramatizing (active-dependent pattern). Charming and sociable, these adolescents are active solicitors of the attention and affection they need. They become bored with routines and form many attachments; however, these are often superficial in nature. Impulsive decision making and exaggerated emotions lead to problems.

5. Egotistic (passive-independent pattern). Often perceived as self-centered and conceited, these adolescents usually have positive self-esteem and view themselves as special. They have a strong need for admiration and may fantasize about future success and power. They often take others for granted and seldom concern themselves with others' problems.

6A. Unruly (active-independent pattern). These adolescents desire autonomy out of a distrust of others. They are typically restless and impulsive with low frustration tolerance and thrill-seeking tendencies. Their actions are often shortsighted with a disregard for social rules or the impact of their behavior on others.

6B. Forceful (active-discordant pattern). These adolescents are strong willed, tough-minded, hostile, and combative. They strive to dominate, humiliate, and abuse others. They lack empathy, compassion, or remorse. Typically, their relationships are marked by power and control issues.

7. Conforming (passive-ambivalent pattern). Responsible and conscientious, these adolescents tend to be serious-minded and emotionally constricted. They act respectfully toward peers and adults. They keep their emotions inside and their self-restraint conceals denied anger. They are rule conscious and try to do what is right.

8A. Oppositional (active-ambivalent pattern). Often feeling misunderstood and unappreciated, these adolescents tend to be discontented, sullen, and passive-aggressive. Their behaviors, thoughts, and feelings are erratic and unpredictable. They are generally confused about their emotions and tend to harbor considerable anger and resentment toward others.

8B. Self-Demeaning (passive-discordant pattern). These adolescents allow others to exploit and take advantage of them. They tend to have poor self-esteem and focus on their worst features. They appear to undermine others' efforts to help them and often sabotage their own chances for success.

9. Borderline Tendency. These adolescents have a more severe level of pathology. They exhibit erratic behavior, experience unstable moods, and have vacillating thoughts. Their sense of self and their identity is uncertain. Object constancy and self constancy are lacking. Repeated failures and inner conflicts can lead to self-destructive ideation and behaviors.

Expressed Concerns

A. Identity Diffusion. High scores on this scale suggest that the adolescent experiences confusion about who they are and what they want and makes megative comparisons between themselves and their peers.

B. Self-Devaluation. Adolescents who earn high scores on this scale tend to have low self-esteem and to be very dissatisfied with their self-image.

C. Body Disapproval. High scores on this scale suggest that the adolescent is dissatisfied with their physical appearance and development.

D. Sexual Discomfort. Adolescents who earn high scores on this scale tend to find sexual thoughts and feelings confusing and often unwelcome.

E. Peer Insecurity. Adolescents who earn high scores on this scale tend to have few friends and do not feel that they "fit in" with or are accepted by their peers.

F. Social Insensitivity. High scores on this scale suggest that the adolescent lacks empathy for others and shows limited concern for the welfare of others.

G. Family Discord. Adolescents who earn high scores on this scale report significant conflict and tension within their families, which can reflect either parental rejection or adolescent rebellion.

(continued)

H. Childhood Abuse. High scores on this scale suggest that the adolescent harbors shame, disgust, or resentment about having been subjected to verbal, physical, or sexual abuse.

Clinical Syndromes

AA. Eating Dysfunctions. High scores on this scale suggest that the adolescent exhibits distinct attitudes, behaviors, and self-perceptions that are consistent with an eating disorder.

BB. Substance Abuse Proneness. High endorsement rates on the items that make up this scale suggest a maladaptive pattern of alcohol or drug abuse as well as attitudes and behaviors often found with substance abusers.

CC. Delinquent Predisposition. Adolescents who earn high scores on this scale often have had run-ins with the law and have conduct-disordered attitudes and behavior patterns.

DD. Impulsive Propensity. High endorsement rates on the items that make up this scale suggest a strong inclination to act without thinking, to have poor frustration tolerance, and to seek immediate gratification.

EE. Anxious Feelings. High scores on this scale may be suggestive of an anxiety disorder, although timid and inhibited adolescents may also earn high scores.

FF. Depressive Affect. Adolescents who earn high scores on this scale often present symptoms suggestive of a depressive disorder with cognitive, mood, and self-image components.

GG. Suicidal Tendency. Adolescents who earn high scores on this scale admit having self-destructive thoughts and plans, which must be carefully monitored and addressed.

TEST ADMINISTRATION

As with most objective inventories, the administration of the MACI is straightforward. It is administered in a booklet format or computerized format, usually individually although the booklet form can be administered in a group setting. The MACI booklet has an advantage over lengthier objective inventories in that the test items and the response spaces are on a single form. The MACI typically requires 20 to 30 minutes to be completed. Before administering it, however, a few caveats must be noted.

Respondents

Respondents must be 13 to 19 years old and have at least a sixth grade reading level. They should be well rested and clear-minded. Severe agitation, drug intoxication, sedation, or a psychotic state can alter test results. If any of these conditions are present, it is advisable to administer the test at a later time.

Testing Environment

The MACI should be administered in a clinical setting that is quiet, has appropriate lighting, and is as free from distraction as possible. The test should not be mailed from or completed at home.

Materials

For the MACI booklet format, the only materials needed are a MACI booklet and a soft-lead pencil. For the MACI online format, clinicians must have the MICROTEST Q system loaded on an IBM or IBM-compatible 486 or higher PC with a Microsoft Windows environment.

Directions

On the MACI cover sheet, the adolescent will be asked to provide certain data. This will include filling out the test date, their birth date, their sex, and grade level. Additionally, they will be asked to identify up to two problems out of 15 choices that "trouble them the most." The clinician is given a section to record an identification number and a section for research purposes.

The test directions are stated in clear and simple terms. Although adolescents can read the directions

DON'T FORGET

Tips for Administering the MACI

- The respondent must be 13 to 19 years old.

- The respondent must have at least a sixth grade reading level.

- The MACI cover sheet must be completed, in particular, the test date, the respondent's birth date, and the respondent's sex.

- Request that the respondent answer all items so that none are omitted and none are double-marked.

CAUTION

Adolescents should be required to complete the MACI in the clinician's office. It should never be mailed to the adolescent or completed at home.

to themselves, it is usually advisable to take the time to read the instructions out loud to them. This will often enhance rapport and cooperation as well as give the clinician the opportunity to emphasize the importance of responding in an honest manner.

After the adolescent completes the test, the clinician should look over the items to make sure that all have been endorsed. If some have not been or if the adolescent endorsed "true" and "false" to the same item, he or she should be encouraged to make one choice. Double-marked items or excessive omissions (10 or more) could invalidate the test. Also, the clinician should check for stray markings and make sure the endorsements were completed with a soft-lead pencil so that the form can be scanned either in the office or at NCS Assessments. Finally, the adolescent's birth date, sex, and the test date must be completed. If not, the scoring program will not know which normative sample to use.

Testing Individuals With Special Needs

MACI administration procedures can be modified to accommodate adolescents with special needs. If an adolescent has poor vision or a reading disability, the MACI can be administered via audiocassette tapes while they record their responses on a separate page. Also, if an adolescent's primary language is Spanish, the Spanish version, either booklet or audiocassette form, can be administered.

SCORING THE MACI

The MACI can be scored with hand-scoring templates through a mail-in service with NCS Assessments or through the in-office MICROTEST Q Assessment System Software package. Whether the MACI is hand scored or computer scored, the clinician must be aware how the BR scores were obtained and whether any scoring adjustments were made. It is generally advised that the clinician gain some experience in hand scoring the MACI in order to understand how it is scored.

As an overview, the necessary materials to hand score the MACI include the scoring templates, a worksheet, and a profile form. Twenty-nine templates are provided (for all scales except the Reliability and Disclosure scales). These templates help tally the raw scores for each scale, which are entered onto the MACI worksheet. A complex formula, taking the raw scores from Scales 1 through 8B and multiplying them by different amounts for each scale, helps establish the raw score value for the Disclosure scale. According to the adolescent's sex and age, these raw scores are then transformed into BR scores, which are also recorded on the worksheet. After this conversion, four adjustments may be made to these initial BR scores according to the adolescent's response style, high-point Personality Patterns Scale, and BR scores on the Anxious Feelings and Depressive Affect scales. The worksheet outlines which scales are subject to which adjustments and facilitates making the proper BR adjustments. When all four adjustments have been completed, the clinician then plots the BR scores on the profile form. The specifics of the scoring procedures (i.e., raw score to BR transformations and subsequent BR adjustments) are described below.

Validity Issues

On the MACI, Scale VV (Reliability) consists of two peculiar items. The probability is very low that either of these items would be endorsed "true" unless the adolescent was not paying adequate attention to the items. If both items are endorsed "false," the test results are valid. If one item is endorsed "true," the tests results may be unreliable. If both items are endorsed "true," the results should be considered invalid. MACI profiles would also be considered invalid if the raw score value of the Disclosure scale (Scale X) is below 201 or above 589. Other invalid conditions can be avoided by ensuring that the adolescent's gender is recorded, that he or she is within the correct age range (13 to 19), and that he or she did not omit 10 or more items.

....

Raw Score Values

Raw score values or item weights (0, 1, 2, 3) have been assigned to all of the MACI items except the two Reliability items. Each is a "prototype" item (3 points) for a single "home" scale and, according to the item statistics conducted during the internal-structural validation phase, lesser weights (2 or 1 points) have been assigned for multiple scales on each item. The vast majority of the items load 3 points on a home scale when the item is endorsed "true." No personality pattern "prototype" items are endorsed in the "false" direction, but 13 Expressed Concerns and three Clinical Syndromes "prototype" items are endorsed in the "false" direction. In many instances, an item can add points to a scale if it is endorsed in the "true" direction and it can add points to other scales if it is endorsed in the "false" direction. There are no negative weights. The total raw score points for any scale are the cumulative number of item weights for all the items on that scale.

Raw Score to Base Rate Score Transformations

Raw score values are converted into BR scores according to the transformation tables for each of the four normative sample groups. Close inspection of the MACI Base Rate Transformation Tables (MACI manual, Appendix C) (Millon, 1993) indicates that a different raw score value for each group will translate into a particular BR score on each scale. For example, the raw score values that translate into a BR score of 85, the prominence anchor point, on the Inhibited scale are 36 points for the 13- to 15-year-old male group, 30 points for the 16- to 19-year-old male group, 46 points for the 13- to 15-year-old female group, and 35 points for the 16- to 19-year-old female group. When comparing the same-sex groups, the younger groups must earn more raw score points to reach the prominence level. When comparing the same-age groups between sexes, the female groups must earn more raw score points to reach the prominence level. Without knowing the specific prevalence rates for the Inhibited personality in each group, the raw score values might suggest that more adolescents within the younger groups possess more characteristics consistent with the Inhibited personality than the older groups; therefore, it requires more raw score points to reach the most prominent level. Additionally, for each age-group pair, it would appear that the females possess more Inhibited personality characteristics since they require more raw score points to reach the same level.

Base Rate Adjustments

After the raw score values have been converted to BR scores, one or more further adjustments may be made in order to "correct" for certain response styles, acute distress states, and personality styles that affect the overall profile. When the MACI is computer scored, a paragraph will state whether adjustments have been made; however, it will not tell the clinician the magnitude of the adjustments. Therefore, it is good practice to then go to the manual and calculate them. It is further recommended that the clinician make notations on the MACI profile indicating how the scales have been adjusted.

Disclosure Adjustment

Scale X (Disclosure) assesses how open and self-revealing or defensive and guarded an adolescent was in responding to the MACI items. Raw score values, derived through a weighted formula for Scales 1 through 8B, that fall between 275 and 400 do not lead to adjustments. On the other hand, low raw scores (below 275) will lead to increases in the BR scores for Personality Patterns Scales 1 through 9 whereas high raw scores (above 400) will lead to decreases on the same scales. The adjustments can be dramatic (up to 25 points) as the Disclosure scale raw scores approach invalid levels.

Anxiety-Depression Adjustment

Some MACI scales can be distorted if the adolescent took the test while in an acute distress state. In these instances, it is probable that elevations will be found on the Anxious Feelings or Depressive Affect scales. Since it has been found that the Inhibited, Doleful, Self-Demeaning, and Borderline Tendency scales are the most affected by psychic turmoil, these scales are adjusted downward if either of the Anxious Feelings or Depressive Affect BR scores are above 85.

Desirability-Debasement Adjustment

The basic response styles captured by the Desirability and Debasement scales may distort MACI results if adolescents attempt to exaggerate how

≡Rapid Reference 3.4

MACI Base Rate Score Adjustments

Adjustment	Situation	Correction
Disclosure	High score (raw score > 400)	Reduces Scales 1–9
	Low score (raw score < 275)	Increases Scales 1–9
Anxiety-Depression	High scores (BR ≥ 85) on Scale EE (Anxious Feelings) or Scale FF (Depressive Affect)	Reduces 2A, 2B, 8B, and 9
Desirability-Debasement	If Scale Y > Scale Z (4 BR points or more)	Increases Expressed Concerns Scales and AA, EE, FF, and GG
	If Scale Z > Scale Y (4 BR points or more)	Decrease Expressed Concerns Scales and AA, EE, FF, and GG
Denial-Complaint	If Scales 4, 5, or 7 are highest Personality Patterns Scale (BR score)	Increases A, B, G, EE, FF, and GG
	If Scales 2A, 2B, or 8B are highest personality pattern scale (BR score)	Decreases A, B, G, EE, FF, and GG

self-confident, socially well adjusted, and morally sound they may be or how troubled and distressed they may be. It is the relative positioning of the Desirability (Scale Y) and Debasement (Scale Z) scales' BR scores that determines whether an adjustment will be made to all of the Expressed Concerns Scales as well as the Eating Dysfunctions, Anxious Feelings, Depressive Affect, and Suicidal Tendency scales. If the adolescent's BR score for Scale Y is 4 or more points higher than the BR score for Scale Z, then the BR scores for the scales just listed will be increased. On the other hand, if the BR score for Scale Z is 4 or more points higher than the BR score for Scale Y, then the BR scores for the same scales will be lowered. The more discrepant the BR scores for Scales Y and Z, the greater the adjustment to these other scales.

Denial-Complaint Adjustment

Certain personality patterns tend to deny psychological problems. If an adolescent's highest Personality Patterns BR score is on the Dramatizing, Egotistic, or Conforming scales, then the BR scores for Identity Diffusion, Self-Devaluation, Family Discord, Anxious Feelings, Depressive Affect, and Suicidal Tendency are increased by 4 BR points. In contrast, other personality patterns tend to exaggerate their problems and weaknesses. If the highest Personality Patterns BR score is on the Inhibited, Doleful, or Self-Demeaning scales, then the same Expressed Concerns and Clinical Syndromes Scales just mentioned are decreased by 4 BR points.

> **DON'T FORGET**
>
> If the clinician receives a computer-generated MACI report that indicates adjustments were made to the profile, it is good practice to calculate the adjustments and make notations on the MACI profile to assess how the scales have been adjusted.

HOW TO INTERPRET THE MACI

Interpretation of the MACI requires that the clinician have familiarity with and working knowledge of several assessment areas. All personality tests, for that matter, all psychological tests, have strengths and weaknesses, assets and liabilities that the clinician must be aware of in order to interpret and utilize the results to a positive end. With the MACI, it is recommended that the clinician be well versed in Millon's personality theory (Millon, 1969, 1981, 1990; Millon & Davis, 1996) since the constructs measured by the Personality Patterns Scales are formulated within that model. Additionally, the test's psychometric properties, especially its theoretically anticipated and empirically derived item overlap and scale intercorrelations as well as the use of BR scores, should be understood. With this prerequisite background knowledge about the instrument, the clinician should then obtain information about the adolescent taking the MACI. Key data would include the adolescent's sex and age (since this determines which normative sample is needed to derive the BR scores) as well as their presenting problems and the purpose for the evaluation.

Step-by-Step Procedures for Test Interpretation

There are numerous steps involved in interpreting the MACI. (For a summary of these steps, see Table 3.1.) The test itself has 31 scales that are divided into four sections. When presented with a MACI profile, it is good practice, as a preliminary step, to visually scan the four sections and make "first time through" associations to it.

Step 1: Assess Test Reliability and Validity

The first true step in the interpretive process of the MACI is to check the reliability and validity of the profile and to assess whether any test-taking distortions occurred. This involves checking the Reliability scale and comparing the Modifying Indices to one another.

Step 2: Gauge Disturbance Level

The second step is to gauge the level of disturbance. This can be determined in various ways and can include, at a general level, summing the number of scales that are elevated (BR of 85 or above); at a more specific level, noting which scales are elevated at or beyond this level; and giving special attention to the Borderline Tendency scale and its BR score.

Step 3: Assess Personality Patterns

Assessing the basic Personality Patterns Scales is the next step. Single-scale elevations suggest a more prototypal clinical presentation related to that particular scale; however, 2-point elevations are not equal to the prototypal presentations of the two separate scales. Instead, the combination of the scales is much more than each alone. For example, a "spike" Scale 4 presentation will be different from Scales 4 to 6A and Scales 4 to 8A presentations, and both will be intensified if the Borderline Tendency scale is elevated.

Step 4: Assess Expressed Concerns

Starting with the Modifying Indices, then analyzing the Personality Patterns Scales, the clinician next encounters the Expressed Concerns section, which assesses the adolescent's perceptions of their progress in key areas of their lives. Many of these scales help assess whether adolescents attribute their troubles to an issue within themselves or to something outside them.

Table 3.1   MACI Interpretive Steps

1. Assess test reliability and validity.

2. Gauge disturbance level.

3. Assess personality patterns.

4. Assess expressed concerns.

5. Assess clinical syndromes.

6. Integrate findings with additional data.

Step 5: Assess Clinical Syndrome

The fifth step involves detecting the presence of specific problems within the Clinical Syndromes section. These scales correspond to several DSM-IV Axis I disorders. Elevations on particular scales may indicate the need for specific consultations (e.g., psychiatric evaluations) or a referral to a specialized treatment program (e.g., eating disorders or substance-abuse programs).

Step 6: Integrate Findings With Additional Data

One of the MACI's distinct advantages is that it assesses Axis I and Axis II symptomatology, and its results can be integrated into a more comprehensive clinical picture. For example, an adolescent with a high score (BR of 85 or above) on the Depressive Affect scale with a basic Personality Patterns profile that reveals elevations on Scales 2A, 2B, and 8B will have a very different presentation, probable cause of onset, and clinical course than an adolescent with a similar Depressive Affect BR score whose basic Personality Patterns profile has elevations on the 6A, 6B, and 8A scales. After reviewing the scale elevations, it is further recommended that the clinician read through all of the MACI items. Although some scales may not have reached prominence or presence

CAUTION

MACI Profile and Interpretive Reports should not be shown to adolescents and their families. The reports are written in clinical and pathological terms rather than toward the adolescent's strengths.

levels, important items for a particular scale (e.g., Childhood Abuse) may have been endorsed. Additionally, there are factor analytically derived content scales for each Personality Patterns Scale, which illustrate various dimensions within a single scale and can lead to further refined interpretations. At the present time, these content scales are not provided in the Interpretive or Profile Reports; therefore, the clinician must hand score them.

Modifying Indices and Base Rate Score Adjustments

The MACI has four scales that assess response style and test-taking attitudes. These scales are Reliability (Scale VV), Disclosure (Scale X), Desirability (Scale Y), and Debasement (Scale Z). Their relative elevations, both in comparison to the normative group and to one another, indicate whether the adolescents were open and forthcoming in their self-assessment, whether they may have underreported and had a tendency to minimize their troubles, or whether they may have exaggerated their current distress and had a tendency to magnify their troubles.

Reliability

The Reliability scale (Scale VV) consists of two items (114: "I have not seen a car in the last 10 years" and 126: "I flew across the Atlantic 30 times last year"), which are quite peculiar. A clinician sitting with an adolescent taking the MACI will often know when they have encountered these items because there will be a chuckle or a spontaneous reading of the item out loud. Nevertheless, although the scale was devised to detect random responding, it could also be indicative of a negative attitude toward taking the test, insufficient attention to the item content, poor reading skills, or mental confusion. The MCMI-III Reliability scale now comprises three items, the same two items on the MACI and one other. Bagby, Gillis, and Rogers (1991) found that when a cutoff of one item is employed, this scale can identify over 95% of all random response sets. As a result, if an adolescent endorses one of those items on the MACI, it challenges the validity of the entire profile, and the clinician should be cautious in interpreting it. When this is brought to the clinician's attention, it is best to review all of the items and compare the adolescent's other responses to what is known about them historically. It is up to the clinician's discretion whether to discuss this finding with the adolescent. If nothing "fits" or contradictory items are endorsed, the profile is probably invalid. If some items "fit," especially if they cluster within specific areas (e.g., anger, impulse control, suicidal ideation), then some data may still be clinically valid.

Disclosure

The Disclosure scale (Scale X) is a measure that assesses how open and self-revealing or defensive and guarded an adolescent was in responding to the MACI items. The Disclosure scale as well as the Desirability (Scale Y) and Debasement (Scale Z) scales are grounded in the research studies conducted in the development of the MCMI-II (Millon, 1987). At that time, BR scores of 85 or above were set to correspond to the highest 10% of the normative sample, BR scores of 75 to 84 corresponded to the next 15%, the BR range of 35 to 74 captured the middle 60%, and BR scores of less than 35 were assigned to the lowest 15% of the sample. These percentages have basically been retained for the entire MACI sample (Millon, 1993) although the formula used to derive the Scale X BR score is much more involved with the MACI than with the MCMI-III (Millon, Millon, & Davis, 1994). The raw score for the Disclosure scale is a weighted combination of the raw scores on Personality Patterns Scales 1 through 8B. In fact, a question could be raised regarding to what extent the very high, positive correlations of the Disclosure scale with the Introversive, Inhibited, Doleful, Unruly, Forceful, Oppositional, and Self-Demeaning scales results from the weighted adjustments for the number of items on a scale themselves. The weights rank these scales, both item-wise and raw score–wise, above the other Personality Patterns Scales that have negative correlations with the Disclosure scale. Furthermore, the Disclosure scale has a negative correlation with the Desirability scale (Scale Y) (−.435) and a very strong, positive correlation with the Debasement scale (Scale Z) (.780). For the clinician, knowing an adolescent's relative position on the Disclosure scale through their BR scores is important; however, at a glance it is easier to remember that raw scores between 275 and 400 do not trigger the disclosure adjustment. Raw scores below 275 will lead to BR increases on the Personality Patterns Scales 1 through 9 whereas raw scores above 400 will lead to BR decreases on the same scales. The amount of the BR increase or decrease depends on how discrepant the Disclosure scale raw score is from 275 or 400. Low scores are often associated with an adolescent who is not forthcoming regarding themselves and the problems that brought them into a mental health setting, although they can also reflect an attempt to appear well adjusted and emotionally healthy, a "blanket" of denial covering all areas, or a lack of insight into one's problems. High scores, on the other hand, suggest adolescents who are open and aware of their problems; however, the higher the scores the more this may reflect that the adolescent may tend to exaggerate their problems or that they are overwhelmed and reaching out.

Desirability

The Desirability scale (Scale Y) is a measure that assesses to what extent adolescents may have attempted to make themselves appear self-confident, socially well adjusted, and morally sound. All 17 items that make up this scale are loaded in the "true" direction and the majority (12) are 3-point items on the Dramatizing, Egotistic, and Conforming scales. The remaining items are 3-point items loaded in the "false" direction on the Identity Diffusion, Body Disapproval, and Social Insensitivity scales where a "true" response then represents a healthier self-perception. As a result, it is common to see the Desirability scale follow the course of the Dramatizing, Egotistic, and Conforming scales and, to a lesser extent, the Submissive scale. Adolescents who obtain high BR scores may be attempting to present themselves in a positive light. The higher the score, the less realistic the overall profile may be.

Debasement

Some adolescents, on the other hand, may attempt to present themselves in a less favorable light or with an emphasis on their problems and negative features. The Debasement scale (Scale Z) assesses to what extent an adolescent may deprecate or devalue themselves. This scale comprises 16 items, all loaded in the "true" direction, that are 3-point items on four Personality Patterns Scales (Inhibited, Doleful, Oppositional, Self-Demeaning), three Expressed Concerns Scales (Identity Diffusion, Self-Devaluation, Body Disapproval), and two Clinical Syndromes Scales (Anxious Feelings, Depressive Affect). High BR scores, therefore, will be indicative of an adolescent who is quite anxious and unhappy, lost and floating, in acute stress with no sense that the future will be different. Under these circumstances, this scale can assist in detecting the adolescent who is psychologically "crying out for help." However, the higher the score, the more difficult it is to identify the underlying personality patterns since the acute condition may exaggerate their pathology.

Modifying Indices

If the Disclosure scale raw score falls between 275 and 400, no disclosure adjustment will be made to the Personality Patterns Scales 1 through 9. If the Desirability and Debasement BR scores do not differ by more than 4 BR points, in either direction, then no desirability-debasement adjustment will be made to Expressed Concerns Scales A through H or Clinical Syndromes Scales AA, EE, FF, and GG. There are four basic Modifying Indices configurations. The first configuration finds all three Modifying Indices falling within the BR range of 35 to 74 and Scales Y and Z within 4 BR points of one another. In these instances, no particular positive or negative response set would appear to exist. A second configuration finds that the Desirability scale (Scale Y) is elevated relative to the Disclosure (Scale X) and Debasement (Scale Z) scales, which visually produces an arrowhead facing right. This array is associated with a positive response style and an adolescent who may be intent on presenting themselves in a favorable light. The greater the discrepancy between the BR scores for Scales Y and Z, the greater the adjustment upward on the Expressed Concerns and Clinical Syndromes Scales noted above. A third configuration finds the opposite array where the Disclosure (Scale X) and Debasement (Scale Z) scales are elevated relative to the Desirability scale (Scale Y), which visually produces the silhouette of an arrowhead facing left. Adolescents who produce this array may have approached the MACI with a negative response style and may be overreporting their problems. In this instance, the greater the discrepancy between the BR scores for Scales Y and Z, the greater the adjustment downward on the same Expressed Concerns and Clinical Syndromes Scales noted above. Finally, in less common numbers, a fourth configuration may be produced where the Desirability and Debasement scales will both be elevated (BR above 75). This pattern often indicates that the adolescent has provided contradictory endorsements on the test that may reflect a nondiscriminating response style where "good" and "bad" features are reported, a vacillating response style where one's self-perceptions are not consistent and one's inner conflicts are not well understood, or a generally healthy adolescent who has suddenly been confronted with significant distress.

Personality Patterns Scales

The MACI has 12 Personality Patterns Scales. Each personality pattern is formulated within Millon's three-polarity personality theory and has a correspondence with particular DSM-IV personality disorders. The following section outlines the personality patterns at this level and describes their primary imbalances or conflicts. Descriptions of the main clinical features associated with high BR scores on each scale will be offered as well as comments regarding early treatment issues with each personality pattern, since it is recommended that the MACI be administered at the beginning of treatment. Additionally, the factor analytically derived content scale for each Personality Patterns Scale will be reviewed with the hopes that some of the details will further enhance the reader's understanding of the underlying theoretical and empirical underpinnings of the test. Table 3.2 presents the content scale names and their alpha values (Millon, 1995).

Introversive

The Introversive scale (Scale 1) is the first of the detached personality patterns. In the DSM-IV, this pattern is associated with the Schizoid personality, and within the Millon theory it is conceptualized as the passive-detached pattern. These adolescents possess a limited capacity to experience both psychic pleasure and pain and have little motivation to seek out rewards through social interactions. High scorers on this scale tend to be passive observers, interpersonally indifferent and aloof, and emotionally bland. On the social periphery, not for protective reasons or out of disillusion, Introversive adolescents are internally unmoved, intrinsically underresponsive to stimulation either physically, emotionally, or socially. They seldom engage in ordinary adolescent activities. Instead, they have few, if any, friendships, have difficulty understanding the nuances of social discourse, and gradually drift further away. Externally and internally "out of touch," these adolescents often live a solitary life, directing their talents and interests toward objects and abstractions. Treatment with Introversive adolescents is challenging since they are

Table 3.2   MACI Personality Pattern Content Scales

Scale	Content Scale	Alpha Value
1. Introversive	Anhedonic Affect	.60
	Social Isolation	.80
	Existential Aimlessness	.80
	Sexual Indifference	.50
2A. Inhibited	Rejection Feelings	.82
	Unattractive Self-Image	.80
	Existential Sadness	.77
	Preferred Detachment	.52
	Sexual Aversion	.60
	Self-Conscious Restraint	.55
2B. Doleful	Brooding Melancholia	.80
	Social Joylessness	.55
	Self-Destructive Ideation	.69
	Abandonment Fears	.67
3. Submissive	Attachment Anxiety	.59
	Guidance Seeking	.41
	Authority Respect	.61
	Social Correctness	.55
	Pacific Disposition	.75
	Deficient Assertiveness	.70
4. Dramatizing	Attention Seeking	.50
	Convivial Sociability	.82
	Attractive Self-Image	.80
	Optimistic Outlook	.67
	Behavioral Disinhibition	.54
5. Egotistic	Admirable Self-Image	.84
	Superiority Feelings	.55

(*continued*)

Table 3.2   (continued)

Scale	Content Scale	Alpha Value
	Social Conceit	.53
	Confident Purposefulness	.72
	Self-Assured Independence	.58
	Empathic Indifference	.44
6A. Unruly	Impulsive Disobedience	.76
	Callous Manipulation	.60
	Authority Rejection	.64
	Socialized Substance Abuse	.75
	Unlawful Activity	.60
	Sexual Absorption	.50
6B. Forceful	Intimidating Abrasiveness	.78
	Precipitous Anger	.79
	Empathic Deficiency	.45
7. Conforming	Responsible Conscientiousness	.51
	Rule Adherence	.58
	Interpersonal Restraint	.78
	Social Conformity	.64
	Emotional Rigidity	.80
8A. Oppositional	Resentful Discontent	.77
	Self-Punitiveness	.74
	Angry Dominance	.74
	Social Inconsiderateness	.52
	Contrary Conduct	.50
8B. Self-Demeaning	Undeserving Self-Image	.57
	Self-Ruination	.73
	Low Self-Valuation	.84
	Hopeless Outlook	.72

Table 3.2 (continued)

Scale	Content Scale	Alpha Value
9. Borderline Tendency	Uncertain Self-Image	.78
	Empty Loneliness	.72
	Capricious Reactivity	.70
	Suicidal Impulsivity	.63

Note. From Millon (1995).

difficult to engage, have limited self-awareness and insight, and must be "jump-started" into a more active stance.

The Introversive scale has four content scales that represent the core dimensions of this pattern. The first content scale, Anhedonic Affect, comprises five items tapping the intrinsic deficit in the Introversive adolescent's capacity to experience pleasure and pain. Three of these items are 3-point, prototype items on the Introversive scale itself. The second and largest content scale (eight items), Social Isolation, addresses the detached quality of their lives and the sense of not "fitting in." Four of these items are 3-point items on the Peer Insecurity scale. A third content scale, Existential Aimlessness, highlights that Introversive adolescents may be less mature and less sure of themselves and their futures than other adolescents. This scale consists of six items; five are 3-point items on the Identity Diffusion scale. A fourth content scale, Sexual Indifference, illustrates how uncomfortable Introversive adolescents may be in their developing sexuality. Three of the four items that make up this scale are 3-point items on the Sexual Discomfort scale.

Inhibited

The second detached personality pattern, represented by the Inhibited scale (Scale 2A), is associated with the DSM-IV Avoidant personality. In the Millon schema, the Avoidant personality is conceptualized as the active-detached pattern. Although these personalities also possess a limited capacity to experience pleasure, they are differentiated from their passive counterparts by their hypersensitivity to anticipated pain. It is the imbalance of diminished psychic pleasure and anticipated psychic pain that is at the core of this pattern. High scores on the Inhibited scale, therefore, are achieved by those adolescents who tend to be apprehensive, socially ill at ease, and withdrawn. These adolescents have learned that the most effective means of avoiding rejection or humiliation is to be alert to the signs that might forewarn their occurrence. There is a tendency to "test the waters" until they validate a core belief that others cannot be trusted and will eventually hurt them. Their perceptions and cognitive processes have a distinct negative valence toward others as well as toward themselves. High scores on the Inhibited scale, in turn, are found with adolescents who have poor self-esteem and who often view themselves and their actions more critically than others do. Inhibited adolescents are able to derive limited pleasure and comfort from any source, from without or within, which leads to an undercurrent of tension, sadness, and anger. In the beginning phase of their treatment, Inhibited adolescents will experience a struggle between their wishes for acceptance and solace versus their beliefs that others cannot be trusted. Clinicians may initially be granted a temporary free pass if they are able to help alleviate some of the adolescent's psychic pain that prompted seeking help. Thereafter, however, progress is often slow and arduous.

Six content scales have been statistically derived from the Inhibited scale item pool and represent core dimensions for this pattern. The first and largest content scale (nine items), Rejection Feelings, addresses the detached quality of their lives and the sense of not "fitting in." This dimension is very similar to that measured by the Social Isolation content scale of the Introversive scale since they share seven items. The Rejection Feelings content scale is differentiated from the Social Isolation content scale by two prototype Inhibited scale items ("I'm very uncomfortable with people unless I'm sure they really like me" and "I won't get close to people because I'm afraid they may make fun of me"), which capture the core conflict for this personality pattern. A second content scale, Unattractive Self-Image, relates to their negative self-perceptions. Of the seven items, two are 3-point items on the Inhibited scale, three are 3-point items on the Body Disapproval scale, and two are 3-point items on the Self-Devaluation scale. Existential Sadness, the third content scale, consists of five items that convey a sense of despondency and discouragement. They are 3-point items on the Doleful, Self-Demeaning, and Self-Devaluation scales. Preferred Detachment, the fourth content scale, assesses the Inhibited adolescent's preference for social distance. Of the four items, three prototype items from the Introversive scale are loaded with a "true" response and one prototype item from the Dramatizing scale is loaded with a "false" response. The fifth content scale, Sexual Aversion, shares four of its five items with the Sexual Indifference content scale from the Introversive scale. Also, four of the five items that constitute the Sexual Aversion content scale are 3-point items on the Sexual Discomfort scale. Finally, the sixth content scale, Self-Conscious Restraint, comprises four "false"-loaded items, which suggest that Inhibited personalities generally have adequate impulse control. These items are "true"-loaded, on the other hand, on the Dramatizing, Unruly, and Impulsive Propensity scales.

Doleful

The third detached personality pattern, the Depressive personality, is the most recent personality construct to be introduced in the DSM-IV and formulated within the Millon schema. Conceptualized as the passive-pain pattern, Depressive personalities experience pain as a permanent fixture in their lives. There is an overemphasis on pain and anguish as well as a sense that the person has "given up," virtually succumbing to what is believed to be a future filled with more suffering and despair. The key distinction between the Avoidant and Depressive personalities resides within the pain dimension where the Avoidant personality takes an active stance in order to minimize and avoid pain whereas the Depressive personality remains passive and surrenders to it. On the MACI, the Depressive personality is represented by the Doleful scale (Scale 2B). High scores on this scale are found with those adolescents whose moods are characteristically depressed, dysphoric, and morose. They typically possess defeatist and fatalistic attitudes about the present and the future. The "weight of the world" seems to be on their shoulders and they doubt that they can affect positive change. Their pessimism translates into low self-esteem and guilt regarding their inadequacies. These adolescents have few friends since interacting with them is seldom rewarding and is more often draining. With few positive expectations, these adolescents are resigned to their plight. From these descriptions, it would be anticipated that therapeutic work with Doleful adolescents is very demanding. Their pervasive dysphoric state, disheartened outlook, and worthless self-image are formidable obstacles to clinical gains. Considerable joint efforts must be put forth to lessen their dysphoria, strengthen their motivation for rewarding experiences, and develop more active and adaptive coping responses.

Four content scales have been statistically derived from the Doleful scale item pool and represent primary facets for this pattern. The first and largest content scale (12 items), Brooding Melancholia, addresses the Doleful adolescent's intense psychic pain, both in the present and toward the future. Social Joylessness, a second content scale, taps the somber views these adolescents often entertain whether prior to or after potentially positive experiences. Three of the four items that make up this content scale are prototype Doleful scale items. Self-Destructive Ideation, a third content scale, addresses the depths of the Doleful adolescent's pain and the desperate measures they may consider. Two of the items are 3-point items on the Suicidal Tendency scale; the third item is a 3-point Depressive Affect scale item. A pervasive sense of aloneness is denoted in the Abandonment Fears content scale where three of the five items are prototype Doleful scale items and the other two items are 3-point Submissive and Family Discord scale items.

Submissive

The Submissive scale (Scale 3) is the first of the MACI dependent personality patterns. It is designed to measure the attributes associated with the DSM-IV Dependent personality, which within the Millon schema is formulated as the passive-dependent pattern. Dependent personalities have imbalances on the active-passive and self-other polarities. Their existence is dependent on secure attachments with significant others whose needs and desires they place first and foremost. In this way they seek to assure themselves of affection and protection and avoid abandonment. High scorers on this scale tend to be passive and submissive in their relationships. They are cooperative and noncompetitive with strong needs for support and guidance. Submissive adolescents tend to focus on their perceived weaknesses and view themselves as fragile and inferior, "not as good as" others. A lack of confidence also leads them to be indecisive, and they will often seek out others' opinions. They avoid conflict and subordinate their desires since they do not want to annoy or disappoint others, lest they threaten an important relationship. If deprived of affection and nurturance, they experience marked discomfort, sadness, and anxiety. Submissive adolescents are usually very receptive to the talking therapies. They gravitate toward the supportive and caring clinician who becomes a new source of protection and reassurance. A positive start to the treatment is anticipated since Submissive adolescents are typically trusting and willing to participate, which, as they are quick to recognize, provides the clinician with what they need. Treatment with Submissive adolescents will initially seem to proceed at a rapid pace. They will listen and learn, develop new coping skills and improve their self-esteem; however, when it is time to work on becoming more assertive and autonomous, the process is much slower.

The Submissive scale has six content scales that represent the core dimensions to this pattern. Attachment Anxiety, a content scale comprising four items, addresses the Submissive adolescent's significant dependency needs as well as his or her fears of being alone. Two of these items are prototype Submissive scale items; the two other items are 3-point Inhibited and Anxious Feelings scale items. Guidance Seeking, a second content scale comprising four items, highlights that the Submissive adolescent seeks assistance and direction from others. Three of these items are prototype Submissive scale items and the fourth item is a prototype Inhibited scale item. The third and fourth content scales, Authority Respect and Social Correctness, illustrate that Submissive adolescents emphasize harmonious relationships and prosocial behavior. The largest content scales, Pacific Disposition (seven items) and Deficient Assertiveness (six items), comprise "false"-loaded items on the Submissive scale. The majority of these items, on the other hand, are 3-point "true"-loaded items on the Unruly and Forceful scales. These personality patterns are virtually diametrically opposed theoretically from the Submissive personality, and their MACI scales have very strong negative correlations (–.70 or stronger) with the Submissive scale.

Dramatizing

The second dependent personality pattern, represented by the Dramatizing scale (Scale 4), is associated with the DSM-IV Histrionic personality. In the Millon schema, the Histrionic personality is formulated as the active-dependent pattern. Histrionic personalities also have imbalances on the active-passive and self-other polarities; however, this personality takes the initiative and is much more solicitous in ensuring the attention and affection it craves. Additionally, while the Dependent personality is usually satisfied with a single attachment object, the Histrionic personality seeks constant stimulation and excitement from multiple attachment objects, which often results in a seductive and capricious presentation. On the MACI Dramatizing scale, high scores are often found with adolescents who are gregarious and sociable.

Through their charming and ingratiating manner, they develop many friendships and typically have very active social lives. They enjoy being the "center of attention" and are enchanting with their propensity for spontaneous adventures and shortsighted hedonism. Dramatizing adolescents need to solicit attention and praise to meet their dependency needs as well as to maintain a positive sense of self. Their external reality is filled with ever-changing images, objects, and social relationships, which mirrors their fleeting and unintegrated inner world. As a result of their attractive social facades, their relationships tend to be more entertaining than sustaining. Fickle and impetuous moods can further dull the luster of their charms, and impulsive decision making can sometimes lead to negative consequences. To ward off uncomfortable experiences (i.e., anxiety or sadness), these personalities employ repression, externalization, and dissociation. Although Dramatizing adolescents are not difficult to engage in the treatment process, maintaining them for a sufficient time to produce real change is another story. Their constant seeking of excitement and stimulation and their "live for the moment" attitude, for example, demand quick solutions and relief. Additionally, their overemphasis with external reality and their limited reflective and introspective capacities do not bode well for extended self-examination. Instead, these personalities seem to offer a narrow window of time within which to help them.

The Dramatizing scale has five content scales that represent the core dimensions to the pattern. The Attention Seeking content scale, comprising three prototype Dramatizing scale items and one prototype Egotistic scale item, contains a primary active-dependent feature related to these adolescents' dramatic, attention-seeking manner. A second content scale, Convivial Sociability, captures their active and rewarding social lives. The 2 "true"-loaded items on this content scale are prototype Dramatizing scale items; the remaining 10 items are "false"-loaded on the Introversive, Inhibited, and Peer Insecurity scales. A third content scale, Attractive Self-Image, relates to their physical appearance while Optimistic Outlook, a fourth content scale, relates to their positive mental outlook. Finally, a fifth content scale, Behavioral Disinhibition, indicates that a certain group of Dramatizing adolescents will use their thrill-seeking tendencies and social skills to more devious ends. The majority of the items on this content scale are 3-point items on the Unruly, Forceful, and Delinquent Predisposition scales.

Egotistic

The DSM-IV Narcissistic personality is the construct measured by the MACI Egotistic scale (Scale 5). This personality is formulated within the Millon schema as the passive-independent pattern where the imbalance resides on the active-passive and self-other polarities. The Narcissistic personality has learned to turn inward for gratification. With significant others who have continually and, often unconditionally, showered them with praise, these personalities have learned that they are special and have an excessive appreciation of their self-worth. They believe that they just need to be themselves in order to feel content and secure. Therefore, high scorers on the MACI Egotistic scale portray themselves as self-confident and self-assured. Their high self-esteem extends from a blind and naive belief that they are superior in their talents and abilities. Although their arrogance may be benign, they do, nevertheless, expect that others will recognize their strengths and stroke them. As a result of their exaggerated self-focus, Egotistic adolescents have difficulty empathizing with others and seldom concern themselves with others' problems. In their relationships, there is a passive exploitiveness in the form of taking others for granted and expecting others to do more for them than they will do or give in return. Typically, their moods are relaxed and positive until their high self-worth has been challenged or undercut. In these instances there can be rapid mood changes that may vacillate between unbridled rage and intense dejection. For Egotistic personalities, all is well until they experience failure or suffer rejection or loss. Such events can throw them into a tailspin, propelling them to seek treatment. Egotistic adolescents will often make quick progress initially since talking about themselves and recalling their competencies will restore their self-confidence. When they regain their psychic balance, they will see little reason to continue treatment.

Six content scales have been statistically derived from the Egotistic scale item pool and represent primary facets for this pattern. The first and largest content scale, Admirable Self-Image, contains seven items that address the positive self-perceptions Egotistic adolescents possess, in particular, regarding how they feel about their appearance. A second content scale, Superiority Feelings, contains five items that address how self-confident and self-assured these adolescents feel regarding their talents and abilities. Three of these items are prototype Egotistic scale items, and the other items are 3-point, "false"-loaded items on the Self-Devaluation scale. Social Conceit, a third content scale, contains six items that address the Egotistic adolescent's need to be the center of attention. Of the five "true"-loaded items, three are prototype Dramatizing scale items and two are prototype Egotistic scale items. Confident Purposefulness, a fourth content scale, contains four items, half "true"-loaded and half "false"-loaded, that relate to their self-confidence regarding a direction for their future. All of these items are 3-point Identity Diffusion scale items. Self-Assured Independence contains six "false"-loaded items from five other scales. As it has been labeled, this content scale addresses the Egotistic adolescent's comfort with his or her autonomy and self-sufficiency. Finally, items that make up the sixth content scale, Empathic Indifference, highlight these adolescents' tendencies to use others in order to pursue their personal desires. These characteristics assume more deviant levels in the Unruly and Forceful personality patterns.

Unruly

The second independent personality pattern, represented by the Unruly scale (Scale 6A), is associated with the DSM-IV Antisocial personality. Within the Millon schema, the Antisocial personality is formulated as the active-independent pattern. Antisocial personalities also have imbalances on the active-passive and self-other polarities. While they are similar to their passive-independent counterparts in having learned to rely on themselves for gratification and security, their experiences and motivations could not be more diverse. Narcissistic personalities, having been indulged and pampered, are confident, content, and secure just being themselves. Antisocial personalities, on the other hand, often having experienced the world as an uncaring, ungiving, or even hostile place, have learned to mistrust others and must be vigilant of the environment lest they be harmed or exploited. The Antisocial personality, therefore, is proactive in meeting its wants and desires through whatever means, both legal and otherwise. High scorers on the Unruly scale are restless and impulsive with low frustration tolerance and thrill-seeking tendencies. Their "live for the moment" motto reflects their need for immediate gratification and their actions are typically shortsighted and imprudent. Since they either disregard social rules or fail to heed to the possible consequences of their actions, they often present with conduct problems. When confronted about their actions, they will usually minimize or externalize responsibility for them. No genuine remorse is forthcoming from these adolescents. Driven by a need for power and control, Unruly adolescents do not know how to have mutually rewarding, intimate relationships. Instead, they value autonomy and will not tolerate feeling confined. Therefore, freedom and self-determination are important rights for them and those who interfere in any way will experience their wrath. Unruly adolescents usually are not willing participants in the treatment process. In many instances, they are referred by schools or the court. They do not trust others, especially those in authority positions, and they see the clinician as an extension of a large network trying to control them. Some Unruly adolescents will be direct and blunt in stating their hostility and resentment, others will take more subtle approaches, sometimes charming the clinician into believing they are no longer acting out. The clinician's most effective tactic is to point out how the Unruly adolescent's actions will undermine him in the long run. It is also key not to become entangled in power struggles with these adolescents or to react out of anger or frustration.

Six content scales have been statistically derived from the Unruly scale item pool and represent its primary facets. The first content scale, Impulsive Disobedience, consists of eight "true"-loaded items that highlight the Unruly adolescent's impulsive, defiant, and rebellious tendencies. Three of the items are prototype Unruly scale items, four items are 3-point Impulsive Propensity scale items, and the last item is a 3-point Dramatizing scale item. Callous Manipulation, the second content scale, consists of seven "true"-loaded items from the Unruly (three), Forceful (two), and Egotistic (two) scales that capture their dislike for rules as well as their cunning and exploitive attitudes. A set of five "false"-loaded items and one "true"-loaded item that convey similar features constitute the Authority Rejection content scale. A triumvirate of content scales, Socialized Substance Abuse, Unlawful Activity, and Sexual Absorption, illustrate the primary acting out behaviors associated with this personality pattern.

Forceful

The Forceful scale (Scale 6B) represents the Sadistic personality, which was introduced into the nomenclature through its presence in the DSM-III-R appendix. Although the construct was then dropped from the DSM-IV, it has remained in the Millon inventories because it has been theoretically derived within the three-polarity model as the active-discordant pattern. It has been assigned to the 6B position since the Aggressive-Sadistic personality was originally formulated as a variant of the Antisocial personality (Millon, 1969, 1981). Within the evolutionary model (Millon, 1990; Millon & Davis, 1996), it became clearer that a reversal within the pleasure-pain polarity illuminated a significant distinction between the two types. Whereas the Antisocial personality emphasizes protecting and maintaining its autonomy and independence out of mistrust and fear that they will be harmed or exploited, the Sadistic personality purposefully engages in ruthless and malicious behaviors in order to demean and dominate others. The Antisocial personality seeks to preserve itself, the Sadistic personality, in its most extreme form, seeks to psychologically annihilate others. On the MACI, high scorers on the Forceful scale are strong-willed and assertive. They are socially arrogant and provocative, willing to say whatever comes to their mind and act however they want. In those instances where the Forceful adolescent feels he or she is in control or "untouchable," objections and consequences will be dismissed as a joke. On the other hand, when confronted in a manner where his or her self-determination or freedom are threatened, he or she may become furious, combative, and vindictive. In their social relationships, these adolescents are insensitive and cold. They lack empathy or compassion and will often prey on these "weaknesses" if they are perceived in their peers since they derive much pleasure from controlling and dominating others. Uncontrolled rages represent significant lapses in control and judgment and will most often be the primary reason these adolescents have been brought for treatment. Their perspective of the world, however, runs counter to the therapeutic process. Cooperation and support and trust, sensitivity and empathy, self-exploration and self-awareness are all foreign concepts that could threaten the stability and integrity of their existence or, in other words, the worldview that drives their current behaviors, thoughts, and feelings. As a first step, treatment should focus on helping these adolescents gain better control over their eruptive tempers. Progress in this area might make other issues more accessible.

The Forceful scale has three content scales representing its core dimensions. The first content scale, Intimidating Abrasiveness, contains seven items that address the theoretically derived notion of a reversal within the pleasure-pain polarity. The Forceful adolescent's core issue is exhibited in their power and dominance orientation in their day-to-day interactions. Six of these items are "true"-loaded, prototype Forceful scale items; the remaining item is a prototype Egotistic scale item. The second content scale, Precipitous Anger, reflects the

Forceful adolescent's impulsive and defiant nature. These seven items are "true"-loaded, 3-point items on the Unruly scale (three items) and the Impulsive Propensity scale (four items). Finally, Empathic Deficiency, comprising four items, highlights the Forceful adolescent's callousness and insensitivity. The majority of these items are 3-point Social Insensitivity scale items.

Conforming

The Conforming scale (Scale 7) is the first of the MACI ambivalent personality patterns. It corresponds to the attributes associated with the DSM-IV Obsessive-Compulsive personality. Within the Millon schema, it is formulated as the passive-ambivalent pattern. Obsessive-Compulsive personalities have a conflict within the self-other polarity that basically relates to whether they should turn to themselves or turn to others in order to find the reinforcement and security they desire. An intense conflict ensues internally where the Obsessive-Compulsive personality must essentially choose between obedience (i.e., becoming other oriented and accommodating to others' desires) and defiance (i.e., expressing their autonomy and pursuing their self-interests). On the surface, these personalities appear to have resolved the conflict through obedience. They repress their urges for independence and act in responsible and conscientious ways, following a strict set of rules regarding what is right and wrong, proper and improper. At a deeper level, however, they are harboring tremendous anger and resentment. They wish or fantasize that they could find an outlet for these urges, but fears of negative repercussions and punishments trigger anxiety reactions. In a self-perpetuating manner, their restrained and conforming existence is a massive effort to bind their anger and anxiety. At the adolescent level, high scorers on the MACI Conforming scale tend to be serious-minded and emotionally constricted. They are disciplined and regimented, following directives and meeting others' expectations, often pursuing achievement-oriented goals. They act respectfully to their peers and especially to authority figures. Conforming adolescents can be "counted on" to meet their obligations because they conduct themselves in a dependable and responsible manner. Good planning and organization skills are typically present in these hardworking and industrious teens. In many respects, they are "model citizens," but their inner lives are often tense and grim. Many who observe their peers acting and relating in spontaneous and carefree ways wish they could do the same, yet seldom do. Conforming adolescents represent one of the less common groups who will present for treatment. When they do, however, it is often due to distress and pressure, which may surface in a mixture of anxiety, sadness, and tension. A frequent scenario is that they find themselves overcommitted, running here, there, and everywhere, spending inordinate amounts of time studying, eventually questioning why and for whom they're doing these things. Individual and family work can relieve their pressures, help them become more assertive, and help them assume more active control of their lives.

Among the five Conforming scale content scales, Responsible Conscientiousness and Rule Adherence highlight key social and moral features for this pattern. On the former scale, three of the four items are 3-point "true"-loaded Conforming scale items while the fourth is a 3-point "false"-loaded Unruly scale item. On the latter scale, four of the five items are 3-point "true"-loaded Conforming scale items while the fifth is a 3-point "false"-loaded Oppositional scale item. The other three content scales consist of "false"-loaded items for the Conforming scale. The content scales labeled Interpersonal Restraint and Social Conformity essentially measure the same issues through "false"-loaded items. Conforming adolescents are reflective; they think and plan before they act, and they adhere to society's rules. The fifth and largest content scale (10 items), although labeled Emotional Rigidity, appears to reflect that Conforming adolescents do not present with identity issues or serious depressive states that may be common to many adolescents and that, despite their often grim and tense presentation, they have some confidence in their abilities and have a generally positive outlook regarding their future. Since the majority of the "true"-loaded items on these content scales are 3-point Conforming items themselves and the majority of the remaining items on these scales are "false"-loaded, it is noteworthy that the Conforming scale has negative correlations with the vast majority of the other MACI scales with the exceptions of the Submissive, Dramatizing, Egotistic, Sexual Discomfort, and Anxious Feelings scales.

Oppositional

The second ambivalent personality pattern, the DSM-IV Negativistic personality, is an expansion of the former passive-aggressive personality. According to Millon's theory, the Negativistic personality is conceptualized as the active-ambivalent personality, and, similar to the Obsessive-Compulsive personality, its passive-ambivalent counterpart, the primary conflict resides within the self-other polarity. Again, this is an intense struggle between obedience and defiance, but Negativistic personalities are much more obvious in their failure to have resolved it. Their ambivalence is pervasive, intruding into all aspects of their lives. They display fluctuating moods, vacillating object relations, contradictory thoughts, and erratic behaviors, all stemming from the same source. Their lives are often filled with discontent and they make the lives of those around them the same way. The Negativistic personality is much more than a proclivity to interact in a passive-aggressive manner, and the MACI Oppositional scale (Scale 8A), in a similar way, is much more than a measure of the features associated with the DSM-IV Oppositional Defiant Disorder. True, high scorers on the MACI Oppositional scale are often defiant, argumentative, and hostile. They are also irritable, lose their temper, and do not comply with requests. In addition though, adolescents who attain high scores on this scale often harbor considerable anger and resentment toward significant others yet, at the same time, need to be close to the same people for support and security. Their resentment takes various forms: procrastination, inefficiency, and obstinence. All create anger in those involved with or relying on them. Oppositional adolescents also experience general confusion about their feelings and are often "out of sync" with them. Their unstable mood and impulsive and often explosive reactions make it difficult to establish and maintain relationships with these personalities. Oppositional adolescents feel misunderstood and unappreciated. They will complain that they've been cheated of the "good things" that others have. One moment they're envious, the next they're guilty. Here, the ambivalence reflects a conflict whether they truly deserve better or that they're fated to a miserable life. In many respects, they serve as their "own worst enemy." Since Oppositional adolescents "wear their emotions on their sleeves," it is not difficult to assess their moods, however, intervening is akin to shooting at a moving target. In the early stages, these personalities often use the session time to complain about others and maintain their negative worldview. They will attempt to drag the clinician through their ambivalence-mined lives. Although the Oppositional adolescent will often divert attention away from the clinician's attempts to connect with them and to address issues clinically, the MACI Expressed Concerns and Clinical Syndromes Scales may provide areas where the clinician and adolescent can become allies in a common cause. Progress is slow, halting, filled with starts and stops. The clinician must teach them how to stay the course and gradually develop inner stability and constancy.

The Oppositional scale has five content scales that represent its core dimensions. Resentful Discontent, the largest content scale (13 items), contains items that capture Oppositional adolescents' displeasure with themselves and their lives as well as their negative attitudes in the present and toward the future. Six of these items are prototype Oppositional scale items; the other items are 3-point items for seven other scales. The six items on the next content scale, Self-Punitiveness, when endorsed with the items from the Resentful Discontent content scale, reveal that Oppositional adolescents can experience severe depressions with serious self-destructive ideation. This content scale consists of 3-point items from the Suicidal Tendency (three items), Depressive Affect (two items), and Self-Demeaning (one item) scales. These first two content scales appear to indicate that the turning inward of the Oppositional adolescent's resentment and anguish can reach serious depths. The three remaining content scales, on the other hand, appear to capture Oppositional adolescents' tendency to direct their anger outward. These content scales, labeled Angry Dominance, Social Inconsiderateness, and Contrary Conduct, have strong connections with the Unruly, Forceful, Social Insensitivity, Delinquent Predisposition, and Impulsive Propensity scales. All 16 items that make up these three content scales are 3-point items on these MACI scales. With this basic division, it is important for the clinician to assess which of these content scales contribute to any elevations on the Oppositional scale.

Self-Demeaning

The Self-Demeaning scale (Scale 8B) represents the Self-Defeating personality, which was also introduced into the nomenclature in the DSM-III-R appendix, but like the Sadistic personality it was dropped from the DSM-IV. This construct was retained, however, in the MCMI-III, now labeled the Masochistic personality, because it has been theoretically formulated as the passive-discordant pattern. Within Millon's three-polarity model, the major distinguishing feature of the Masochistic personality is a reversal within the pleasure-pain polarity, which indicates that the person has learned to prefer experiences of psychic pain over experiences of psychic pleasure. From the active-passive polarity, the passive component indicates that there may be an acceptance of psychic pain as a viable and realistic choice. Given their life experiences and their subsequent perspective of the world, they have learned to tolerate discomfort since it may serve as a preamble to acceptance and affection. On the MACI, high scorers on the Self-Demeaning scale tend to act in a self-effacing and self-denigrating manner. They often present themselves in an inferior light, avoiding positive attention and giving off messages that they are undeserving of praise and recognition. Self-Demeaning adolescents undermine their own good fortunes, spoiling what limited pleasures may come their way. Their self-esteem is very poor, and they often perceive themselves as weak, inadequate, and helpless. Harboring so many self-doubts, even when they do succeed, they tend to gradually undo their accomplishments. Success also does not enhance their self-confidence but instead sets in motion a tendency to increase expectations, often to unreasonable heights, that only triggers anxiety reactions that immobilize them. In their relationships, Self-Demeaning adolescents tend to take on inferior and subservient roles. Submissive and self-sacrificing, these adolescents, especially females, tend to recreate past experiences and choose partners who are demanding and exploitive. In a common manifestation of the reversal on the pleasure-pain polarity, they will often stay in these relationships despite being mistreated because, periodically, they do receive love and affection. Self-Demeaning adolescents also internalize their distress, which results in a chronic anxious and dysphoric condition. Many will exhibit somatic issues. Self-Demeaning adolescents seek treatment because their pain and suffering has exceeded even their thresholds. As a result, the clinician is often initially faced with chronic and severe Axis I conditions that must be addressed. This is a challenge because the Self-Demeaning adolescent tends to perpetuate unpleasant situations and experiences out of their identity as a sufferer and their role as a victim. Treatment of these adolescents requires an extensive time period where work can be done to identify their strengths and resources, adjust their negative perceptions and thought processes, develop a more adaptive and positive self-image, and make healthier object choices where love and affection are not contingent on self-sacrifice and abuse.

Four content scales have been statistically derived from the Self-Demeaning item pool and represent primary facets of this pattern. The first content scale, Undeserving Self-Image, comprises five prototype Self-Demeaning scale items. These items highlight these adolescents' perspective that they deserve to suffer and appears to capture their conflict on the pleasure-pain dimension. Suffering is a resigned choice in the matter. Self-Ruination, the second content scale, addresses the related feature that much of their suffering is self-inflicted. The seven items that make up this scale are 3-point items on the Self-Demeaning (three items), Identity Diffusion (two items), Doleful (one item), and Self-Devaluation (one item) scales. Low Self-Valuation, the third content scale, comprises seven items that illustrate their negative self-perceptions and low self-esteem. These seven items are 3-point items on the Self-Devaluation (three items), Body Disapproval (three items), and the Inhibited (one item) scales. Finally, the fourth content scale, Hopeless Outlook, appears to speak to their pessimism and future despair. This content scale comprises seven items. Three items are prototype Doleful scale items and all are loaded on the Doleful scale's Abandonment Fears content scale; the other four items are prototype Oppositional scale items and all are loaded on the Oppositional scale's Resentful Discontent content scale. This finding creates an interesting dilemma since these three personality pattern scales also have high correlations with one another suggesting a high probability that they will often be comorbid with one another.

Borderline Tendency

The Borderline Tendency scale (Scale 9) was constructed to measure the DSM-IV Borderline personality. Since it helps identify adolescents with more serious problems, it is a severity gauge. It was constructed later in the MACI development process, so it does not have its own 3-point items. It is a compilation of 21 items from 10 scales that address many of the core features of the Borderline personality. Within the Millon schema, the Borderline personality is conceptualized as a more severe pattern where a conflict is present within all three polarities. These conflicts contribute to their intense ambivalence, labile moods, unpredictable behaviors, capricious thoughts, split object relations, and identity diffusion. In other words, there is a pervasive instability and inconstancy that permeates all aspects of their lives. Adolescents who attain high scores on the Borderline Tendency scale experience periods of marked behavioral and emotional dysregulation. Their instability may be indicative of defective psychic structures and the failure to develop internal cohesion. Their sense of self and identity is uncertain. These adolescents have great difficulty maintaining relationships since their perceptions of significant others are wide ranging and ever changing from idealization to devaluation. Many Borderline adolescents have dependency needs that have never been met, and although they need attention and affection many cannot tolerate closeness. So, while fears of separation and abandonment can lead them to act in desperate ways to hold on and save them from ensuing aloneness and emptiness, fears of engulfment can contribute to their angry explosions, which drive others away. Life is a constant struggle with frequent upheavals. At the behavior level, Borderline adolescents are impulsive and often engage in risky acting-out behaviors (e.g., drug use, promiscuity). There is little planning preceding their actions, and they are unable to focus on more ordinary adolescent concerns (e.g., school, work). Their inner turmoil leaves them ill prepared to take on new challenges and responsibilities; therefore, these adolescents have tremendous difficulty with life's transitions, whether in school settings (e.g., from middle or junior high school to high school or from high school to college) or home settings (e.g., moves to another home, parents' separation or divorce). Repeated conflicts and failures gradually intensify into a pained and desperate existence, which leads to self-destructive thoughts and, in some Borderline adolescents, self-mutilating behaviors and suicide attempts. At any age, Borderline personalities are challenging, requiring tremendous time, energy, and resources. Clinicians must remain supportive and consistent in their interventions. Primary treatment goals include stabilizing their moods, improving their impulse control, and developing object and self-constancy.

The Borderline Tendency scale has four content scales representing some of its core features. The first content scale, Uncertain Self-Image, comprises five 3-point Identity Diffusion items that highlight their immature and wavering sense of identity. They have difficulty maintaining a stable sense of who they are and the direction they're going in. The second content scale, Empty Loneliness, and the third content scale, Capricious Reactivity, comprise items that appear to be opposite points within the internalizing-externalizing dimension. The former content scale comprises 3-point items on the Doleful (three items), Submissive (one item), Self-Demeaning (one item), and Self-Devaluation (one item) scales; the latter content scale comprises 3-point items on the Unruly (one item), Forceful (one item); Oppositional (one item), and Impulsive Propensity (three items) scales. This finding, especially relevant to the Borderline Tendency scale and the Borderline personality construct, raises the notion of personality subtypes. Millon and

Davis (1996) wrote about integrating stylistic polarity features (e.g., personality patterns presented by MACI Scales 1 through 8B) within the context of structural Borderline defects (e.g., represented by MACI Borderline Tendency scale). Finally, Suicidal Impulsivity, the fourth content scale, highlights the self-destructive ideations and suicide attempts that are so prevalent with this group. These items are 3-point Suicidal Tendency scale items and a fourth item is a 3-point Impulsive Propensity scale item.

Expressed Concerns Scales

The MACI has eight Expressed Concerns Scales that focus on some of the primary developmental issues adolescents face. These scales assess adolescents' self-perceptions regarding their progress in these areas, which they may compare to their image of what or how they would like to be or through their comparisons to their peers. Since these are subjective impressions, elevations on these scales often provide insights into the issues that adolescents may wish to address in their therapy. Therefore, the clinician may use elevations on the Expressed Concerns Scales to develop early treatment plans.

Identity Diffusion

The Identity Diffusion scale (Scale A) assesses concerns that adolescents may have about who they are and what the future holds in store for them. Adolescence represents a transition period from childhood to adulthood, and some adolescents believe they are well equipped to handle it. High scorers on this scale, on the other hand, are very confused about who they are, what they stand for, and what they want. They report feeling lost and aimless, uncertain about the future, and unsure how to set and pursue goals. They also see their peers as more mature and focused than they are. Anxiety and sadness are often present.

Self-Devaluation

The Self-Devaluation scale (Scale B) basically assesses the adolescent's views of his or her self-esteem. Some adolescents progress through this period essentially unscathed, feeling comfortable about their appearance, abilities, and social status. High scorers on this scale, however, are not in this group. In contrast, they are dissatisfied in these key areas and have very low self-esteem.

They are unhappy with themselves and often fear that they will fall short of their goals. A mixture of jealousy and despair may be present.

Body Disapproval
The Body Disapproval scale (Scale C) assesses concerns that adolescents have about their physical development and appearance. High scorers are often dissatisfied with the way their bodies have been developing and believe that they are unattractive. Preoccupations with their weight and the need to diet may be prominent. Body image disturbances may be detected by this scale, especially when a high BR score is also found on the Eating Dysfunctions scale. Adolescents who are displeased with their appearance and question their attractiveness tend to be very self-conscious and have poor self-esteem.

Sexual Discomfort
Adolescents with high scores on the Sexual Discomfort scale (Scale D) are reporting that their sexual thoughts and feelings make them uncomfortable or confuse them. In some instances, elevations on this scale may reflect a teenager who is sexually immature, inexperienced, or disinterested. However, at another level, all four 3-point Childhood Abuse items load on the Sexual Discomfort scale. Two of these items specifically address sexual abuse and the other two items address abuse that could be interpreted as sexual abuse. Although all these issues could lead to elevations on this scale, Scale D does not address an adolescent's sexual orientation.

Peer Insecurity
The Peer Insecurity scale (Scale E) measures adolescents' perceptions of their social relationships. High scorers on this scale often feel that they do not "fit in" with their peers. A common pattern finds that they hesitate to initiate contact with others since they fear rejection; at the same time, they feel that others do not seek them out. As a result these adolescents often have few friends and miss out on common social experiences. In many instances they feel sad and alone.

Social Insensitivity
Adolescents with high scores on the Social Insensitivity scale (Scale F) indicate that they are not concerned about their callous indifference regarding

others' welfare. Instead, elevations on this scale reflect their bravado, a brazen attitude, and a flaunting of social rules and graces. These adolescents lack empathy and can be very manipulative and exploitive. With conduct-disordered adolescents, it is very common to find this scale elevated with the Unruly, Forceful, Delinquent Predisposition, and Impulsive Propensity scales.

Family Discord

Adolescents with high scores on the Family Discord scale (Scale G) report that their family relationships are tense and conflicted. There is a general sense of estrangement from their parents. In some instances a high score may reflect an adolescent's rebellion toward his or her family, its structure, and rules; in other instances it could be indicative of much deeper family pathology. Additionally, some adolescents with limited insight into their own problems will blame their families. Either way, there is often a chasm between family members.

Childhood Abuse

High scores on the Childhood Abuse scale (Scale H) suggest that an adolescent is reporting shame and disgust about having been subjected to verbal, physical, or sexual abuse. The long-term repercussions of these experiences can be far-reaching. Adolescents with high scores on this scale may have chronic depressive or anxious moods, poor self-esteem, and difficulty trusting others. High incidences of eating disorders and substance abuse indicate that these issues need to be monitored carefully.

Clinical Syndromes Scales

The MACI has seven Clinical Syndromes Scales that assess symptoms adolescents often present with in clinical settings. Although many of the scales are associated with DSM-IV diagnostic categories, all represent significant problems that are disruptive to the adolescent's healthy development and smooth path toward adulthood. Elevations on these scales provide guidance regarding specific treatment targets as well as the need for specialized programs and consultations.

Eating Dysfunctions

The Eating Dysfunctions scale (Scale AA) measures symptoms related to anorexia, bulimia, and overeating and assesses the likelihood that an adolescent has an eating disorder. High scorers engage in various eating disorder behaviors and often have body image disturbances, poor self-esteem, and depressive symptoms. These adolescents often have a preoccupation with food, caloric intake, and fears over gaining weight. A high score may suggest the need for a consultation with a clinician who has an expertise in eating disorders.

Substance-Abuse Proneness

The Substance-Abuse Proneness scale (Scale BB) measures an adolescent's admission of persistent drug and alcohol abuse. High scores on this scale may be indicative of substance abuse as well as dependence. When taking the test, adolescents often ask the clinician if their parents will see the test results when they encounter the first of these items. Although experimentation is a common occurrence in the adolescent population, significant elevations on this scale indicate that the test taker is probably well beyond experimental and social usage. Depending on the clinician's expertise in the substance-abuse field, these adolescents should be candidates for an evaluation at a substance-abuse program.

Delinquent Predisposition

Conduct-disordered adolescents will typically earn high BR scores on the Delinquent Predisposition scale (Scale CC). High scorers have probably had repeated run-ins with the law since they tend to break social norms and rules. These adolescents tend to be impulsive and shortsighted. They are self-centered and exhibit little remorse and regard for others. This scale has high correlations with the Unruly and Forceful scales as well as the next scale, the Impulsive Propensity scale.

Impulsive Propensity

Conduct-disordered adolescents will also earn high BR scores on the Impulsive Propensity scale (Scale DD). High scorers have great difficulty controlling their impulses. They are inclined to act out without thinking ahead. This feature can be present in many contexts with a bottom line on frequent episodes of behavioral and emotional dysregulation. Not only do these adolescents act without thinking about the probable consequences for themselves, but they also do not consider the impact of their decisions and actions on others.

Anxious Feelings

The Anxious Feelings scale (Scale EE) addresses symptoms consistent with an anxiety disorder. Several items address physical symptoms and general apprehension; however, over two thirds of the items on this scale are "false"-loaded. If this scale has a BR score of 85 or above, the clinician, before offering an anxiety disorder diagnosis, should double-check the items that contributed to the elevated score. As a reminder, during the development of the MACI, this scale had a very poor correlation with the BAI.

Depressive Affect

The Depressive Affect scale (Scale FF) assesses symptoms associated with a mood disorder. High scorers often feel sad and discouraged. They have negative thoughts about the present and a pessimistic outlook for the future. With their low self-confidence and frequent withdrawal from others, these adolescents perceive few supports. At more serious levels, passive suicidal ideation may be present and this scale should be carefully considered in conjunction with the Suicidal Tendency scale. High BR scores of 85 or above on the Depressive Affect scale should prompt a psychiatric evaluation.

Suicidal Tendency

The Suicidal Tendency scale (Scale GG) assesses suicidal ideation and planning. Adolescents who score high on this scale may contemplate suicide as a viable option to end their pain and suffering. Their depressive states are often quite severe with the adolescent losing sight of any reasons to live. Although the items on this scale generally assess passive ideation, the clinician must assess further the possibility of the adolescent's actual intent, their impulse control, and whether they have access to the means to commit the act. The inability to contract for their safety may necessitate a psychiatric admission.

STRENGTHS AND WEAKNESSES OF THE MACI

Several characteristics of the MACI, which highlight its major strengths and weaknesses relative to similar self-report inventories, follow.

Strengths

1. *Theory-Based Assessment.* The MACI is grounded in Millon's theory of personality (1969, 1981). The three-polarity model generates and defines personality constructs in a logical and systematic manner. The model is coordinated with the current nomenclature, the DSM-IV, yet extends well beyond it in many significant ways. For example, Millon's personality theory delineates characteristics specific to each personality in eight clinical domains (Millon, 1990; Millon & Davis, 1996). Additionally, the theory provides insight regarding how personality patterns are developed (e.g., characteristic experiences) and sustained (e.g., self-perpetuating tendencies) as well as guidance regarding the link between Axis I and II symptoms and, most important, treatment interventions.

2. *Sequential Construction and Validation.* This strength follows from the first one since few instruments have been developed with an underlying theory, no less a theory as comprehensive as Millon's. The MACI was developed in accordance with Loevinger's (1957) three stages of construction and validation. In the theoretical-substantive stage, items were generated and selected to operationalize the personality patterns recognized with the Millon model as well as the adolescent concerns and syndromes that were to be measured. In the internal-structural stage, extensive analyses were conducted to ensure that the individual scales were internally reliable and valid and that the interscale correlations were consistent with theoretical expectations. Finally, in the external-criterion stage, the MACI was compared with other measures to evaluate its convergent and discriminant validity (Campbell & Fiske, 1959). Although all the Millon inventories adhere to this three-stage process, the majority of other instruments have been validated through the latter two stages.

3. *Large Normative Sample and Clinician Involvement.* The MACI was normed on a large clinical sample. Over 1,000 adolescents participated

from over 25 states and Canada. The age range was 13 to 19 years with 56% males and 44% females. All major ethnic groups were included (e.g., 79% White, 8% Black, 5% Hispanic, 3% Native American, and 5% other or not reported). These numbers allowed for four separate norm groups to be established in order to set the initial raw score to BR score transformations as well as to have large cross validation samples. From its initial stages, the development of the MACI involved experienced clinicians who offered numerous suggestions and provided valuable clinical data.

4. *Base Rate Scores.* BR scores, in contrast to standardized T or Z scores, are the preferred reporting statistic when the constructs that an instrument measures have different prevalence rates in the population. The BR scores, as they are constructed on the MACI, inform the clinician that if an adolescent scores at a BR score of 85 or above on a particular scale they have endorsed items at a level consistent with members of the normative sample that had been rated most prominent on that scale by their clinicians. In other words, they have scored at a level within the prevalence rate of the criterion group. Similar comments apply to BR scores 75 to 84, but at a presence level or second most prominent level. This reporting method facilitates identifying the most salient clinical data.

5. *Assesses Axis I and Axis II Symptoms.* The MACI is the only inventory that assesses personality patterns, expressed concerns, and clinical syndromes specific to an adolescent population. Separate scales have been developed for the more stable personality patterns as well as more transient clinical syndromes. Personality patterns provide the context within which Axis I symptoms manifest themselves and valuable insight into developing treatment interventions.

6. *Modifying Indices and Adjustments.* The Modifying Indices help identify test-taking attitudes that may distort the overall profile. BR adjustments are made when adolescents appear to have been guarded and defensive or overly revealing in their self-assessments (Disclosure scale) as well as when they may have attempted to present themselves in a more favorable light than may be realistic or to have exaggerated their symptoms (Desirability–Debasement scale comparisons). Additionally, acute clinical conditions may exaggerate one's underlying personality style (anxiety-depression adjustment) or one's underlying personality

style may either minimize or magnify one's clinical condition (denial-complaint adjustment).

7. *Quick Administration.* With its 160 items at a sixth grade reading level, the MACI usually requires 20 to 30 minutes to complete, which is much less time than other popular adolescent objective inventories (e.g., MMPI-A). Also, the booklet form is user-friendly in that the "true" and "false" choices are next to the items and answers do not have to be transferred to a separate answer form. When administered as part of a battery, the MACI is a reliable and valid personality measure that does not exhaust time and energy resources, both in its administration and scoring, especially in comparison to projective personality measures.

8. *Straightforward, Nonthreatening Items.* Adolescents are usually not threatened or put off by the MACI. The items are face valid and the adolescent recognizes what they are revealing about themselves. There is no guessing or questioning why particular items are present.

9. *Computerized Administration, Scoring, and Interpretation.* The Millon inventories have been at the forefront of computerized personality assessment. Through NCS Assessments' state-of-the-art technologies, the MACI can be administered and scored via the MICROTEST Q system and can be scored and returned via mail-in service. The interpretive reports are comprehensive and written in easy-to-read narrative form. Separate sections address elevations on the Personality Patterns, Expressed Concerns, and Clinical Syndromes scales, noteworthy responses, diagnostic hypotheses, and prognostic and therapeutic implications.

10. *Suitability for Research.* The MACI is well suited for research, in particular, treatment outcome work. It is comprehensive, yet brief, so it can be readministered without much objection. Its scales address pertinent clinical areas, and, theoretically, the Expressed Concerns and Clinical Syndromes Scales have been developed to be sensitive to changes in their state while the Personality Patterns Scales were constructed as more enduring traits and styles.

Weaknesses

1. *Respondent's Interpretation of the Items.* One of the drawbacks to any objective inventory is that the respondents have to interpret the items.

As a result, objective inventories, including the MACI, are not as "objective" as one often assumes. Respondents, for example, must decide what the terms *often, sometimes,* and so forth mean to them. Although the clinician, as an observer, would set the threshold at one point, the respondent may choose a very different point.

2. *Respondent's Awareness and Insight.* Some respondents have very poor awareness and insight into their problems. This issue may be global or it may be specific to a particular problem area. In these instances the MACI profile may not be able to identify and provide, with an adequate degree of reliability and validity, any useful clinical data.

3. *Severe Clinical Symptoms.* The MACI does not assess severe Axis I pathology, which would include psychotic disorders, bipolar disorders, delusions and hallucinations, and paranoid states. Although these conditions are prevalent in psychiatric inpatient settings and after-care day treatment programs, they are much less common in outpatient settings. If the adolescent is in one of the former settings and has any of these conditions, it is probable that they have been detected through observations and interviews; therefore, it would not be necessary to identify them through an objective inventory. In an outpatient setting, if these issues are in question, the MACI can still be administered to provide a context within which the more florid issues are found and it may be advisable to administer projective tests, in particular, the Rorschach.

4. *Interpretive Limits.* In the majority of its cases, the MACI will provide useful clinical data. However, the interpretations in the narrative report should not be considered stated facts. The report comprises probabilistic statements that must be combined with other clinical data to more fully assess their accuracy. The report is considered a "professional-to-professional consultation" (Millon & Davis, 1993). Also, it is "a supplement, not a substitute" for clinical judgment. A word of caution should also be noted here: The MACI Profile and Interpretive Reports should never be shown to adolescents and their families.

5. *Limited Research.* Since its introduction, the MACI has generated modest research activity. While this has hampered further clarification of the test's external validity, some necessary and creative research has been conducted and is beginning to appear in the literature. For example, Murrie and Cornell (2000) compared the MACI with the Psychopa-

thy Checklist-Revised (PCL-R) in regard to its ability to identify adolescents with conduct disorders and, more specifically, psychopathic traits. Six MACI scales (Unruly, Forceful, Social Insensitivity, Substance Abuse Proneness, Delinquent Predisposition, and Impulsive Propensity) had strong correlations with the PCL-R, and the authors then generated a twenty item Psychopathy Content Scale for the MACI. Hiatt and Cornell (1999) studied the concurrent validity of the MACI with the Children's Depression Inventory (CDI) and clinicians' diagnoses. They found that the Doleful and Depressive Affect scales had stronger correlations and diagnostic agreement with the CDI than the clinicians' diagnoses. These results were similar to what was found during the MACI's development. Also, Romm, Bockian, and Harvey (1999) conducted an impressive study that addressed the MACI's underlying factor structure and generated five factor-based prototypes in a residential treatment referred sample.

6. *Cost.* For some clinicians and agencies, in the current economic environment, the MACI is one of the more expensive tests to administer. This may be a major setback regarding its usage, both clinically and empirically.

CLINICAL APPLICATIONS OF THE MACI

The MACI's appropriate use is in a clinical setting and it should be administered only by clinicians with at least a master's degree in a mental health field. Its normative sample includes all major treatment sites—inpatient, residential, and outpatient facilities. It is often administered as a component during a psychological evaluation or during the initial treatment phase. Although not reported in the literature at this point in time, the MACI can also be used to assess treatment outcome.

Personality Assessment and Treatment Planning

Personality assessment and treatment planning are interdependent processes. If the clinician's role is as an evaluator and consultant, the MACI can be administered as part of a comprehensive battery to assess the adolescent's personality style, strengths and weaknesses, conflicts and coping strategies, and so on. The MACI should not be asked to stand on its own; other measures, such as the Rorschach and Thematic Apperception Test (TAT), should be administered to supplement and complement one another. Since the MACI has the benefit of being the instrument with the underlying theory, it often serves as the best place to start the interpretive and integrative process. The end result of an evaluation should be to outline problem areas and specific treatment recommendations which, under the initial premise, would be conducted by another therapist. If the clinician's role with the adolescent, on the other hand, is as an evaluator and therapist, the MACI can be administered initially to outline the above personality issues as well as to identify specific concerns and possible diagnostic syndromes. These latter issues may be the first targets of the treatment, but the clinician, at an early treatment stage, will have gained valuable insight into the adolescent's personality style and can address his or her particular vulnerabilities and tendencies to perpetuate their problems. Each personality pattern has its own underlying conflicts and configuration of responses that may be more or less adaptive to their circumstances. The benefit to this knowledge is that the clinician can help the adolescent prevent recurrence by effecting changes and developing strengths at a more enduring level.

Treatment Outcomes

Although no studies are available at this time, it is believed that the MACI can serve as a clinically relevant treatment outcome measure. On an individual case basis, the MACI can be administered at the beginning of treatment as well as toward the end. A comparison between the profiles would provide some measure of treatment relief and effectiveness. The MACI could also be applied on a broader level, in particular, in specialized treatment settings (e.g., eating disorders and substance-abuse programs). Since adolescents with different personality styles can develop these disorders, it may be possible to separate the clinical population into different groups according to the high-point personality patterns scales (e.g., the two highest scales) and determine which group benefited most from the treatment offered. A third area, focused on the Borderline Tendency scale, would identify adolescents with elevations on this scale and track them through adolescence and, perhaps, into early adulthood. In clinical settings, the prevalence of the Borderline personality in adolescents seems to be rising. However, for what percentage of adolescents might this pattern be a reaction to acute and overwhelming distress that disorganizes them during this time period and for what percentage does it become an enduring pattern? Are there reparative factors that can be identified that help some with this pattern recover and become higher functioning adults?

Adolescence is a period of transition and change and growth, typically filled with challenges and setbacks, accomplishments and failures. Its very nature is questionable, therefore, regarding stability and consistency for all adolescents, but especially for those who struggle and find themselves in clinical settings. The evaluation of these adolescents and its connection to treatment interventions as well as the outcome issues raised above requires instruments that are sufficiently robust to provide confidence that the results are clinically reliable for a period of time yet are also sufficiently sensitive to detect changes that may occur through treatment. To this point in time, test-retest estimates, reported in the MACI manual (Millon, 1993), have only addressed the first aspect of this issue. Table 3.3 reveals that these estimates, obtained between two test administrations 3 to 7 days apart, ranged from .57 (Scale E, Peer Insecurity) to .92 (Scale 9, Borderline Tendency) with a median stability coefficient of .82.

ILLUSTRATIVE CASE REPORTS

The Case of C. G.

C. G., a 17-year-old female, was seen for a psychological evaluation because of her acting-out behavior, truancy, lying, and poor school performance. Her parents were concerned that her poor attitude toward school and learning was a reaction to an underlying learning disability. During her grammar school years, C. G. was a fair student although she possessed high average intellectual abilities and no learning disabilities. She emphasized the social aspects of school and never worked up to her potential. At the time of the evaluation, she was in her senior year and was failing all of her classes. She didn't complete her work and often didn't attend class. She had poor motivation and rejected efforts to help her.

Through C. G.'s adolescent years, her behavior problems escalated. Her

Table 3.3   MACI Test-Retest Correlations

Modifying Indices	Test-Retest Correlation
X. Disclosure	.86
Y. Desirability	.71
Z. Debasement	.84

Personality Patterns	
1. Introversive	.63
2A. Inhibited	.70
2B. Doleful	.83
3. Submissive	.88
4. Dramatizing	.70
5. Egotistic	.82
6A. Unruly	.79
6B. Forceful	.85
7. Conforming	.91
8A. Oppositional	.76
8B. Self-Demeaning	.88
9. Borderline Tendency	.92

Expressed Concerns	
A. Identity Diffusion	.77
B. Self-Devaluation	.85
C. Body Disapproval	.89
D. Sexual Discomfort	.74
E. Peer Insecurity	.57
F. Social Insensitivity	.83
G. Family Discord	.89
H. Childhood Abuse	.81

Table 3.3   (continued)

Clinical Syndromes

AA.	Eating Dysfunctions	.78
BB.	Substance-Abuse Proneness	.90
CC.	Delinquent Predisposition	.80
DD.	Impulsive Propensity	.78
EE.	Anxious Feelings	.85
FF.	Depressive Affect	.81
GG.	Suicidal Tendency	.91

Note. 3 to 7 days between test administrations; $N = 47$. From Millon (1993), p. 34.

parents gradually lost control over her. She broke rules and curfews, often lied, and was very sly and manipulative. The more her parents tried to contain her, the more she rebelled. She spoke disrespectfully toward her mother, cursing and taunting her, until her father intervened. On more than one occasion, he and his daughter had physical altercations. C. G.'s unpredictable moods and behaviors created tremendous tensions in the home and put the entire family "on edge." C. G. lived with her parents and younger brother. She had a conflict-ridden relationship with her parents. She felt that her mother wanted her to be "just like her" and would become angry and disappointed if she wasn't. They were enmeshed and struggled with separation issues. Her father, on the other hand, was detached and very passive until moved to protect his wife. C. G. reported and her parents confirmed that their son was the "good child" and C. G. was the "bad child."

   In addition to her school problems, she had social problems and had not met many adolescent responsibilities. She had many friends; however, she didn't trust them. Friendships with females, in particular, were often intense and fleeting while friendships with males were more stable but often filled with flirtation. She was participating in gang fights as well as beginning to use drugs and alcohol. She did not hold a job and did not participate in organized extracurricular activities. In 11th grade, she had been transferred to an alternative school-based program, but she was reinstated in the mainstream for the beginning of 12th grade.

Cognitive testing revealed average to above average intellectual abilities (WAIS-R Full Scale IQ = 108; Verbal IQ = 104; Performance IQ = 115) and above average academic skills with the exception of written expression. All language and memory scores were within the high average range. Therefore, no learning disability or processing deficit was detected that could account for her academic problems.

The MACI was administered in conjunction with the Rorschach, TAT, and Sentence Completion Test. Figure 3.3 presents C. G.'s MACI profile. A quick look through the profile suggests that she is experiencing tremendous conflict and distress. A review of the reliability and validity measures reveals that it is a valid profile (Reliability, Scale VV) and that she was open and revealing in her self-report (Disclosure scale raw score = 426). As a result, 4 BR points have been deducted from Scales 1 through 9. Additionally, there was a large discrepancy between the Desirability (Scale Y) and Debasement (Scale Z) scales, which led to a 3-point BR deduction on the Expressed Concerns Scales as well as the Eating Dysfunctions, Anxious Feelings, Depressive Affect, and Suicidal Tendency scales. No anxiety-depression adjustment was made since neither scale exceeded a BR score of 85 or above, and no denial-complaint adjustment was made because her highest Personality Patterns Scale was the Forceful scale (the Borderline Tendency scale is not considered in this adjustment). The level of disturbance is severe. Three scales have BR scores of 85 or above, led by the Borderline Tendency scale (BR = 98) and followed by the Forceful and Unruly scales. Meanwhile, there are eight other scales with BR scores in the presence range.

In this case, the interpretive process begins with the Borderline Tendency scale. Elevations at this level are very severe and suggest that C. G. possesses an internal instability that may result from defective psychic structures as well as a failure to develop inner cohesion. She has an uncertain sense of self and deep-seated confusion. She is prone to experiencing pervasive ambivalence, labile moods, unpredictable behaviors, and capricious thoughts. Her inner turmoil leaves her ill prepared to handle ordinary, age-appropriate demands. Within the context of C. G.'s Borderline personality structural defects, her profile elevations reveal the Anger-Hostility Triad associated with conduct-disordered adolescents. She displays a non-empathic and self-centered attitude. Her anger is projected outward and is expressed in impulsive, unpredictable, and often explosive outbursts. Much

Personality Code: 96B**6A48A*2B8B//G**FA*-//-**DDCCFF*BB//

Valid Report

Category		Score		Profile of BR Scores				Diagnostic Scales
		Raw	BR	0 60 75 85 115				
Modifying Indices	X	426	75					Disclosure
	Y	7	35					Desirability
	Z	9	67					Debasement
Personality Patterns	I	22	38					Introversive
	2A	20	37					Inhibited
	2B	25	74					Doleful
	3	30	34					Submissive
	4	52	78					Dramatizing
	5	38	54					Egotistic
	6A	50	82					Unruly
	6B	28	95					Forceful
	7	21	21					Conforming
	8A	38	77					Oppositional
	8B	31	65					Self-Demeaning
	9	29	98					Borderline Tendency
Expressed Concerns	A	29	78					Identity Diffusion
	B	27	48					Self-Devaluation
	C	0	1					Body Disapproval
	D	26	43					Sexual Discomfort
	E	2	8					Peer Insecurity
	F	42	82					Social Insensitivity
	G	35	102					Family Discord
	H	14	45					Childhood Abuse
Clinical Syndromes	AA	3	3					Eating Dysfunctions
	BB	31	72					Substance Abuse Proneness
	CC	34	81					Delinquent Predisposition
	DD	28	82					Impulsive Propensity
	EE	22	41					Anxious Feelings
	FF	21	77					Depressive Affect
	GG	10	26					Suicidal Tendency

Figure 3.3 MACI Profile for C. G., a 17-year-old female.

of her aggressive demeanor is genuine and serves to intimidate and control others. Underneath her brazen exterior, however, there lies an immature, insecure, and vulnerable child who craves attention and affection. She becomes angered when others fail to meet her needs, and she then uses her moods and threats as a means to fight off her separation anxiety as well as to retaliate against those who have disappointed her. C. G.'s tenuous control in all spheres, internally and externally, wreaks havoc in her life leaving her angry, depressed, and lost.

The Expressed Concerns section reveals elevations on three scales. The Family Discord scale is consistent with her history and suggests serious family problems. She experiences tension, conflicts, poor communication, and a lack of support in her family. The Social Insensitivity scale often co-occurs with the Anger-Hostility Triad. Again, the elevation reflects her bravado and self-centered attitude. The third scale, Identity Diffusion, suggests that despite the chaos that she experiences and, in many instances creates, she is aware that she has a poor sense of who she is and what her future holds.

The final section, the Clinical Syndromes section, contains three elevations. The Delinquent Predisposition and Impulsive Propensity scales were consistent with her impulsive and hostile behavior, which were often seen in rebellious acts and angry noncompliance. Her inner turmoil is found with the elevation on the Depressive Affect scale, which indicates that although there is tremendous acting out underneath the behavior problems she is sad. Finally, it was later discovered that her drug and alcohol use was more than reported on the Substance-Abuse Proneness scale.

Results from the projective tests complemented and supplemented the MACI findings. C. G. harbors considerable anger and negativism toward the world. Under nonstressed conditions, she demonstrates adequate reality testing and an ability to perceive her environment in an ordinary way. When she becomes angry, on the other hand, she can experience cognitive distortions, which may lead to outbursts and impulsive actions. Four out of five space responses were minus form quality responses, which accounted for half of her total minus form quality responses. Unable to tolerate frustration, she shows a proclivity to physically acting out her anger. On the Sentence Completion Test, she admitted, "I am very . . . aggressive and opinionated."

C. G. is a persistent seeker of attention, stimulation, and excitement. She often acts in immature, seductive, and dramatic ways. She has a penchant for shortsighted, pleasure-oriented adventures, and she pursues them without much thought given to negative outcomes or the amount of risk involved. C. G. also has an intense need for acceptance and affection from others and takes the initiative in securing these reinforcements. She seeks constant nourishment and possesses a fear of aloneness. Several TAT stories addressed this theme, as did the following Sentence Completion Test responses: "My greatest fear . . . is being alone" and "At home . . . I get very bored because I'm alone."

C. G. has an immature self-image and life perspective for her age. Among her Rorschach percepts, she described "two kids playing pat-a-cake," "two bunny rabbits," and "a face of a teddy bear." She does not appear to be well equipped to resolve the "adult" problems she has created. Her flighty cognitive style limits her capacity to develop insight into her problems and to make the needed changes in her life. Her thinking is not complex; instead, she tends to handle stimuli at a simple level.

Finally, significant family conflicts are present that appear to revolve around issues of trust, separation-individuation, and poor communication. Her internalized images of her parents are contradictory. A lack of consistency and predictability would appear to characterize her relationships with her parents. Numerous aggressive and cooperative behaviors on the Rorschach further suggest that conflicts and confusion pervade her relationships.

The Case of A. N.

In the following case illustration, the MACI results are presented in an integrated fashion with other personality instruments. A. N. is a 16-year-old male who was seen for a psychological evaluation. At the time of the evaluation, he had just completed his junior year at a prestigious high school where he had taken numerous Advanced Placement classes. The evaluation was prompted when A. N.'s guidance counselor expressed concern regarding his stress levels and social functioning. When A. N. was interviewed, he reported having experiences he called "time skips," episodes in which he would seem to lose time and could not remember things. They had been occurring during the past school year. A. N. also described in vague terms and with bland affect other uncommon experiences involving both auditory and visual perceptions. Additionally, there were possible ideas of reference and depersonalization.

A. N. comes from an intact family. He lives with his parents and a younger sister. Family conflicts were denied and A. N. reports generally positive interactions and relationships with other family members. On the other hand, historically he has had difficulty making friends and has often felt uncomfortable in social situations. He has had a few dating experiences, none long-term. A. N. summarized his social difficulties in these words: "I know people but I don't know where I stand."

The MACI was administered as one part of a comprehensive evaluation. Figure 3.4 presents A. N.'s MACI profile. Since the MACI does not assess A. N.'s more bizarre presenting problems, projective tests, in particular the Rorschach, were administered to assess his perceptual abilities and his thought processes. A. N.'s intellectual abilities were found to reside in the very superior range (WAIS-R Full Scale IQ = 133; Verbal IQ = 125; Performance IQ = 134). His memory abilities were also within the very superior range (WRAML Screening Memory Index = 138) and his abstract reasoning abilities were at a similar level (Raven's Standard Progressive Matrices = 99+ percentile, 60/60). A. N.'s responses on the MACI and the Rorschach, TAT, and Sentence Completion Test, in stark contrast to his tremendous intellectual abilities and academic achievements, suggest that he is an internally troubled and worried adolescent. A. N.'s overall profile suggests that he is clinically depressed with a sad mood, psychomotor retardation and slow speech, diminished interest in and pleasure derived from activities, a sense of fatigue and boredom, and difficulty thinking and concentrating. The MACI Doleful and Depressive Affect Scales were at clinically significant levels and the Rorschach Depression Index was positive. Significant concerns were raised by the formal test data because of A. N.'s weak perceptual abilities, limited coping resources, poor interpersonal relatedness, and negative self-esteem. In this author's experiences, when the MACI profile includes elevations on the Personality Patterns Scales 1, 2A, 2B, 8A, and 8B, which is found in this case, it is common to find a significant Coping Deficit Index on the Rorschach. This was a positive finding in this case. In these instances, the adolescent often experiences considerable stress, both chronic and situationally based, and he is vulnerable to becoming overwhelmed. A. N.'s defense was to simplify his perspective and attempt to make the world more manageable. This strategy appeared to help him maintain contact with reality and prevent his thought processes from becoming disorganized.

Personality Code: -**2B2A18B*8A39//E**GBA*-//FF**-*EE//

Valid Report

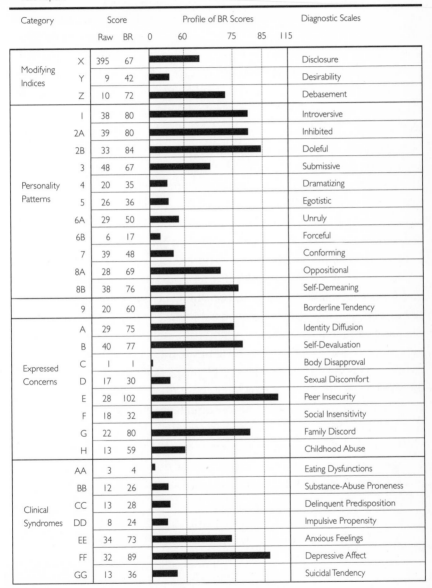

Figure 3.4 MACI Profile for A. N., a 16-year-old male.

A. N. often misperceives and misinterprets his environment. A state of hyperalertness exists where he shows a marked tendency to narrow and simplify ambiguous situations as well as to perceive the world in an idiosyncratic way. He appears to invest excessive mental energy scanning and surveying his world. There is a significant drive to be vigilant, and trust is a primary issue for him. This preoccupation, however, is believed to interfere with his participation in the natural give and take of social interactions. Interpersonally, A. N. acknowledged that he has difficulty "fitting in," both in the present as well as in the past. He is less socially aware and mature than might be expected for his age. He tends to be cautious in developing relationships, instead often maintaining a peripheral stance, more observer than participant. To this point in his life, A. N. has gained limited experience in close relationships and finds it difficult to understand others as well as to be understood. He seems to lack the know how and the initiative to develop close contacts. Among the MACI Expressed Concerns Scales, there is a a second poor sign regarding A. N.'s coping resources and support network. He has significant elevations on the scales that relate to self (Identity Diffusion and Self-Devaluation) and others (both Peer Insecurity and Family Discord). As a result, it appears that A. N. does not have a "place to turn" for a sense of support, security, and reinforcement. Additionally, A. N. is preoccupied with feelings of inadequacy and weakness. He experiences low self-worth, which is both a source and sign of his distress. His displeasure with himself colors his perceptions so that he is inclined to discount his real achievements. He worries that others may have a similar low opinion of him, so his social difficulties may contribute to his poor self-esteem. His self-esteem issues may also stem from feeling confused and uncertain regarding his future. He seems to believe that others have a surer sense than he does of their identity and life goals. He seems upset by his struggle to achieve a greater clarity in this regard.

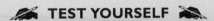

TEST YOURSELF

1. **Which of the following MACI features represent significant changes from the MAPI?**

   (a) The MACI and MAPI share only 49 items.

   (b) The MACI is normed on a clinical sample.

   (c) Ten new clinical scales were developed.

   (d) all of the above.

2. **What was the three-step sequence in the MACI's construction and validation?**

   (a) item selection, empirical keying, external validity

   (b) theoretical-substantive, internal-structural, external-criterion

   (c) internal consistency, convergent-discriminant validity, post-hoc theory

   (d) set item-to-scale relationships, determine item weights, transform to BR scores

3. **The MACI and all Millon Clinical inventories use which reporting statistic?**

   (a) *T* scores

   (b) *Z* scores

   (c) scaled scores

   (d) base rate scores

4. **Which base rate score represents the "prominence" level on a scale?**

   (a) 70

   (b) 75

   (c) 85

   (d) 100

5. **What subject data are needed to convert raw scores to base rate scores?**

   (a) age and sex

   (b) name and date

   (c) setting and presenting problems

   (d) ethnic background and marital status

(continued)

6. **The personality patterns that are most associated with symptom overreporting are**

    (a) Inhibited, Doleful, and Self-Demeaning.

    (b) Dramatizing, Egotistic, and Conforming.

    (c) Introversive, Submissive, and Egotistic.

    (d) Unruly, Forceful, and Oppositional.

7. **A valid MACI profile cannot be obtained if**

    (a) the test taker is younger than 13 or older than 19.

    (b) both validity items are endorsed in the "true" direction.

    (c) more than 10 items are omitted or double-endorsed.

    (d) all of the above.

8. **Clinicians should interpret the _____ scale with caution since the majority of its items are "false"-loaded.**

    (a) Identity Diffusion

    (b) Anxious Feelings

    (c) Depressive Affect

    (d) Suicidal Tendency

9. **Anecdotally speaking, comorbid elevations on the MACI Introversive, Inhibited, Doleful, and Self-Demeaning scales appear to have an association with a positive Rorschach_____ score.**

    (a) Hypervigilance Index

    (b) Coping Deficit Index

    (c) Schizophrenia Index

    (d) Suicidal Constellation

10. **Research indicates that an adolescent's MACI profile is a stable reflection of their personality and psychopathology and can be considered valid for up to 3 years.** True or False?

Answers: 1. d; 2. X; 3. d; 4. c; 5. a; 6. a; 7. d; 8. b; 9. b; 10. False

Four

ESSENTIALS OF PACL ASSESSMENT*

Stephen Strack

INTRODUCTION

The Personality Adjective Check List (PACL) is a 153-item self-report and rating measure of Theodore Millon's (1969/1983b) eight basic personality patterns for use with normal adults and counseling or psychotherapy clients. It features a Problem Indicator scale that may be used as a measure of personality problems. PACL personality scales assess theoretically derived, *normal* versions of the character types most frequently seen in clinical settings. Test results yield rich descriptions of respondents in a language that closely resembles that found in the *Diagnostic and Statistical Manual of Mental Disorders* (DSM-IV; American Psychiatric Association, 1994). The measure is frequently used by therapists and personnel psychologists who work with relatively high functioning individuals and who want to understand the strengths of their clients as well as their weaknesses. The PACL has been used in numerous research studies with normals and patients that ad-

---

DON'T FORGET

Purposes and Uses of the PACL

- Provides personality assessment in normal individuals and counseling or psychotherapy clients 16 years of age and older
- Identifies individuals with personality problems who may warrant further testing for personality disorder
- Assists in treatment planning for therapy clients
- Helps clients make vocational choices
- Aids in personnel selection

---

*Preparation of this manuscript was supported by the U.S. Department of Veterans Affairs. I am grateful to the late Maurice Lorr for consultation and advice.

≡ Rapid Reference 4.1

Personality Adjective Check List (PACL)

Author: Stephen Strack, Ph.D.

Publication date: 1991

What the test measures: Millon's eight basic personality styles and general personality problems

Age range: 16 years and older

Administration time: 10–15 minutes

Qualification of examiners: Graduate training in psychometrics and personality assessment

Publisher: 21st Century Assessment
P.O. Box 608
South Pasadena, CA 91031-0608
Phone: 800-374-2100
Fax: 626-441-0614
Web site: http://www.21stcenturyassessment.com

Start-up kit (includes manual, scoring keys, 50 test sheets, 50 profile sheets), $85; software with narrative interpretations (unlimited uses), $425 (as of January 2001); test administration, scoring, and interpretation via web site, $50 for 5 uses.

dressed a variety of empirical, theoretical, and diagnostic issues (e.g., Hyer & Boyd, 1996; Millon & Davis, 1994; Strack, 1991c, 1993, 1997; Strack & Guevara, 1999; Strack, Lorr, & Campbell, 1989, 1990). Rapid Reference 4.1 provides basic information on the PACL and its publisher; Rapid Reference 4.2 summarizes the personality styles measured by the PACL.

HISTORY AND DEVELOPMENT

The PACL originated at the University of Miami in the early 1980s in a research group led by Theodore Millon, Catherine Green, and the late Robert Meagher, Jr. This was an important time in the development of Millon's work. DSM-III (American Psychiatric Association, 1980) had just been published, and the new multiaxial diagnostic system incorporated much of Millon's (1969/1983b, 1981) personality theory into its taxonomy of character disorders (Axis II). The Millon Clinical Multiaxial Inventory (MCMI; Millon,

≡ Rapid Reference 4.2

Summary of PACL Scales

Introversive. Aloof and solitary by nature, these individuals prefer limited social involvement. They are easygoing, slow paced, and retiring. They rarely show strong emotion and may appear to others as dull and lacking in spontaneity.

Inhibited. Shy and sensitive to criticism, these individuals keep others at an arm's distance and remain on the periphery of social gatherings. They are typically kind and considerate and do not like to draw attention to themselves. They are wary of novelty and seek stable rather than changeable environments.

Cooperative. These individuals value communality and seek others' approval. They are docile, obliging, and agreeable. They tend to think poorly of their own skills and seek stronger individuals to lean on.

Sociable. Active and extraverted, these individuals seek high levels of stimulation and attention. They are often spontaneous, colorful, and dramatic. Their interests and emotions change frequently and others may experience them as shallow and fickle.

Confident. Typically bold and self-assured, these individuals think highly of themselves and expect others to cater to their wishes and demands. They can be charming and manipulative, and others may see them as lacking empathy.

Forceful. Assertive and socially dominant, these individuals are adventurous, competitive, and nonconforming. They persevere in difficult circumstances but can be inconsiderate of others' needs. They are often brusque and insensitive in their tactics and downplay the value of tender emotions.

Respectful. Rule bound and conscientious, these individuals are hardworking and respectful of those in authority. They tend to be perfectionistic and emotionally constricted. They are methodical and persistent but can be too rigid and moralistic in their efforts to live up to conventional standards.

Sensitive. Unconventional and moody, these individuals march to the beat of a different drummer and are not happy with the status quo. They are often loyal and forthright with their opinions but are also awkward, changeable, and fault finding.

Problem Indicator. Items for this scale were compiled from adjectives measuring Millon's (1969/1983b) schizoid, cycloid, and paranoid personalities. Individuals who score high on this scale may possess personality disorder traits, low ego strength, and emotional instability. They often appear anxious, fretful, and moody and may openly express dissatisfaction with themselves and others. They tend to be inflexible and unable to adjust to the life circumstances they find themselves in.

1977), Millon Adolescent Personality Inventory (MAPI; Millon, Green, & Meagher, 1982a), and Millon Behavioral Health Inventory (MBHI; Millon, Green, & Meagher, 1982b) were just becoming widely known in psychiatric and medical settings. Unfortunately, up to that time very little empirical work had been accomplished with Millon's model of personality and we sought ways of changing this. Many theses and dissertations were spawned in the research group, including *Development of the Personality Adjective Check List and Preliminary Validation in a Normal College Population* (Strack, 1981). The purpose of creating the PACL was to open the door for measurement of Millon's personalities in normal subjects. Although Millon's model posits a direct link between normal and abnormal personalities, the MCMI, MAPI, and MBHI were designed for clinical populations. Our long-term goals included building an analogue model of personality disorders among normals and demonstrating the inherent continuity between the normal and abnormal domains of personality functioning.

The PACL was developed using a method outlined by Loevinger (1957), and which was used by Millon and his colleagues for creating his clinical measures. In this method test construction is theory driven and follows a three-step process with development and validation occurring together.

In the first stage of development, called *substantive validity*, 405 theory-derived adjectives were selected to measure normal versions of Millon's (1969/1983b) eight basic and three severe personality styles. Items were drawn from numerous sources, including *Modern Psychopathology* (MP), and were selected based on rater judgments that each item had a clear best-fit for one style (see Strack, 1987, 1991c, for details).

The second, *structural validity*, phase of test construction involves creating scales that match the underlying theory. Toward this end, the 405-item experimental check list was given to 207 men and 252 women from colleges in Ohio and Florida. Preliminary scales were created from items that were endorsed by at least 5% and no more than 80% of subjects; had minimum item-scale correlations of .25; and maximum within-scale item-item correlations of .49 (to prevent redundancy; Strack, 1987, p. 577). Using these criteria, measures were created for each of Millon's eight basic styles that had satisfactory internal consistency and temporal reliability. Alpha coefficients ranged from .76 to .89 (new sample Median = .83; Strack, 1987, p. 578), while test-retest correlations over a three-month period ranged from .60 to .85 (Median = .72 across sexes;

Rapid Reference 4.3

Test Development Strategy of the PACL

Using Loevinger's (1957) method of test construction, PACL scales are developed in a three-stage process based on Millon's (1969/1983) original model of personality. The theory was used throughout test construction as a gauge of validity.

Stage 1: Substantive Validity

A pool of 405 items was generated to measure each theory-defined construct.

Stage 2: Structural Validity

Scales were constructed to match criteria defined by Millon (1969/1983). For example, Millon sates that personality scales must demonstrate high internal consistency, test-retest reliability, and a specific pattern of correlations with other scales.

Stage 3: External Validity

Sometimes called convergent-discriminant validity, final scales were associated with other measures and self-reports of behavior to demonstrate theoretically-appropriate relationships.

Strack, 1987, p. 578; see Rapid Reference 4.3). Additional data showed the scales to be relatively free from social desirability bias (Strack, 1987, p. 581).

Unfortunately, measures could not be developed for the three severe schizoid, cycloid, and paranoid personalities because of extremely low endorsement rates ($< 5\%$) for most keyed items. Rather than throw away the handful of good items that remained for these measures, they were combined into an experimental problem indicator scale, PI, which we thought might be useful in identifying individuals with personality disorders.

In addition to the personality and experimental scales, I developed three response bias indices to aid in the detection of faked protocols (Strack, 1991d), namely, Random (R), Favorable (F), and Unfavorable (UF). Separate groups of college students were asked to complete the PACL randomly, or with intent to give an overly favorable or overly unfavorable self-report. Discriminant function analyses were used to distinguish the faked tests from PACLs completed under the normal instructional set. Equations were derived from these analyses (separately for men and women) and were cross-validated with independent samples. The equations were able to correctly identify a large majority of faked (75%-91%) and normal tests (60%-94%).

In accordance with the third, *external validity*, stage of test development, extensive data were gathered by myself and a number of independent researchers in the form of correlations with tests of personality, mood, and dispositional variables, and reports from subjects about current and past behavior (Chung, 1993; Durff, 1994; Guevara & Strack, 1998; Horton & Retzlaff, 1991; Pincus & Wiggins, 1990; Strack, 1987, 1991b, 1991c, 1994; Strack & Guevara, 1999; Strack & Lorr, 1990b; Strack, Lorr, & Campbell, 1989; Wiggins & Pincus, 1989, 1994). My own research demonstrated that each PACL scale is in line with theoretical expectations and measures milder versions of Millon's (1969/1983b) pathological styles. For example, the scale measuring the avoidant personality (Inhibited) was positively associated with measures of shyness, submissiveness, and social anxiety, and negatively associated with measures of sociability, dominance, and emotional well-being (Strack, 1991d). The scale measuring aggressive traits (Forceful) was positively linked to measures of arrogance, dominance, assertiveness, and autonomy, and negatively linked to measures of deference, submissiveness, and conscientiousness (Strack, 1991d). In a study comparing the PI scores of psychiatric patients (n = 124) and normal adults (n = 140) who completed the PACL using standard instructions, I (Strack, 1991a) found that 84% of the PI scores T = 60 and above were obtained by patients (only 16% of the normals had scores over 59).

Other investigators have reported expected relationships between PACL scales and a variety of measures. For example, Horton and Retzlaff (1991) correlated the PACL with Moos' (1974) *Family Environment Scale* in a sample of 65 undergraduates. They found that family cohesion and expressiveness were strongly associated with cooperative and sociable personality styles, while conflict was most prevalent in the families of sensitive and forceful persons. High scores on the Respectful scale were linked to family environments in which cohesion, organization, and religiosity were salient features.

Wiggins and Pincus (1989; Pincus & Wiggins, 1990) examined the PACL in the context of *Minnesota Multiphasic Personality Inventory* (MMPI) personality disorder scales (Morey, Waugh, & Blashfield, 1985), Big Five *Interpersonal Adjective Scales* (IAS-B5; Trapnell & Wiggins, 1988), the *NEO Personality Inventory* (NEO-PI; Costa & McCrae, 1985), and a circumplex version of the *Inventory of Interpersonal Problems* (Alden, Wiggins, & Pincus, 1990). PACL scales exhibited anticipated relationships with each of the tests in correlational, canonical, and factor analyses. For example, PACL Introversive and Sociable were loaded (in opposite directions) on a factor that included the MMPI Schizoid and Histrionic scales, NEO-PI Extraversion, and IAS-B5 Dominance. PACL Forceful was correlated .59 with interpersonal problems associated with dominance behavior, while PACL Cooperative was correlated .48 with problems involving exploitation by others.

The PACL was recently correlated and factor anlyzed with MMPI-2 scales in independent samples of psychiatric patients ($N = 196$) and normal adults ($N = 124$) (Strack & Guevara, 1999). Consistent with previous research, PACL scales measuring Millon's neurotic, introverted styles (Introversive, Inhibited, Sensitive, PI) were positively associated with MMPI-2 scales measuring introversion (Si), affective states (D, Pt), and disturbed thinking (Sc), while PACL scales measuring extraverted, socially dominant Millon styles (Sociable, Confident, Forceful) were negatively associated to the same MMPI-2 scales. PACL and MMPI-2 scales were reliably associated along two bipolar dimensions measuring *Neuroticism/Introversion versus Extraversion* and *Emotional Distress versus Emotional Stability*, that accounted for 45% of the variance. A third *General Distress* factor loaded only MMPI-2 scales. Congruency coefficients indicated that the factors for patients and normals were very similar. Results highlighted the consistency of the links between MMPI-2 basic scales, the PACL, and other Millon instruments, as well as the utility of the PACL as a measure of Millon's personality styles in a mental health population.

T Scores and Norms

In keeping with the emphasis on normality, PACL scales were normed as T scores rather than as base rate (BR) scores, which Millon used for his clinical tests. Normative data (Strack, 1991c) were obtained from 2,507 normal adults between the ages of 16 and 72. Subjects were sampled between 1980 and 1986, with 90% coming from colleges and 10% from businesses. Men made up 47.4% of the sample and women 52.6%. Ethnicity was 65.2% non-Hispanic White, 17.3% Hispanic, 9.1% Black, 7.6% Asian, and 0.8% Native American Indian or Eskimo (see Table 4.1).

Available Test Forms

The PACL is available as a paper-and-pencil measure that can be hand scored or entered into a computer file via optical scanner. Computerized versions of the checklist for Windows (WinPACL; Robbins, 1998b) and DOS

Table 4.1   Breakdown of Subjects Composing the PACL Normative Sample by Ethnicity and Sex and Comparison With U.S. Census Figures for Enrollees in Institutions of Higher Education

Demographic Feature	Percentage in Sample	
	PACL	U.S.
Ethnicity		
Non-Hispanic White	65.2	82.9
Black	9.1	10.0
Hispanic	17.3	3.8
Asian	7.6	2.7
Native American Indian/Eskimo	0.8	0.6
Sex		
Male	47.4	48.3
Female	52.6	51.7

Note. Reprinted from Strack (1991c, p. 7).

(AUTOPACL; Robbins, 1998a) are available that permit computer administration of the test, scoring, and printing of profile plots of scores as well as narrative interpretations. These programs allow for unlimited uses on a single computer and, as an aid to researchers, can produce exportable files containing test data for multiple subjects. The internet now makes it possible to securely administer and score the PACL, and produce interpretive reports, via the publisher's web site (see Rapid Reference 4.1). PACL computer programs and the web-based scoring service utilize narrative interpretations that were written for counseling and personnel settings, and were based on Millon's writings, empirical information obtained during test construction and validation, and clinical experience with the test.

THEORETICAL AND RESEARCH FOUNDATION

The PACL is based on the comprehensive personality theory of Theodore Millon. Millon (1969/1983b) presented his original biosocial-learning theory in

Modern Psychopathology. Millon's assumptions about normal personality were outlined as follows: (a) Normal and abnormal personality are shaped according to the same basic processes and learning principles; (b) normal personality is on a continuum with pathological personality; (c) no sharp dividing line exists between normal and abnormal personality types; and (d) normal personality patterns may be distinguished from pathological patterns by their adaptive flexibility and balance on the active-passive, pleasure-pain, and self-other polarities. Millon noted: "When an individual displays an ability to cope with his environment in a flexible and adaptive manner and when his characteristic perceptions and behaviors foster increments in personal gratification, then he may be said to possess a normal and healthy personality pattern" (1969/1983b, p. 222).

Although *Modern Psychopathology* clearly addressed both normal and abnormal character types, the focus of that text on personality disorders overshadowed healthy personality development. Normal personality styles were not described there or in Millon's (1981) subsequent text, *Disorders of Personality*. In the early 1970s Millon (1974) and his colleagues developed the Millon Personality Inventory, which assessed normal and abnormal personality traits. It was used primarily by students and was not widely distributed, but it did signal Millon's early interest in normal traits and served as a springboard for development of later measures.

Nondisordered personality styles were not disseminated to a large audience until the publication of the MAPI (Millon, Green, & Meagher, 1982a) and MBHI (Millon, Green, & Meagher, 1982b). These instruments were developed and normed for use in health care settings and presented personalities that were different from personality disorders. Curiously, Millon did not alert test users to the essential differences between these styles and personality disorders. Nevertheless, careful readers could grasp the differences by comparing them with the personalities described in earlier texts and the MCMI (Millon, 1977, 1983a). Significantly, Millon gave different names to the normal styles (Table 4.2) and used terminology

> ### DON'T FORGET
>
> Normal and disordered personalities of the same type are essentially the same in basic trait makeup. There is no sharp dividing line between the two. The major difference is that disordered individuals are rigid and maladaptive in their attitude and behaviors whereas normal persons are flexible and adaptive in responding to their environment.

Table 4.2 Comparable Personality Scales on Millon Instruments

Millon's Original Names	PACL	MCMI-III	MAPI	MACI	MBHI	MBMD	MIPS
Asocial (passive-detached)	Introversive	Schizoid	Introversive	Introversive	Introversive	Introversive	Retiring
Avoidant (active-detached)	Inhibited	Avoidant	Inhibited	Inhibited	Inhibited	Inhibited	Hesitating
Submissive (passive-dependent)	Cooperative	Dependent	Cooperative	Submissive	Cooperative	Cooperative	Agreeing
Gregarious (active-dependent)	Sociable	Histrionic	Sociable	Dramatizing	Sociable	Sociable	Outgoing
Narcissistic (passive-independent)	Confident	Narcissistic	Confident	Egotistic	Confident	Confident	Asserting
Aggressive (active-independent)	Forceful	Antisocial	Forceful	Unruly	Forceful	Forceful	Dissenting
Conforming (passive-ambivalent)	Respectful	Compulsive	Respectful	Conforming	Respectful	Respectful	Conforming
Negativistic (active-ambivalent)	Sensitive	Passive-Aggressive	Sensitive	Oppositional	Sensitive	Oppositional	Complaining

Note. PACL = Personality Adjective Check List; MCMI-III = Millon Clinical Multiaxial Inventory–III; MAPI = Millon Adolescent Personality Inventory; MACI = Millon Adolescent Clinical Inventory; MBHI = Millon Behavioral Health Inventory; MBMD = Millon Behavioral Medicine Diagnostic; MIPS = Millon Index of Personality Styles.

that was much less severe than that used for the personality disorders. For example, normal introversive personalities were described in the MBHI manual as "colorless," "quiet," and "unconcerned about their problems" (Millon, Green, & Meagher, 1982b, p. 2), while Millon (1983a) reported in the MCMI manual that disordered schizoid (asocial) persons demonstrated "an inability to display enthusiasm or experience pleasure," "obscure thought processes," and a "lack of vitality" (p. 4).

The first published work devoted exclusively to Millon's healthy personality styles was an article describing the development and validation of the PACL (Strack, 1987). The instrument provided self-report and rating measures of Millon's basic eight personality patterns and was normed solely on normal adults. In that initial report and several subsequent articles (Strack, 1991a, 1992, 1993, 1994; Strack & Lorr, 1990a, 1990b; Strack, Lorr, & Campbell, 1990), my colleagues and I provided considerable empirical evidence in support of Millon's proposition that his normal styles are quite similar to their personality disorder counterparts.

In the mid-1980s Millon (1986a, 1986b, 1987, 1996, 1997; Millon & Davis, 1994) began altering his model and clinical measures to accommodate changes in DSM Axis II (American Psychiatric Association, 1987, 1994). He also widened his focus by placing his model in an evolutionary framework (Millon, 1990). From a structural perspective these changes resulted in the addition of a discordant reinforcement strategy (where pleasure and pain have reversed value) and three abnormal personality styles: depressive, aggressive-sadistic, and self-defeating.

The dimensional approach to normal personality presented by Millon in 1990 was his first effort to delineate healthy character styles outside the domain of psychopathology. It was followed in 1994 with the publication of the manual for the Millon Index of Personality Styles (MIPS; Millon, 1994b), a measure for use with normal adults that assesses his trait dimensions as well as character styles.

Millon's new perspective was developed without reference to disorder but borrowed many concepts from his original model of personality. In this approach Millon considered the universe of traits and interpersonal styles that exist in the normal population and came up with three sets of personality variables to define and measure them. The first set, called *motivating aims,* represents his three basic axes in evolutionary form. The original pleasure-pain polarity was called enhancing-preserving, active-passive was modifying-accommodating, and self-other was individuating-nurturing. The second set of variables, which were borrowed from Jung (1936/1971), were termed *cognitive modes*. For Millon cognition means an individual's primary source of obtaining information and the means by which that information is processed or transformed. Preferred sources of information can be the self (internal) or others (external), and either tangible or intangible. Preferred means of transforming information can be intellectual or affective and assimilative versus imaginative. The last set of variables describe 10 common *interpersonal behaviors* or styles. Eight of the 10 personalities are essentially the same as those measured by the MAPI, MBHI, MBMD, and PACL, and are empirically related to PDs. See Table 4.2. Two additional styles, doleful and self-demeaning, are hypothesized to be related to the depressive and self-defeating PDs, but empirical evidence is needed to verify this.

COMPARISON OF THE PACL WITH OTHER MILLON INSTRUMENTS

The eight personality styles measured by the PACL are also measured by the MCMI-III, MAPI, MACI, MBHI, MBMD, and MIPS. The MCMI-III and MACI assess disordered versions of these personalities types; the PACL, MAPI, MBHI, MBMD, and MIPS assess normal variants. The MCMI-III, MAPI, MACI, MBHI, and MBMD were developed and normed on individuals seeking psychological or medical help. Because of this, Millon recommends that these instrument *not be used in normal populations*. The PACL and MIPS are the only Millon instruments developed and normed on normal adults. The PACL and MIPS differ significantly in that the PACL is an adjective measure whereas the MIPS is a questionnaire measure. The PACL is faster to administer than the MIPS, can be more readily used as a rating instrument, and has a more extensive research base. At the same time, the MIPS assesses many personality components not tapped by the PACL (six motivating aims, eight cognitive styles, and two additional interpersonal styles) and has more thorough norms.

TEST ADMINISTRATION

The PACL was developed for use with individuals 16 years of age and older who possess English reading skills at the eighth grade level. The checklist may be administered to individuals or groups using a paper-and-pencil test form or via personal computer using one of the IBM-compatible programs currently available, or the publisher's secure internet web site. Administration time for all forms of the PACL is 10 to 15 minutes.

Administering the Paper-and-Pencil Form

The paper-and-pencil form is administered in a manner common to most objective personality instruments. Directions for completing the checklist, space for entering identifying information, the test items, and space for giving responses are provided on the single-sheet test protocol. Instructions are concise, clear, and were designed to be self-explanatory. For all but a few handicapped respondents, little or no special attention is required for test completion. The PACL has proved itself to be interesting and nonthreatening to nearly all respondents and can be easily introduced as "a measure of personality style."

After the test form and No. 2 pencils have been handed out, respondents should be given a few moments to look over the format of the checklist and to complete the sections asking for identifying information. The examiner may also ask respondents to give other personal data in the section marked "optional" (see the section Optional Identifying Information, below).

Next, respondents should be asked to turn the form over, carefully read the instructions for completing the checklist, and begin answering the items. If there are questions about the meaning of individual items, examiners may either

> ## DON'T FORGET
>
> ### Tips for Administering the PACL
>
> - Providing a No. 2 pencil allows respondents to mark their answers clearly and to erase completely any errors.
> - If respondents have questions about the meaning of individual items, give standard definitions for the words. Avoid giving examples of word usage.
> - If the meaning of an item remains unclear to a respondent after giving a definition, instruct the individual to leave the item blank as if it did not apply.
> - When the test is complete, check to make sure that all identifying information has been entered accurately and that responses are clearly marked.

give standard definitions for these words or simply ask the respondent to leave blank any items they are unsure about. In practice, very few respondents request help with word definitions. If an individual has questions about several test items, this may indicate a reading comprehension problem. In such cases, the examiner must decide if the respondent has enough facility with the language to complete the checklist in a valid manner.

When examinees have finished the test it is advisable to carefully check to see that identifying information has been entered correctly and that responses are clearly marked. The most frequent errors are item responses that overlap or are marked too lightly.

Optional Identifying Information

For some purposes examiners may wish to gather information about respondents beyond basic demographics. The portion of the answer sheet marked "optional" gives space for recording a nine-digit identification number, a five-digit research code, years of education, ethnicity, marital status, and religion. The identification number and research codes are defined by the examiner, for example, social security number, driver's license, and diagnosis.

ADMINISTERING THE PACL BY COMPUTER

The PACL can be administered to individuals or groups by personal computer using any of the software programs available for IBM-compatible computers running DOS or Windows operating systems, or via the publisher's secure internet web site. Procedures for giving the test are essentially the same for all computerized versions. The directions given here are from WinPACL 2.0 (Robbins, 1998b).

1. Start the software program prior to seating the respondent in front of the computer. From the start-up menu, select Data Entry and then choose Single Administration. The respondent data input screen will be displayed. See Figure 4.1.

2. Enter the demographic information desired, then click the OK button. A screen with instructions for completing the test will be displayed. See Figure 4.2.

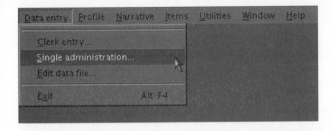

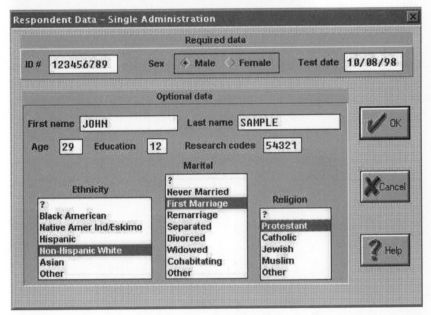

Figure 4.1

3. Seat the respondent in front of the computer and familiarize him or her with use of the keyboard and mouse. Next, go over the instructions with the respondent to ensure that he or she is comfortable with the task. Click the OK button to display the first page of test items. See Figure 4.3.

4. Items are endorsed by using the left mouse button to click on the check box next to each word. When the respondent is finished with the first group of words, he or she clicks on the Page 2 button to move to the next group. The test is completed when the respondent has gone through all of the items in the second group.

This list consists of words which people use to describe themselves. Read each word and decide whether or not it describes you.

If the word describes you, use the mouse to click on the box next to the word. A check mark will appear in the box. To correct an error, click on the box again to erase the check mark.

If the word does not describe you, simply leave the box empty and go on to the next word.

Some of the words may sound alike, but it is important that you check all the words that describe you. Also, do not worry about contradictions or inconsistencies in your reporting.

The words are presented on two "pages." When you have given your answers to the first eighty words, click on the "Page 2" button to go to the second page.

Click on the "Done" button when you are finished. This button appears only when you are on page 2. Note that you may go back to page 1 from page 2.

Although there is no time limit for completing the list, it is best to work as rapidly as is comfortable for you. There are 153 words in all. You may ask for help at any time.

Click the OK button to begin.

✓ OK

Figure 4.2

Page 1

✓ 1. playful	21. competitive	41. apathetic	61. fearless
2. self-satisfied	22. industrious	42. fluctuating	62. baffling
3. reserved	23. uneasy	43. agreeable	63. neat
4. consenting	24. chaotic	44. peppy	64. solitary
5. ignored	25. gregarious	45. temperamental	65. touchy
6. insecure	26. arrogant	46. self-centered	66. secretive
7. boastful	27. fragmented	47. testy	67. outgoing
8. strict	28. afraid	48. depressed	68. traditional
9. extravagant	29. yielding	49. unemotional	69. subdued
10. oversensitive	30. virtuous	50. fearful	70. fickle
11. apprehensive	31. sluggish	51. overconfident	71. animated
12. careful	32. upright	52. annoyed	72. moody
13. intimidating	33. selfish	53. lively	73. talkative
14. bubbly	34. worried	54. rigid	74. nagging
15. edgy	35. straight-laced	55. naive	75. decent
16. remote	36. aggravated	56. irritable	76. expressionless
17. courageous	37. precise	57. shy	77. conforming
18. timid	38. cool	58. disciplined	78. coy
19. erratic	39. vivacious	59. uninspired	79. dramatic
20. innocent	40. daring	60. excluded	80. militant

▶ Page 2   ? Help

Figure 4.3

Appropriate Testing Conditions

Respondents

To complete the checklist in a reliable and valid manner, respondents should be alert, well oriented to their surroundings, have a clear grasp of the nature of the task, and understand what the test data will be used for. Persons who are unduly fatigued, apprehensive, apathetic, or sedated will not be able to complete the test properly and should be examined at another time when they are not affected by these conditions.

Testing Environment

The PACL may be administered in a variety of settings depending on the types of individuals who will be examined and how the test data will be used. The PACL has been successfully administered in office reception rooms, classrooms, auditoriums, and homes. The setting should be relatively quiet, free of unnecessary distractions, and have ample light. Those completing the paper-and-pencil form will need desk space or a clipboard on which to place the test protocol while giving responses. Enough physical space is needed to make respondents feel comfortable and to ensure confidentiality.

Supervision of the Testing

Most respondents require little or no supervision to complete the checklist. In clinical and personnel settings, where individuals may have special needs due to age and emotional or medical handicaps, and where data are used for treatment planning, career or job counseling, and access to various services, direct supervision of respondents is often necessary to ensure confidentiality and standardized test administration.

Testing Individuals With Special Needs

Administration procedures can be altered to accommodate those who are hard of hearing, or have poor vision or poor motor control. It is advisable to learn as much as possible about the respondent's impairment prior to testing so that proper accommodations can be considered and made. The PACL can be administered to hearing-impaired individuals by giving instructions in American Sign Language. Visually impaired persons and those with motor-control problems can be assisted by reading aloud the instructions and test items and by having a proxy record their responses on the test protocol or computer.

The effects of altered test administration procedures on PACL results are unknown. However, objective personality assessments are typically reliable under varied data collection conditions. As a rule, the more one deviates from standard administration procedures, the more likely it is that unwanted errors will accrue. For this reason it is important to note in any report of test findings the nature of the respondent's impairment and the changes that were made in test administration to accommodate him or her.

SCORING THE PACL

The paper-and-pencil version of the PACL may be hand scored and plotted using template keys and a profile sheet provided by the publisher. It may also be computer scored through the publisher's secure web site, or by entering test data manually or through optical scanner into one of the software programs available for this purpose. When the PACL is administered by computer it is scored automatically.

Scoring the PACL by Hand

To score the PACL by hand, (a) calculate raw scores for each of the test's nine scales, (b) add up the number of items endorsed across all 153 items, and (c) convert the raw scores into T scores. Most users will then want to plot the T scores on the profile sheet. To calculate the raw scores, use the key templates provided for this purpose by the publisher. There are nine templates in all, one for each scale. Simply align each template on the test form as instructed and count the number of items endorsed for the scale. Record the raw score in the appropriate box found in the lower portion of the profile sheet. The number of adjectives checked is determined by counting the items

> **CAUTION**
>
> ....
>
> T scores for PACL scales are calculated separately for men and women by five groups based on the number of adjectives checked across the test. When scoring the PACL by hand, you must accurately note the respondent's sex and norm group or you will obtain the wrong values.

endorsed across the test. This value is recorded in the same section as the test scales.

To obtain T scores, use the conversion tables presented in Appendix E of the test manual. First, determine the respondent's norm group using the number of adjectives checked. There are 10 groups in all, 5 each for men and women. Use the respondent's norm group number and raw scale scores to locate the appropriate T scores. Record these values on the profile sheet in the space provided; then plot the scores on the graph. Plotting the scores allows you to quickly grasp how far above and below the mean ($T = 50$) the respondent falls on each scale. Figure 4.4 shows a completed profile sheet.

Validity Indices

The PACL's three Validity Indices are scored when a respondent is suspected of completing the checklist incorrectly by randomly endorsing items as self-descriptive or by giving an inordinately favorable or unfavorable self-impression. They are calculated by inserting the appropriate raw scale scores into the following formulas:

For men,

Random = ((Introversive × .31) + (Cooperative × −.11) + (Forceful × .08) + (Respectful × −.18) + 0.98) × 10

Favorable = ((Introversive × −.16) + (Sociable × .07) + (Sensitive × −.28) + (Problem Indicator × −.33) + 0.64) × 10

Unfavorable = ((Inhibited × .12) + (Cooperative × −.19) + (Sociable × −.13) + (Confident × .08) + 0.82) × 10

For women,

Random = ((Introversive × .32) + (Sociable × −.11) + (Confident × .42) + (Forceful × −.13) + (Number of Adjectives Checked × −.08) + 2.51) × 10

Favorable = ((Introversive × .22) + (Inhibited × −.11) + (Problem Indicator × −.43) + 0.90) × 10

Unfavorable = ((Cooperative × −.18) + (Sociable × −.23) + (Number of Adjectives Checked × .03) + 1.64) × 10

Scores from these indices are recorded on the profile sheet in the space provided.

PACL

Personality Adjective Check List

Stephen Strack, Ph.D.

Name or ID: **C. W.**   Sex: M (F)   Age: **30**

Date: **10/10/98**   Education: **B.A.**   Ethnicity: **NHW**   Marital Status: **M**

Religion: ———   Research Codes: ———   Examiner: ———

Scale	T Score	T Score Profile
1 - Introversive (IN)	43	
2 - Inhibited (IH)	41	
3 - Cooperative (CO)	53	
4 - Sociable (SO)	66	
5 - Confident (CN)	52	
6 - Forceful (FO)	67	
7 - Respectful (RE)	40	
8 - Sensitive (SE)	42	
9 - PI	48	

30   40   50   60   70   80   90   100

Raw Scores			Validity Indices
1 - IN **1**	4 - SO **16**	7 - RE **6**	R = ———
2 - IH **3**	5 - CN **6**	8 - SE **3**	F = **-0.7**
3 - CO **15**	6 - FO **11**	9 - PI **2**	UF = ———
	Number of Adjectives Checked	**54**	

Figure 4.4 Example of a Completed Profile Sheet

Note. © 1991 Stephen Strack, Ph.D. All Rights Reserved.

Computerized Scoring Procedures

Data from paper forms may be entered manually or by optical scanner into any of the software scoring programs available from the publisher or through the internet scoring service. To scan the forms, follow the instructions provided by the manufacturer of the scanner. Once the forms are scanned, data are automatically recorded in the computer and can then be read by the PACL scoring program.

For manual entry of test data, start the computer program and go to the initial working menu. Select the Data Entry item and then Clerk Entry. This will bring up a screen for entering demographic information. Complete the desired sections and click on the OK button if you are using a Windows program or F10 if you are using a DOS program. This will move you to a screen where you will be able to enter individual responses. When you have finished entering all of the item endorsements, click on OK (Windows program) or Q (DOS program) to end the routine. Data are automatically scored and recorded in individual computer files. The files can be called up to print or be displayed on the computer monitor.

HOW TO INTERPRET THE PACL

The task of interpreting PACL scale scores is like that of interpreting most other objective personality measures and involves knowledge from a number of different domains. To adequately interpret the test, examiners must be familiar with the assets and limitations of self-report measures of personality in general and, in particular, with the assets and limitations of the PACL (see the section Strengths and Weaknesses of the PACL on page 193). An understanding of basic psychometric theory is needed, as is familiarity with Millon's (1969/1983b) original model of personality. Examiners also need to know some things about the individual taking the test and about the validity of the respondent's test protocol. In particular, they should know the respondent's sex, age, ethnic background, and educational level, since each of these characteristics is used to evaluate the fit of the respondent with the normative sample on which the standardized T scores are based.

Other factors influencing judgments about the test scores are the particular setting in which the test is given, the reasons for giving the test, and the kinds

> ## DON'T FORGET
> ....
> Accurate test interpretation requires a valid test protocol obtained from a respondent who fits the characteristics of the test's normative group.

of questions to be answered by the interpretation. It is assumed that persons interpreting the PACL will have the special knowledge required to apply test results to their particular settings, for example, personnel selection and vocational counseling. It is also assumed that examiners will utilize additional test or interview data to make decisions about the respondent that cannot be made based on results from the PACL alone, for example, determining the presence of a personality disorder.

Test Validity

Prior to interpreting PACL results the examiner should assess whether the test responses are valid. To accept that a given PACL protocol is valid, the checklist must have been completed according to the instructions provided on the answer sheet by an alert, willing respondent who is not affected physically or mentally in a manner that would seriously hamper his or her ability to complete the test. Test instructions may of course be altered by the examiner to accommodate individuals with special needs, to obtain observer ratings, or another type of assessment other than basic self-report. However, it should be noted that the norms for the PACL are based on self-reports using the standard instructional set found on the PACL answer sheet.

In nearly all settings, respondents are willing and able to complete the PACL in a valid manner. However, there are instances where the validity of test results may come into question. The question of validity may arise when an individual checks very few or very many adjectives as being self-descriptive or when a respondent is suspected of having answered the PACL randomly or in an overly positive or negative manner. Each of these threats to validity is discussed below.

Number of Adjectives Checked

For men in the normative sample, the mean number of adjectives checked on the PACL was 47. For women, the mean was 50. The standard deviation for men was 19.6 and for women it was 19.0. Although individual differences in the number of adjectives checked is expected, and is controlled for in the standardized T scores, the checking of exceptionally few or many items is cause for concern. As a general rule, protocols with fewer than 10 or more than 120 items checked should be considered invalid. Protocols with 10 to 19 or 111 to 120 adjectives checked should be considered questionable and deserving of closer scrutiny.

CAUTION

Tests that are invalid due to random, favorable, or unfavorable responding often do not show a distinct score profile. To assess for these types of bias, calculate the appropriate validity index and use the recommended cutoff score.

Random Responding

Respondents may occasionally attempt to defeat the purpose of the test by randomly checking items as self-descriptive. When viewing the profile of scores for such tests they are often distinguishable from those answered accurately. If an individual is suspected of random responding, calculate the Random score (see the section Validity Indices on page 173) according to the appropriate formula for men or women. Scores above 0.0 suggest that the individual answered the test randomly. The higher the score, the more likely it is that the test is invalid.

Favorable Responding

Some individuals may be motivated to present themselves in an especially favorable light. Such persons often exaggerate their socially desirable traits and downplay their negative qualities. To identify tests that may be invalid owing to biased responding, calculate the Favorable score (see the section Validity Indices on page 173) for men or women, as appropriate. Scores above 0.0 suggest a favorable bias. The higher the score is above 0.0, the more likely it is that the test is not interpretable.

Unfavorable Responding

There are circumstances where respondents may attempt to present themselves in an especially negative light. Test protocols that are suspected of being biased because of an unfavorable response set can be distinguished from unbiased protocols using the Unfavorable index (see the section Validity Indices on page 173). Scores above 0.0 suggest a bias owing to negative self-presentation, with larger values indicating a greater probability that the results have been unduly affected and may be uninterpretable.

Step-by-Step Procedures for Test Interpretation

Valid PACL results can be interpreted according to the following procedures.

Step 1: Determine Highest Scale Scores

Identify the highest two or three scale scores from among the eight basic personality styles. Although highly elevated Problem Indicator scores should be noted at this time, do not include this scale in determining the highest two or three scale scores because it does not measure a single personality style. Interpretation of the Problem Indicator scale will come later, after interpretation of the basic personality scales.

Step 2: Order Prominent Scales

Order the prominent scales from highest to lowest, noting their elevation above the mean and vis-à-vis each other. The highest scale serves as the base for the overall interpretation; the second-highest scale is given secondary importance; the third-highest scale is given tertiary importance.

Step 3: Determine Characteristic Personality Styles

Synthesize descriptions of the two or three prominent personality styles represented in the profile to create a picture of the individual's typical manner of interacting with others, as well as his or her feelings, attitudes, and response behaviors toward given situations, persons, and environments. Experience with the PACL and with Millon's theory will enhance your ability to accurately bring together aspects of different personalities to form a cohesive and comprehensive picture of a respondent. In general, the approach is an additive one, where characteristics of the most prominent personality style are used as an outline, and features of the other prominent styles are brought in to fill in the picture. It is important to remember that with increasing elevations above 50, the likelihood that an individual will demonstrate the behaviors and characteristics represented by a given personality scale also increases. A T score of 70, for example, implies that the respondent possesses more traits of the given personality than 98% of the population and, therefore, that these characteristics will appear quite dominant from an interpersonal point of view. The same thing cannot be said about an individual with a T score of 55 since this score would mean that the person possesses about the same number of personality traits as the average respondent. Be aware too that scales with similar elevations (i.e., those within 5 points of each other) should be given more equal weighting in the interpretation than scales that have quite different elevations. Noting the standard error of PACL scales will help you judge when two scales are approximately equal and when they are likely to be significantly different. (See Rapid References 4.4 and 4.5.)

Once a personality description has been generated using the two or three highest scales, other information about the respondent should be brought in to complete the interpretation, as outlined in the next steps.

≡Rapid Reference 4.4

Understanding T Scores and Percentiles

T score distributions have a mean of 50 and a standard deviation of 10. In this distribution, approximately 70% of all respondents will have scale scores falling between 40 and 60. Only 15% of respondents will have scale scores of 60 or above, and only 15% will have scale scores of 40 or below.

T Score and Corresponding Percentile

T Score	Percentile
70	98
60	85
55	71
50	50
45	29
40	15
30	2

Step 4: Interpret Low Scale Scores

Low scale scores may be interpreted as indicating that the respondent has *few* of the traits being measured. For example, low Cooperative scores imply that the respondent has little need for approval and affection and will *not* appear especially docile, obliging, and so forth. It is important to remember that a low score does not indicate the *opposite* of the scale name, just low levels of the traits being measured. (For more details, see Rapid Reference 4.6.)

≋ Rapid Reference 4.5

Understanding Standard Error of Measurement

The standard error of a scale score is an estimate of the variability that can be expected in the score due to imperfect measurement. The standard error for a particular scale is a function of its standard deviation and internal consistency. Scales with low standard deviations and high internal consistency will have lower standard errors than scales with high standard deviations and low internal consistency. Scores for any PACL scale are likely to vary up or down by the number of points listed in the standard error table below *simply because of measurement error*. The chances are 2:1 that a respondent's "true" score lies somewhere within the interval obtained by adding and subtracting the appropriate standard error value from his or her obtained scale score. As an example, suppose that a man obtained an Introversive *T* score of 60. According to the table, the standard error is 5.1. There is a 2:1 chance that his "true" score lies somewhere between 54.9 and 65.1.

Standard Errors for PACL Scales by Sex of Respondent

Scale	Men	Women
Introversive	5.1	4.7
Inhibited	3.7	3.5
Cooperative	4.5	4.4
Sociable	4.4	3.9
Confident	4.4	4.3
Forceful	3.9	4.2
Respectful	4.3	4.3
Sensitive	3.9	4.0
Problem Indicator	5.6	5.7

Note. Reprinted from Strack (1991c, p. 27).

Step 5: Interpret High Problem Indicator Scores

Scores of 60 or above on the Problem Indicator scale should be noted and discussed in the interpretation. As was noted in Rapid Reference 4.2, the Problem Indicator scale measures aspects of Millon's three more severe styles and may be considered an indicator of maladaptive personality characteristics. It should be clear, however, that although scores of 60 or above may suggest the presence of a personality disorder, further testing is necessary before this conclusion can be made.

Step 6: Integrate Other Test Results

Take into account results of other tests, demographic information, and special knowledge of the respondent and his or her environment. The personality description developed up to this point is "blind" with respect to extratest data. At this time, the test interpretation should be altered to reflect knowledge of the respondent from other sources.

Counseling/Psychotherapy Presentation Features and Treatment Issues

The following scale summaries outline (a) the typical features of individuals who score high on various PACL scales during the initial evaluation phase of counseling or psychotherapy and (b) the vocational interests and work behaviors most frequently associated with various Millon personality types as measured by the PACL. Since most individuals score high on more than one scale,

---

≡Rapid Reference 4.6

Interpreting Low Scale Scores

Consider the following information when a respondent obtains a *T* score of 40 or below.

Cooperative	Low need for dependency and approval; is not a "people pleaser"
Sociable	Not socially oriented; may lack social skills; may not be appropriate for group interventions
Confident	May devalue personal skills and accomplishments; may have low self-confidence and self-esteem
Forceful	May have trouble being assertive; may be thin-skinned
Respectful	Low need for approval; may lack organizational skills; may have trouble keeping appointments and completing work assignments

the descriptions fit best when they are blended with descriptions from associated personality styles.

Introversive

Counseling/Psychotherapy Evaluations   These individuals frequently break down when they have to adjust to major environmental changes and extreme shifts in their usual responsibilities. Their typical response to stress and pressure is to withdraw and shut down their feelings. In doing this, they may become insensitive and detached from themselves and others. In these circumstances, introversive individuals may present themselves for help when others goad them into it. They may not fully appreciate why others have become concerned with their well-being; nor may they be aware of how their behavior has changed. Sometimes these individuals may experience an uncharacteristic surge of emotions. They may feel acutely tense, anxious, hypomanic, or depressed. Their distress is all the more painful, since they are not used to handling strong feelings. Others may experience little change in their emotions but an increase in somatic symptoms such as headaches, vague bodily pain, gastrointestinal ailments, and so forth.

Regardless of presentation, introversive individuals typically tend not to be intuitive and are usually awkward in the world of feelings. They may not have the words to precisely report their internal experiences. They may have difficulty in establishing a therapeutic relationship and may expect therapy to offer a quick fix. Often they will leave treatment once they are able to resume their usual routine without undue difficulty. They are usually receptive to medical explanations for their difficulties and may welcome anxiolytic or antidepressant medication. Supportive therapy that aims at counteracting withdrawal and shoring up self-esteem can also help. Reconstructing the circumstances that led to their current problems may also be beneficial. Assisting these individuals to learn more proactive coping skills is a frequent therapeutic goal. Behavioral techniques are especially well suited to these individuals. Group therapy is often not well tolerated, though it may be useful for motivated clients who want to develop their interpersonal skills.

Vocational Interests/Work Behaviors   Individuals with this personality style are frequently attracted to intellectual or mechanical occupations that allow them to be on their own. They often pursue goals that permit them to regulate the amount of information and stimulation they receive. Given a choice, they seek a stable work environment with few people and little commotion. Nevertheless, most of these individuals perform well in noisy, stimulating environments, if they are allowed to work independently at a pace they set for themselves. These individuals are usually reliable and dependable employees who are not bothered by repetitive tasks. They are quiet, slow paced, pleasant, nondemanding, and usually keep a calm demeanor. They do not respond well if asked to assume leadership positions or participate actively in groups. At times coworkers may find these individuals frustrating to be with, because they often tune out those around them and may seem insensitive to their needs.

Inhibited

Counseling / Psychotherapy Evaluations   Individuals with this personality style are most likely to seek help when they become overwhelmed by painful feelings of anxiety, depression, inadequacy, and helplessness. They may feel fragile and unable to regulate their emotions or personal defenses. They may have experienced a failed relationship or have been unable to handle interpersonal demands at home or the workplace. They may even blame others for their problems. Alternatively, they may turn on themselves and become overly critical and disparaging of their ability to cope with life.

When faced with stress, these individuals often respond by withdrawing and becoming more distrustful. In therapy they are likely to be wary and fearful of intrusion. It is best to take a direct but nonthreatening approach with these individuals and to take time to build rapport. Because they are withdrawn, therapists will do well regularly to seek their feedback about the relationship and proposed tasks. Even when they appear to be open, they are likely to keep their true feelings to themselves, often appearing to be happy but actually feeling quite differently.

Supportive individual or group therapy aimed at shoring up defenses and building self-esteem is recommended. Once a working alliance has been established, cognitive and interpersonal techniques may be used to develop adaptive defenses and realistic appraisals of self and others. For example, these individuals may not be aware that their sensitivity can be an asset as well as a liability. Since they feel things strongly, they can tune into the subtle messages and responses from others, which gives them an edge in dealing with people, if they can learn to modulate their feelings and remain objective about their experience. Behavioral techniques may be useful here in controlling anxious arousal and generalized avoidance. Since these individuals have a habit of keeping others at a distance, they may have deficient interpersonal skills. Because of this, learning about people and how to manage conflicts is often an important therapeutic goal.

Vocational Interests/Work Behaviors   Individuals with this personality style frequently seek intellectual, conventional, and artistic occupations that permit them to regulate the amount of stimulation and information they receive from their environment. They prefer stable work settings where they can operate alone or with a few close associates. They do not thrive in busy, social environments, which they frequently find too taxing of their personal resources. In a stable, safe environment, these personalities are known for being kind, considerate, and loyal. They are often perceptive and tuned in to the feelings and thoughts of others. However, they are typically slow in adjusting to change and find it difficult to be assertive or active in group situations. Supervisors will do well to appreciate their sensitivity and need for interpersonal space. Since these individuals are usually not forthcoming with their feelings, it is important to request regular feedback from them about their work experiences.

Cooperative

Counseling/Psychotherapy Evaluations   Emotional and interpersonal conflicts are often responded to by these people with denial; overconventional thinking; and feelings of helplessness, powerlessness, and failure. They may become morose, complain excessively, and cling to those they view as stronger and more capable. They may seek help for physical rather than emotional symptoms and resist psychological explanations for these difficulties. Problems often arise because their success in eliciting support from others perpetuates their weak self-image and inhibits the acquisition of proactive coping skills.

Those who score high on this scale are likely to seek treatment willingly and be trustful and self-disclosing right from the start. Unfortunately, they also tend to be naive, dependent, and resistive of therapeutic efforts that guide them toward autonomy. A nondirective approach may foster growth and independence better than more directive techniques. Helping these individuals typically involves bolstering their self-worth and self-esteem, exploring problem-solving techniques, and encouraging them to try new behaviors. Cognitive techniques also may be useful in counteracting self-defeating thoughts and attitudes. Since these people value communality over independence and self-

assertion, it can be useful to frame therapeutic tasks methods to increase interpersonal competence and manage conflicts before they get out of hand. In
this regard, group therapy may provide an arena for these persons to learn better social skills, test new behaviors, and bolster self-confidence.

Vocational Interests/Work Behaviors   Cooperative individuals are known as
team players who thrive in large, social work environments. They perform
best in supportive work roles under the guidance of strong leaders. They are
cordial, agreeable, and reliable and strive to get along well with colleagues.
They enjoy many conventional, social, and intellectual occupations. Their
cheerful optimism helps them weather workplace stress and change relatively
well. They are thoughtful of others, willing to please, and good at smoothing
over conflicts and disagreements. When things are gloomy and the going gets
tough, they can often find the silver lining. These individuals are usually uncomfortable being assertive; they prefer to avoid problems rather than to face
them head on. They are followers rather than leaders and struggle when asked
to act independently or be on their own.

Sociable

Counseling/Psychotherapy Evaluations   When presenting for help, these individuals may appear dramatically distressed, depressed, exhausted, or scattered. They may be enraged at the people they feel have caused them trouble
or, alternately, appear emotionally shut down, bored, and disinterested in life.
They are probably uncomfortable with seeking treatment and may have difficulty grasping their role in a therapeutic relationship. Although they are likely
to have long-standing problems with self-doubt and low self-esteem, they will
probably expect a quick fix and may not be inclined to stay in therapy for
more than a few sessions. They may come across as psychologically naive and
view the therapist as having somewhat magical powers to solve their problems quickly. They may demonstrate a superficial understanding of people
and emotions and be lacking in insight. They are likely to resist delving into
personal material and may take a dependent stance in hopes that the therapist
will fix them without much effort on their part. In this regard they may prefer
medication and behavioral techniques for managing emotions than interventions that require self-focus.

Nevertheless, a direct, supportive approach that steers clear of their dependency maneuvers should be useful. Immediate goals may include reduc-

ing histrionic emotional reactivity, counteracting negative thinking, and accurately assessing the situations that got them into trouble. These individuals may also benefit from a reexamination of their perceived need for high levels of attention and stimulation and by learning about their quickly shifting emotions as well as how to manage them. Fickleness and boredom can be reduced by helping them see and appreciate the nuances and complexities in people and situations that they usually take for granted. Since they are used to fleeing problem situations and relationships rather than face them, they are likely to be deficient in the mature coping skills that would allow them to manage conflicts effectively and build self-esteem. Cognitive and group therapies may prove useful with these individuals in building and reinforcing interpersonal problem-solving skills.

Vocation Interests/Work Behaviors   Individuals with this personality style often seek social, enterprising, and artistic occupations in which they can exercise their need for stimulation and attention. Easily bored with repetition, they enjoy unusual duties and tasks that change frequently. They do well in large groups and seem to thrive in boisterous environments with little structure. They are extraverted, lively, and energetic. They often enjoy working with the public and make good salespersons. They are attentive to their appearance and keep a cheerful optimism, even in difficult circumstances. However, these individuals can be exasperating to some colleagues, because of their quickly shifting interests and emotions. They find it difficult to stick with something once they have lost interest and seldom hesitate to change loyalties if an alternative gives them more of what they want. Attitudes and feelings can likewise vacillate from intense enthusiasm to disgruntled negativism in a short span of time. However, angry outbursts are just as short-lived as intense reactions in the other direction. When the air has cleared, these individuals return to their upbeat disposition, as if nothing had happened.

Confident

Counseling/Psychotherapy Evaluations   Individuals with this personality style frequently experience problems when they fail to achieve important goals or step on others' toes through arrogance and neglect. Unrealistic expectations and inflated self-worth may contribute to interpersonal conflicts. These individuals often harbor deep-seated feelings of guilt and inadequacy. They often doubt themselves and struggle under the heavy weight of self-imposed demands for achievement and perfection. However, even when asking for help, these individuals usually deny or downplay their turmoil and fear. They frequently blame others for their problems and can get worked into a rage when discussing the abuse they believe they have endured. They are often disdainful of seeking help and typically find it difficult to settle into a client role, which they view as passive and submissive. They may be unwilling to face personal responsibility for problems and may seek to outwit the therapist and sabotage treatment efforts.

It's not surprising that these individuals usually stay in therapy only long enough to restore lost self-esteem. Therapists will do well to take a firm yet supportive stance and to avoid power struggles. These individuals will welcome the therapist's appreciation of their suffering as well as their talents and accomplishments. By framing change techniques as methods for mastering difficult situations, therapists can ally themselves with the need these individuals have to be dominant and self-directed. If amenable to more than supportive treatment, these individuals are likely to benefit from a reappraisal of their expectations for themselves and others. They may need to learn how to contain their feelings and be less angry and judgmental. They also may need to learn to be less self-focused and more empathic toward others. Some individuals may appreciate the increased interpersonal effectiveness they will obtain from use of cooperative, prosocial methods.

Vocational Interests/Work Behaviors Confident individuals are frequently attracted to enterprising occupations that give them the status and power they seek. They are self-driven and work hard to attain their goals. They are competitive and shrewd. They do equally well on their own and in social settings, but in groups they have a need to be one up and will often resist roles that place them in an equal or deferential position. The self-assured, bold style of these individuals often wins them leadership positions. Colleagues frequently feel secure that these individuals will work hard to succeed and will accomplish their objectives in spite of obstacles. On the negative side, these individuals are usually more concerned with themselves than with others and can be insensitive and uncaring about the effects of their behavior on coworkers. Their need for success and tribute may, at times, take precedence over company rules, ethics, and social propriety.

Forceful

Counseling/Psychotherapy Evaluations　When they feel overwhelmed by interpersonal and emotional difficulties, these persons are likely to exaggerate their usual methods of maintaining distance from others, being excessively defensive, angry, gruff, and reckless. They may also withdraw into bitterness and self-pity or use alcohol or drugs to soothe themselves. They will typically perceive that they have been outwitted or undone by vindictive others, and will downplay or deny personal responsibility for their failures. At the core, though, they are likely to doubt themselves and feel weak, vulnerable, and inadequate.

Because of their general distrust, disdain for the world of emotions, and awkwardness in a help-seeking role, these persons are unlikely to enter treatment on their own. To obtain their interest and cooperation, therapists will do well to take a firm yet supportive stance. These persons are most likely to respond positively when the therapist is authoritative and allows them to be on an equal footing in the relationship. However, even with good rapport, these persons are likely to be reserved and uncomfortable discussing intimate feelings. They may attempt to challenge the therapist's competence and control, especially if they feel threatened. An immediate goal is to permit venting of frustration so that they can regain their sense of self-control and competence. They may then be receptive to problem-focused treatment, including a review of their problems from a cognitive point of view. Behavioral methods may be useful for anger and stress management. Getting them to change is often a matter of convincing them that doing so will increase their competence and control over harsh circumstances. If amenable to long-term therapy, goals may include softening their rigid defenses and intense emotional responses, increasing empathic regard for others, and resolving the feelings of inadequacy that lead to overcompensation. Toward these ends, these individuals may respond well to modeling techniques in a one-on-one or group setting.

Vocational Interests/Work Behaviors　Forceful people often aspire to mechanical and enterprising occupations that give them independence and a sense of being in control. Their strong competitive spirit gives them an edge in jobs that require a steadfast pursuit of goals in difficult circumstances. These individuals are known for their hard work, toughness, and determination. Although they can tolerate group settings, they prefer to be outside the bounds of community rules and regulations. They are self-oriented and do not readily consider the needs of others. They can be gruff and insensitive to colleagues and seldom hesitate in stepping on toes, if doing so helps them achieve their ends. Their assertive, forthright style and desire to win typically earns them confidence and respect from colleagues. In many job situations, their lack of sensitivity and warmth may be overlooked because of their perseverance and ability to succeed in spite of opposition.

Respectful

Counseling / Psychotherapy Evaluations   Emotional and interpersonal problems that arise in these individuals can often be traced to attitudinal and behavioral rigidity. When things go wrong, their instinct is to constrict their feelings and hold fast to whatever rules apply to their situation. They may seek help for anxiety and tension complaints and for psychosomatic ailments such as headaches and gastrointestinal upsets. They may also be angry and bitter at those they feel have let them down. If they perceive that their trouble is due to their own failure, they may become clinically depressed. A common thread to their symptoms is their tendency to be overly critical: Someone or something must be blamed and punished for the problem. Although they will probably be highly defended in their view of whatever trouble they are in, a sense of worry, fearfulness, and inadequacy often permeates their demeanor.

These individuals are likely to view the therapist as an expert and will be superficially cooperative in an effort to obtain his or her approval. They will be punctual and carry out homework tasks with fervor. At the same time, they tend to be uncomfortable with strong emotions and are likely to resist letting down their defenses in order to explore potential shortcomings. A supportive, problem-focused approach may be useful in exploring their difficulties and restoring self-efficacy. They tend to get lost in nondirective therapy, so it is usually best to keep the level of structure fairly high. They are likely to be receptive to medication and behavioral methods for reducing anxiety, depression, tension, and stress reactivity. When their defenses are eased, these individuals may benefit from a rational exploration of dysfunctional thoughts and attitudes, especially their excessive criticalness and rigid acceptance of certain standards and rules. They may also gain from learning how to be less perfectionistic and black-and-white in their judgments. In this regard they may respond well to interpersonal modeling techniques in either one-on-one or group settings.

Vocational Interests / Work Behaviors   Individuals with this personality style are frequently attracted to conventional, mechanical, and intellectual occupations that offer a structured work environment and clear guidelines for performance. Given a job to accomplish, they use their organizational skills and strong work ethic to see that it gets done accurately and on time. In the workplace, they are often prized for their loyalty, conscientiousness, and willingness to persist at difficult, even repetitive, tasks. They take their responsibilities seriously and are motivated to please supervisors and respected colleagues. These individuals do well on their own, but they are also good team players and thrive in group settings. They are willing to cooperate and follow the lead of others. They are astute at recognizing the implicit rules of the workplace and will internalize these quickly. It is difficult for these individuals to operate successfully if tasks and goals are not well defined and when a freewheeling, unstructured approach is required. They are uncomfortable making decisions on their own and asserting a point of view that is not shared by others. Coworkers often value their ability to keep their nose to the grindstone and emotions under wrap, but some individuals may come across as so task oriented and constricted that they are viewed as impersonal, insensitive, and uncaring. They can be tough on subordinates, whom they hold to the same perfectionist standards they have for themselves.

Sensitive

Counseling / Psychotherapy Evaluations   These individuals often arrive in treatment displaying a plethora of emotions and negative attitudes. They may feel angry at a world they experience as arbitrary and unjust. They may feel scattered, depressed, and drained, ready to give up hope of happiness. Dependency conflicts and feelings of inadequacy are often present. In therapy these persons are likely to shift between compliance and resistance, hope and disillusionment. Affective expression may be controlled and sensible one moment, then shift to irrationality. Therapists may feel their patience being tested by these persons as they can make even the most carefully crafted interventions seem futile and may complain excessively about every detail of the professional relationship.

Success with these persons entails an appreciation of their brittle ego, emotional sensitivity, quickly shifting moods, and need for clear but flexible boundaries. Initially, therapists will do well to let them vent their frustrations by being supportive and nondirective, but unsentimental. Medication and behavioral interventions may be needed to help stabilize their thoughts and feelings. Once the initial storm has cleared, it is important to obtain a rational understanding of the problem situation. This may take some time, since these persons often have trouble separating their own view of a situation from its objective characteristics. A practical, problem-solving approach may then be useful in teaching self-control and general coping skills. Cognitive therapy may assist them in gaining a more realistic appraisal of themselves and the world. Additionally, interpersonal and group therapy can often be employed to increase self-awareness, behavioral consistency, and social maturity.

Vocational Interests/Work Behaviors   Artistic and intellectual occupations are frequently favored by people with this personality style. They seek loosely structured work environments that allow them freedom and autonomy in interpreting task requirements. They do not respond well to strict rules and regulations. They like to determine the pace at which they work and choose the goals they strive for. Although they appreciate stable group settings and can operate successfully within them, these individuals tend to be freethinking and not inclined to follow group norms. Their sensitive, temperamental nature requires a measure of tolerance and support from supervisors and colleagues. Since they often react quite negatively to criticism and heavy-handed authority, these should be avoided or downplayed. The talents of these persons are most likely to be realized in a workplace that is nurturing and supportive of their individuality.

Problem Indicator

Counseling/Psychotherapy Evaluations   Elevations of T scores of 60 or above suggest the presence of a moderate level of personality disturbance and psychiatric symptoms. People with high Problem Indicator scores may have significant difficulty getting along with others and adjusting to the demands of work, school, family, and friends. They may feel overwhelmed by life circumstances and be unable to perform satisfactorily in major life areas. They may have low self-esteem and be pessimistic about the future. They may experience high levels of stress, anxiety, dysphoria, restlessness, and tension. A referral for additional testing, psychotherapy, or medication may be appropriate.

Vocational Interests/Work Behaviors   Since this scale does not measure a single personality style, there are no associated vocational interests. In the workplace, individuals with elevated Problem Indicator scores are likely to be poor performers who have high absentee rates and significant interpersonal problems with coworkers and supervisors. They tend to be self-absorbed, moody, and thin-skinned. Regardless of the actual workload, they often feel stressed and pressured by the demands placed on them. Since the workplace problems these individuals have are not likely to remit on their own, a referral for employee assistance or counseling may be appropriate.

Computer Interpretation of the PACL

Narrative interpretations of PACL test results can be generated from software programs available for IBM-compatible personal computers running Windows or DOS, or from the publisher's internet scoring service. The procedures used by these programs to interpret test scores are similar to those just presented. The major differences are that the computer programs always calculate, print, and interpret the three Validity Indices and provide interpretations for only a subset of different combinations of high scale scores.

Since the programs provide validity scores for all respondents, they use more lenient cutoff scores for determining biased protocols than those given previously. Instead of the above 0.0 cutoffs, a statement indicating that the examiner should consider possible response bias is printed when Random or Favorable are between 5.00 and 10.99 and when Unfavorable is between 0.00 and 4.99. A statement indicating that response bias is likely is printed when Random or Favorable is 11.00 or greater, and Unfavorable is 5.00 or greater.

As there are more possible combinations of 2-point and 3-point high scale scores than narrative reports, some tests with different high scale combinations will receive the same narrative. Decisions about which score profiles receive the same or different narrative interpretation were based on theoretical similarities and differences between personalities as outlined by Millon (1969/1983b) and by expected rates of occurrence for various code types in counseling and personnel settings. Rarely occur-

> ## DON'T FORGET
> ....
> PACL Validity Indices are most accurate in identifying problem tests when they are applied only to forms that are suspected of being invalid. Because PACL software programs calculate these indices for all respondents, they use higher cutoff scores for identifying biased tests than those originally developed by Strack (1991c). The higher cutoff scores help reduce the chances of incorrectly identifying a test as biased when it is not.

ring but theoretically similar code types were grouped together, while separate narratives were created for the most frequently occurring codes.

STRENGTHS AND WEAKNESSES OF THE PACL

Several characteristics of the PACL, which highlight its major strengths and weaknesses relative to similar self-report inventories, follow.

Strengths

1. *Quick and Comprehensive Assessment.* The PACL takes just 10 to 15 minutes to complete and measures Millon's eight basic personality styles along with an indicator of personality problems that can be useful in identifying persons with possible character disorders. On its own, the PACL is a fast and economical screening device. As part of a test battery, it is a reliable and valid personality measure that will not tax valuable time resources.

2. *Interesting and Nonthreatening to Respondents.* Most people are interested in the topic of personality and enjoy describing themselves on the PACL. Test items are nonthreatening and are well tolerated by many individuals who cannot or will not complete a questionnaire measure (e.g., adolescents, medically ill persons, the elderly).

3. *Useful as a Self-Report Form and Rating Inventory.* The same instrument may be used for self-report, and for rating individuals, groups, objects, concepts, or anything else.

4. *Availability of Validity Indices to Help in Identifying Biased Tests.* Three empirically based indices were developed to assist in identifying PACL protocols that may be biased because of random, favorable, or unfavorable responding.

5. *Theory-Based Measurement.* Unlike most assessment devices, the PACL is grounded in a comprehensive theory. Its development and validation were guided by Millon's (1969/1983b) model of personality, which is interpersonally oriented and cast in a biopsychosocial framework. As such, each PACL scale measures theory-derived characteristics directly and quantifiably. Since the scales are anchored in a comprehensive theory, a rich picture can be generated of persons completing

the measure. Furthermore, results from the PACL can be readily compared with results from any other Millon inventory.

6. *Sequential Development and Validation.* All phases of test construction and validation followed a step-by-step, theory-based schedule, as suggested and described by Loevinger (1957). In the substantive validity phase, items were generated and selected to fully represent the personalities under consideration. In the structural validity phase, scale construction was carried out to meet both the general psychometric criteria for internal validity (e.g., high alpha coefficients) and criteria for validity as described by Millon's theory (e.g., hypothesized scale intercorrelations). In the final external, convergent-discriminant validity phase, extratest validity was established for each scale through correlations with other measures and life data. Here the scales had to be correlated or uncorrelated with other constructs as predicted by theory. Using sequential development and validation helped ensure that scale items would meet validity criteria at each successive phase of development, thereby resulting in more precise, theory-true measurement.

7. *Extensive Sampling.* Development, validation, and standardization of scale scores were accomplished separately for men and women based on the responses of over 2,500 persons from across the United States comprising twenty separate samples. Subjects were between 16 and 72 years of age, represented all major ethnic groups (i.e., Black, Native American Indian or Eskimo, Hispanic, non-Hispanic White, Asian), and were drawn from all regions of the United States.

8. *Computerized Administration, Scoring, and Interpretation.* In addition to hand scoring, a full-color, computerized version of the PACL is available for IBM-compatible personal computers. This program allows for both computer administration of the test and hand entry of item responses from the paper-and-pencil protocol. Easy-to-read profile plots of scale scores may be printed, as well as narrative interpretations of results. And unlike many other test products, this program allows for unlimited uses. The narratives are based on Millon's (1969/1983b) theory, the extensive empirical database compiled through test development and validation, and over 10 years of clinical use. They are nontechnical, easy to comprehend, and were written with personnel and counseling professionals in mind.

Weaknesses

1. *Nonspecific Assessment.* Adjective measures assess personality more generally than questionnaire measures. On the PACL, respondents can tell us that they are typically "playful," "self-satisfied," and "touchy," but they cannot report on their behavior, thoughts, attitudes, and moods in specific circumstances. Questionnaire measures have an advantage in this area because they can tap more narrowly defined qualities, as in "I like to be the center of attention at parties."

2. *Degree of Measurement.* The PACL's all-or-none response format helps make it one of the quickest personality instruments available, but it sidesteps measurement of the degrees to which various traits apply to the individual. For example, respondents can tell us that they are generally "theatrical" by endorsing that item, but the PACL answer sheet does not allow them to choose between "very theatrical" and "moderately theatrical." Tests that allow for several degrees of measurement can often provide a more finely tuned assessment of traits than the PACL.

3. *Problems With Normative Sample.* The normative sample is less than ideal because (a) most individuals were college students at the time they completed the test, (b) persons 65 years of age and older were undersampled, and (c) there are fewer non-Hispanic Whites but more Hispanics and Asians represented than in the general population.

4. *Few Validity Studies.* Although there is considerable empirical data associating PACL scores with those from other self-report measures of personality, behavior, and mood, only a few validity studies have been conducted in clinical samples and no studies have yet examined the PACL as a rating instrument. While there is a basis for making specific predictions about PACL respondents from Millon's theory, correlational data, and clinical experience with the test, most such predictions have not been tested empirically.

5. *Spanish-Language Norms Needed.* Norms are not yet available for the Spanish-language PACL and for ratings.

6. *Updated Manual Needed.* The test manual needs to be updated to incorporate data from research studies published since 1991.

CLINICAL APPLICATIONS OF THE PACL

The PACL has been successfully employed by therapists working in high school and college counseling centers and employee assistance programs; by vocational counselors, personnel psychologists, marriage and family counselors; by therapists doing custody and worker's compensation evaluations; and by general practitioners who work with relatively high functioning clients. Because the PACL is quick and easy to administer, it is often given during initial screening visits to assess personality style, identify persons who may have more serious character problems, and to help in the development of treatment plans. Clinicians have found it useful with people who cannot or will not complete questionnaire measures (e.g., some medical patients, adolescents, and the elderly).

Personality Assessment and Treatment Planning

The PACL was specifically developed to measure normal versions of Millon's (1969/1983b) eight basic personality styles. Millon's comprehensive theory of personality provides a rich context for understanding how individuals with different traits think and behave in a variety of everyday situations, including close relationships, school, work, and psychotherapy or counseling. In clinical settings, PACL results can tell the examiner how the personality characteristics of individual clients compare with a national sample of normal adults. High scale scores (T score of 60 or above) indicate that an individual possesses more of a particular group of traits than most others (85% or above) in the general population; low scale scores (T score of 40 or below) indicate that an individual has fewer of those traits than most others (15% or below). (See Rapid Reference 4.4 on page 199.)

The personality profile can be used to identify problem areas for

> # CAUTION
>
> High scores on the PACL indicate that an individual possesses *more* of the traits of a particular normal personality style than other adults in the general population. For example, the higher an individual's score is above $T = 50$ on any particular scale, the more likely it is that he or she will fit the prototype descriptions given earlier. The test will not assess disordered personality features beyond those measured by the Problem Indicator scale.

an individual. The Problem Indicator scale can be especially helpful in this regard. *T* scores of 60 or above suggest significant personality problems and the possibility of a diagnosable personality disorder. When the Problem Indicator scale is elevated above 60 additional testing with clinical personality measures such as the MCMI-III or MMPI-2

> **CAUTION**
>
> Separate norms are not yet available for Spanish-speaking clients and observer ratings. Caution must be exercised when applying current norms to these types of cases since the measurement errors in doing so are unknown.

may be warranted to rule out the presence of a disorder.

Each of Millon's personality styles is associated with a set of symptoms that are frequently seen when these individuals present for help. Each style also has a characteristic manner of thinking about and relating to the world, including therapy and the therapist. The scale summaries beginning on page 201 encapsulate these characteristics, offer diagnostic clues, and make specific recommendations for treatment.

Assessing Couples and Families

The relationship problems that confront couples and families can have many sources, including personality style. The PACL can be helpful in assessing the personality fit between individuals in a couple or family. Profiles of individuals may be compared and contrasted by plotting scores for each person on a single profile sheet. Knowing how individuals are the same and different in terms of personality style can help the clinician evaluate the role of individual differences and preferences in relationship problems.

Vocational Counseling and Personnel Selection

Millon's personality styles frequently show preferences for particular types of occupations, job duties, and work environments. In conjunction with other vocational and personnel selection instruments (e.g., Self-Directed Search), the PACL can provide useful information about an individual's likely vocational choices and suitable work settings. (Refer to the scale summaries beginning on page 201.)

Outcome Tracking and Assessing the Effectiveness of Interventions

By definition, personality is a pervasive and ingrained aspect of the self. Longitudinal studies have verified that under normal circumstances an individual's basic personality style remains quite stable after age 18 (e.g., Costa & McCrae, 1984). Nevertheless, there are circumstances where significant personality shifts are expected and can be observed. Individuals who are confronted with traumatic experiences; who battle serious medical ailments; and who endure major psychological problems such as chronic substance abuse or depression often demonstrate significant personality changes as a result of their ordeal or problem and in response to interventions to alleviate their suffering. When employing the PACL with these individuals, test results can be used to document changes in their interpersonal style, social orientation, self-esteem, assertiveness, level of organization, and emotional stability.

For this purpose, two or more score profiles for an individual can be plotted on the same graph to visualize the similarities and differences in test results over time. Chance scores are frequently used to note whether observed differences for a particular scale are statistically significant. Since there are sources of measurement error in all test scores, it is important to be aware of how much variability can be expected simply due to chance before concluding that a particular difference is the result of an intervention. Two statistics that can be helpful in estimating the degree of chance error in PACL scores when observations are made over time are the standard error and test-retest reliability. Rapid Reference 4.5 (page 200) gives standard errors for PACL scales, and Rapid Reference 4.7 gives test-retest correlations over 1 to 3 months. The standard error indicates how much chance variability there is in any particular scale score at any measurement point. The test-retest correlation gives an estimate of the degree of variability in a test score over time in the absence of an intervention. Statistical tests for change scores take measurement errors into account when judging levels of significance. Such tests are strongly advisable if the examiner wishes to make conclusions about the effects of an intervention on an individual's personality profile.

≡Rapid Reference 4.7

Test-Retest Correlations for Scales by Sex of Respondent

Scale	1 Month		2 Months		3 Months	
	Men (94)	Women (86)	Men (77)	Women (66)	Men (81)	Women (72)
Introversive	.62	.60	.68	.73	.69	.72
Inhibited	.75	.82	.70	.77	.73	.70
Cooperative	.69	.74	.71	.68	.60	.64
Sociable	.69	.90	.72	.89	.70	.85
Confident	.69	.81	.66	.77	.71	.80
Forceful	.70	.81	.67	.73	.77	.80
Respectful	.61	.75	.75	.68	.71	.73
Sensitive	.74	.71	.76	.85	.71	.76
Problem Indicator	.66	.55	.67	.63	.67	.63

Note. Numbers in parentheses are *n*s. Reprinted from Strack (1991c, p. 44).

ILLUSTRATIVE CASE REPORT

The case report that follows illustrates how the PACL may be employed in a counseling setting. The PACL results are then integrated with results from the *Symptom Checklist-90-R* (SCL-90-R; Derogatis, 1994).

J. C. is a 19-year-old, single, third-generation Asian American man who is a sophomore at a large state university. He came to the college counseling center at the urging of his girlfriend, who was concerned about his moodiness and tendency to withdraw from those around him. On an intake questionnaire he reported trouble with anxiety, irritability, and an inability to concentrate on his studies. He reported having difficulty getting along with people at his dormitory, whom he described as "gossipers" and "practical jokers." He admitted that his only "real" friend at college is his girlfriend. He feels that he is not coping well with college life and would like help.

The PACL and SCL-90-R were administered during J. C.'s initial visit to the counseling center. His test scores were:

PACL		SCL-90-R	
Scale	T Score	Scale	T Score
Introversive	56	Somatization	47
Inhibited	71	Obsessive-Compulsive	42
Cooperative	48	Interpersonal Sensitivity	63
Sociable	42	Depression	59
Confident	38	Anxiety	64
Forceful	51	Hostility	55
Respectful	59	Phobic Anxiety	53
Sensitive	70	Paranoid Ideation	52
Problem Indicator	65	Psychoticism	62
		Global Severity Index	60

On the PACL, J. C. endorsed 35 adjectives as self-descriptive. This indicates a valid protocol and a willingness to disclose personal information. With regard to the profile, the elevated scores on the Inhibited, Sensitive, and Problem Indicator scales, and a low score on the Confident scale should be noted. The Problem Indicator score indicates the possibility of personality disturbance and suggests the need for further testing to rule out a personality disorder. In terms of general personality characteristics, J. C. reveals himself to be somewhat shy, inhibited, moody, high strung, pessimistic, and lacking in self-esteem. He values his privacy and tends to keep others at an arm's distance. He is likely to be seen by acquaintances as socially awkward, unconventional, self-preoccupied, and easily distracted. He is not likely to work well in groups, instead preferring to operate alone or with one or two others. He tends to brood a good deal, worrying about the stresses and strains of life and may feel inadequate in his ability to cope with general difficulties. He can be opinionated, temperamental, and passive-aggressive at times and may feel and express resentment toward others who are seen as more gifted and powerful. The high Problem Indicator score additionally suggests long-standing adjustment problems. The conflicts he reports with dormitory mates are probably ongoing but recently may have become exacerbated. It is likely that J. C. has never fit into the dormitory culture and may benefit from a transfer to a more private living environment. The low Confident score reinforces the opinion that J. C. is not self-assured or self-confident. He may be genuinely humble and not consider self-advancement a worthy goal or indicator of personal worth. Being mindful of his Asian heritage, it is important to learn more about his family background and value system before making judgments about what may be traits and what may represent cultural preferences.

Concerning positive characteristics, J. C. is probably an empathic and loyal friend who is appreciated for his forthright and, usually accurate, social observations. Individuals with this personality style are often creative and individualistic in their approach to life. They "march to the beat of a different drummer" and frequently offer a refreshing perspective on everyday events. They spice things up with their roller-coaster moods and incisive wit.

The SCL-90-R asks respondents about their symptoms during the past week. The T scores listed are based on a nonclinical normative sample (Derogatis, 1994), so what is seen are deviations from a general population average. J. C.'s Global Severity Index score of 60 is just at the cutoff for clinical significance. It indicates that J. C.'s emotional symptoms, although mild from a clinical perspective, are bothersome enough to interfere with his daily functioning. The most pressing discomforts fall in the areas of Anxiety, Interpersonal Sensitivity, and Psychoticism. Right now J. C. probably experiences pervasive nervousness, apprehension, muscle tension, and anxious rumination. He is likely to feel self-conscious and tentative in his relations with others. There may be moderately strong feelings of inferiority and inadequacy over his skills and abilities. The T score of 62 on Psychoticism probably reflects a sense of social alienation rather than disturbed thinking. Depression just misses the clinical cutoff at $T = 59$. At this time anxiety seems to be J. C.'s primary problem, but any reported symptoms of sadness, hopelessness, and pessimism should be probed during a clinical interview.

Together the personality and symptom data portray J. C. as a private, socially isolated individual who endures a lot of emotional ups and downs and who struggles with self-doubt and self-esteem. J. C. may lack the skills needed to excel in college life and is probably experiencing some recent stressors that have overwhelmed his coping abilities.

Should J. C. follow through with getting help, we may advise his counselor that he is likely to be sensitive and inhibited in expressing his innermost feelings yet quite open in demonstrating anger, hurt, pessimism, and bitterness. Dependency conflicts and feelings of inadequacy may be evident in earnest complaints about how the world is arbitrary and unforgiving. Success with J. C. will require an appreciation of his brittle ego, emotional sensitivity, shifting moods, and need for clear but flexible boundaries. Initially, his counselor will do well to let him vent his frustrations by being supportive and nondirective, but unsentimental. Once the initial storm has cleared, it will be important to obtain a rational understanding of the problems that he faces. This may take some time, since J. C. is likely to have trouble separating his own view of a situation from its objective characteristics. A practical, problem-solving approach may then be useful in teaching emotional control and general coping skills. Cognitive therapy may assist him in gaining a more realistic appraisal of himself and the world. Additionally, behavioral, interpersonal, and group therapies can often be employed to increase self-awareness, behavioral consistency, and social skills.

🦎 TEST YOURSELF 🦎

1. **What were the three steps of PACL test development?**
   - (a) theoretical inference, internal reliability, external validity
   - (b) item development, structural analysis, test-retest reliability
   - (c) substantive validity, structural validity, external validity
   - (d) internal consistency, external consistency, convergent-discriminant validity

2. **According to Millon, normal personality is _____ with abnormal personality.**
   - (a) discontinuous
   - (b) continuous
   - (c) not associated
   - (d) tenuously linked

3. **The Problem Indicator scale measures**
   - (a) personality problems.
   - (b) aspects of Millon's three introverted personality styles.
   - (c) emotional stability.
   - (d) conscientiousness.

4. **The PACL's three Validity Indices are named**
   - (a) Infrequency, Defensiveness, Fake Good.

(b) Reliable, Favorable, Dissimulation.

(c) Disclosure, Desirability, Debasement.

(d) Random, Favorable, Unfavorable.

5. **When scoring the PACL by hand, what information is needed to obtain *T* scores?**

(a) name, date, sex, and age

(b) raw scale scores, number of adjectives checked, and sex

(c) raw scale scores, age, and sex

(d) number of adjectives checked, raw scale scores, and percentile scores

6. **A *T* score of 70 implies that a respondent possesses more traits of a given personality than _____ of the general population.**

(a) 70%

(b) 79%

(c) 89%

(d) 98%

7. **People with low scores (*T* scores of 40 or below) on the Cooperative scale**

(a) are uncooperative.

(b) are docile and dependent.

(c) have little need for approval and affection.

(d) are orderly and methodical.

8. **Describe what needs to be accomplished during the *structural validity* stage of test development.**

9. **When interpreting the PACL, how should an individual be described who has two prominent personality scale elevations that are approximately equal?**

10. **How are Confident and Forceful personalities similar and different?**

Answers: 1. c; 2. b; 3. a; 4. d; 5. b; 6. d; 7. c; 8. Test scales need to be developed that match criteria dictated by the theory on which they are based (e.g., by demonstrating appropriate internal consistency and test-retest reliability); 9. by giving equal weight to the two scales when describing trait features such as interpersonal style, emotionality, work behavior, and therapeutic presentation; 10. Both personalities are interpersonally bold and socially dominant. They can be insensitive, exploitive, and lacking in empathy. Confident individuals tend to feel entitled and may expect others to cater to them. Forceful individuals do not feel this way. They tend to grab for what they want rather than wait for others to provide.

Five

ESSENTIALS OF MIPS ASSESSMENT

Lawrence G. Weiss

INTRODUCTION

The Millon Index of Personality Styles (MIPS) (Millon, Weiss, Millon, & Davis, 1994) is distinct from Millon clinical instruments (Millon Clinical Multiaxial Inventory [MCMI], Millon Behavioral Health Inventory [MBHI], and Millon Adolescent Clinical Inventory [MACI]) in that it measures *normal*-range personality styles. The MIPS is a 180-item, true-false questionnaire designed to measure personality styles of normally functioning adults age 18 and over. Most MIPS items require an eighth grade education to complete. Most individuals finish it in 30 minutes.

The MIPS consists of 24 scales grouped into 12 pairs. Each pair contains two juxtaposed scales. For example, the Retiring and Outgoing scales are considered a pair. As shown in Table 5.1, the 12 pairs of MIPS scales are organized into three major areas: Motivating Aims, Cognitive Modes, and Interpersonal Behaviors. The MIPS also contains a composite of overall adjustment called the Adjustment Index, and three Validity Indicators: Positive Impression, Negative Impression, and Consistency. Rapid Reference 5.1 provides basic information on the MIPS and its publisher.

> DON'T FORGET
> ....
> The MIPS is different from Millon clinical assessment instruments because it measures *normal* personality styles, not clinical disorders.

Although especially useful in organizational contexts, appropriate applications of the MIPS include any settings in which counselors seek to identify, understand, and assist normally functioning adults.

Table 5.1 Organization of the MIPS Scales

Validity Indicators	Motivating Aims	Cognitive Modes	Interpersonal Behaviors
Consistency	Enhancing	Entraversing	Retiring
Positive Impression	Preserving	Introversing	Outgoing
Negative Impression			
	Modifying	Sensing	Hesitating
	Accommodating	Intuiting	Asserting
	Individuating	Thinking	Dissenting
	Nurturing	Feeling	Conforming
		Systematizing	Yielding
		Innovating	Controlling
			Complaining
			Agreeing

≡ *Rapid Reference 5.1*

Millon Index of Personality Styles (MIPS)

Authors: Theodore Millon, Lawrence Weiss, Carrie Millon, and Roger Davis

Publication date: 1994

What the test measures: Normal-range personality traits

Age range: 18 years of age and older

Administration time: 25 minutes

Qualification of examiners: Master's degree in psychology or related field

Publisher: The Psychological Corporation
555 Academic Court
San Antonio, TX 78204-2498
Phone: 800-211-8378

Start-up kits, $99 (mail-in reports) and $199 (computer version); profile reports, $71 for 10; narrative reports, $132 for 10 (as of 2002).

HISTORY AND DEVELOPMENT

Development of the MIPS followed a theory-based strategy outlined by Loevinger (1957) and used by Millon in creating his other instruments. In this method, test development and validation occur together in three stages. During the theoretical-substantive stage, test items that could be answered "true" or "false" were written to measure each construct under consideration according to explicit theoretical definitions. Following this the items were reviewed by experts to assure their theoretical relevance. In the second stage, the internal-structural stage, scales were developed to match criteria specified by theory. For example, Millon's (1969/1983, 1990, 1997) model of personality is polythetic, which means that some personality types share traits. This dictates that scales measuring theoretically similar constructs share items that tap the overlapping traits. Furthermore, in accordance with Millon's taxonomy, traits are divided into three groups for measurement purposes: those that are prototypical for a particular style or construct and those that are moderately or mildly characteristic of a personality or construct. Prototypical features are core aspects that distinguish the personality or construct from all other types or constructs. Traits that are moderately or mildly characteristic are recognizable features of a personality or construct but not definitive of the subject. In the MIPS, items measuring prototypical features are given a weight of 3; items tapping less definitive features are weighted 2 or 1.

Item selections for the scales took place using data from hundreds of subjects gathered in several pilot studies. The final scales contain 4 to 10 prototypical items with 12 to 37 support items. Item overlap percentages range from 0% to 49%. Scale intercorrelations tend to be quite high for theoretically similar and opposite personalities and constructs, ranging from −.87 to .81 for the combined adult sample (Millon, Weiss, Millon, & Davis, 1994).

Internal consistency and test-retest reliability of MIPS scales were found to be very good. Alpha coefficients ranged from .69 for Innovating to .85 for Hesitating in an adult sample ($N = 1,000$; median = .78), and .70 for Intuiting to .87 for Hesitating in a sample of college students ($N = 1,600$; median = .77). Median split-half reliabilities were $r = .82$ and $r = .80$ for the adult and college samples, respectively. Test-retest stability over 2 months was estimated in samples of 50 adults and 110 college students. Correlations corrected for variability of scale scores at first testing ranged from .73 to .91 in the adult sample (median = .85), and .78 to .90 in the college sample (median = .84) (Millon, Weiss, Millon, & Davis, 1994).

MIPS scales were normed on independent samples of 1,000 adults and 1,600 college students from across the United States and Canada. The adult sample, consisting of 500 men and 500 women ranging in age from 18 to 65, closely matches 1988 U.S. census proportions for racial/ethnic group, educational level, region of the country, gender, age, and occupational level.

Using the normative sample, raw scores were transformed into standardized prevalence scores that are calibrated to match hypothesized distributions of various traits in the normal population. Prevalence scores are akin to the base rate scores employed by Millon for the MCMI and are not equivalent to typical percentile scores. Prevalence scores range from 0 to 100 and were anchored at 0, 9, 29, 49, 69, 89, and 100. Prevalence scores of 50 or above indicate that the respondent is a member of the trait group assessed by a particular scale. The higher the scale score is above 50, the more traits of a personality or construct the individual is likely to possess. Tables for converting raw scores into prevalence scores are provided in the test manual.

The final step of test development, called external-criterion, involves validating the scales against other measures of similar personality styles and constructs. Such data are presented in the MIPS manual (Millon, Weiss, Millon, & Davis, 1994) in the form of correlations with six widely used personality measures and one measure of depression. Most notable is a strong similarity of certain MIPS scales with the Myers-Briggs Type Indicator (MBTI; Myers & McCaulley, 1985) (see section Interpret Cognitive Modes Scales on page 235). Validation studies with several large organizations are reported in the manual and summarized in the section Managerial Performance on page 255).

THEORETICAL FOUNDATION

As a group the MIPS scales have a rich theoretical foundation in a model of personality that is deeply rooted in biosocial and evolutionary theory (Millon, 1969/1983, 1990, 1991). (For a synopsis of the MIPS scales, see Rapid Reference 5.2.) Three pairs of Motivating Aims Scales assess the person's orientation toward obtaining reinforcement from the environment. Millonian theorists will recognize these three pairs of scales as normal-range variations of

≡Rapid Reference 5.2

Summary of MIPS Scales

Validity Indicators

Consistency. High scores indicate that the respondent was conscientious and consistent in answering test items. Low scores suggest inconsistent, careless, or confused responding.

Positive Impression. Individuals who score high on this scale answered the test by accentuating their positive characteristics. They may have biased the test by underreporting their personal difficulties.

Negative Impression. High scores indicate that the respondent answered the test by giving an unfavorable impression of his or her personal characteristics. Malingering should be considered.

Motivating Aims

Enhancing. High scorers on this scale tend to look for the bright side of life, are optimistic about future possibilities, find it easy to enjoy themselves, and face the ups and downs of their lives with equanimity.

Preserving. Individuals scoring high on this scale focus on and intensify the problems of life. Perceiving the past as having been personally troubling, they always seem to be waiting for something else to go wrong, and feel that things are likely to go from bad to worse. They are easily upset by minor concerns and disappointments.

Modifying. Respondents scoring high on this scale take charge of their lives and make things happen rather than wait for them to occur. They are busily involved in modifying their environments and arranging events to suit their needs and desires.

Accommodating. High scores on this scale indicate that the respondent will undertake little to shape or alter their lives. They react to the passing scene, accommodating to circumstances created by others; they seem acquiescent, are unable to rouse themselves, lack initiative, and do little to generate the outcomes they desire.

Individuating. Individuals scoring high on this scale are oriented to actualize their own needs and wishes—that is, they seek to fulfill themselves first, worry little about the impact of their behavior on others, and tend to be both independent and egocentric.

Nurturing. Respondents scoring high on this scale are motivated to meet the needs of others first, and to attend to other people's welfare and desires at the expense of themselves. They are seen as nurturing and protective, taking care of others before taking care of themselves.

Cognitive Modes

Extraversing. High scorers on this scale turn to others to find stimulation and encouragement. They draw upon friends and colleagues for ideas and guidance, inspiration and energy, as well as garnering assurances of self-worth from them and taking comfort in their presence.

Introversing. Respondents scoring high on this scale prefer to use their own thoughts and feelings as resources, gaining inspiration and stimulation primarily from themselves rather than from others. In contrast with extraversers, introversers experience greater serenity and comfort by distancing themselves from external sources, preferring to heed the prompting that comes from within.

Sensing. High scorers on this scale gather their knowledge from the tangible and concrete, trusting direct experience and observable phenomena over the use of inference and abstraction. The practical and "real," the literal and factual are what give these individuals comfort and confidence.

Intuiting. Individuals scoring high on this scale prefer the symbolic and unknown to the concrete and observable. They are open to the intangibles of life and are inclined to seek out and enjoy the more mysterious experiences and speculative sources of knowledge.

Thinking. High scorers on this scale prefer to process the knowledge they have by means of logic and analytic reasoning. Decisions are based on cool, impersonal, and "objective" judgments, rather than on subjective emotions.

Feeling. Respondents scoring high on this scale form their judgments by heeding their own affective responses to circumstances, by evaluating subjectively the impact of their actions on those involved, and by following their personal values and goals.

Systematizing. High scorers on this scale are highly organized and predictable in their approach to life's experiences. They transform new knowledge in line with what is known and are careful, if not perfectionistic, in arranging even minor details. As a result they are seen by others as orderly, conscientious, and efficient.

Innovating. Individuals scoring high on this scale are inclined to be creative and to take risks, ready to alter and recast whatever they come upon. They seem discontented with the routine and predictable, spontaneously modifying what is given by following their hunches and seeking to effect novel, unanticipated consequences.

Interpersonal Behaviors

Retiring. Individuals scoring high on this scale are characterized by their lack of affect and their social indifference. They tend to be quiet, passive, and uninvolved; they may be viewed by others as quiet and colorless, unable to make friends, as well as apathetically disengaged.

(continued)

Outgoing. High scorers on this scale seek social stimulation, excitement, and attention. They often react dramatically to situations around them, but typically they lose interest quickly. Colorful and charming socialites, they also can be demanding and manipulative.

Hesitating. Individuals scoring high on this scale are usually shy, timid, and nervous in social situations, strongly wanting to be liked and accepted, yet often fearing that they will be rejected. At the same time that they are sensitive and emotionally responsive, they are mistrusting, lonely, and isolated.

Asserting. Respondents scoring high on this scale tend to feel that they are more competent and gifted than the people around them. They are often ambitious and egocentric, self-assured and outspoken. Others may see them as arrogant and inconsiderate.

Dissenting. Respondents scoring high on this scale tend to act out in an independent and nonconforming manner. They often resist following traditional standards, displaying an audaciousness that may be seen either as reckless or as spirited and enterprising.

Conforming. High scorers on this scale are likely to be upstanding and self-controlled. They relate to authority in a respectful and cooperative manner, tend to behave in a formal and proper manner in social situations, and are unlikely to be self-expressive or to act spontaneously.

Yielding. Individuals scoring high on this scale are their own worst enemies: They are accustomed to suffering rather than pleasure, are submissive, and tend to act in self-demeaning ways. Their behavior renders ineffective the efforts of others to assist them, and causes the yielders to bypass opportunities for rewards and to fail repeatedly to achieve despite possessing abilities to do so.

Controlling. Individuals scoring high on this scale are forceful and often domineering and socially aggressive. They tend to see themselves as fearless and competitive. To them, warmth and gentleness are signs of weakness, which they avoid by being strong-willed and ambitious.

Complaining. Respondents scoring high on this scale are characterized by their tendency to be passive-aggressive, sullen, and generally dissatisfied. Their moods and behavior are highly changeable: At times, they relate to others in a sociable and friendly manner; on other occasions, they are irritable and hostile, expressing the belief that they are misunderstood and unappreciated.

Agreeing. High scorers on this scale tend to be highly likable socially, often relating to others in an amenable manner. They form strong loyalties and attachments to others. They cover any negative feelings, however, especially when these feelings may be viewed as objectionable by the people they wish to please.

Note. © 1994 Dicandrien, Inc. All Rights Reserved.

Millon's pleasure-pain, active-passive, and self-other dimensions. The first pair of scales (Enhancing-Preserving) examines the extent to which the respondent's behavior is motivated by obtaining positive reinforcement (e.g., pleasure) or avoiding negative stimulation (e.g., pain) from the world. The second pair assesses the extent to which the individual's activities reflect an active Modifying or passive Accommodating approach toward the world. The third pair of scales focuses on the source of reinforcement, assessing the extent to which the person is primarily motivated by Individuating (referring to self) or Nurturing (referring to others) aims.

Four pairs of Cognitive Modes Scales examine styles of information processing. The first two pairs of scales in this area, Extraversing-Introversing and Sensing-Intuiting, assess information-gathering strategies. The second two pairs, Thinking-Feeling and Systematizing-Innovating, assess different styles of processing information once it has been gathered.

The astute reader will observe that the Cognitive Modes Scales are highly consonant with the model formulated by Jung (1921/1971a) and subsequently popularized in the MBTI. The MBTI's Judging and Perceiving scales have been renamed Systematizing and Innovating in the MIPS to more accurately capture the original Jungian meaning. More important, however, Millon has recast these Jungian constructs in terms of their influence on one's cognitive style of dealing with the voluminous influx of information required for daily living in the information age. This is an important contribution because cognitive differences in how individuals respond to information and the manner in which they are expressed in daily life have been much overlooked in generating and appraising personality traits.

Five pairs of Interpersonal Behaviors Scales assess the person's style of relating to others. Millonian theorists will recognize these five pairs of scales as normal-range variations of the Millon's 10 personality disorders. The MIPS Retiring and Outgoing interpersonal styles are the normal variants of the Schizoid and Histrionic personality disorders, respectively. The Hesitating and Asserting styles are related to the Avoidant and Narcissistic disorders. The Dissenting and Conforming personality styles are consonant with the Antisocial and Obsessive-Compulsive disorders in the pathological range. The Yielding and Controlling styles are the normal-range variants of the Self-Defeating/Masochistic and the Sadistic disorders. Finally, the interpersonal styles characterized by the Complaining and Agreeing scales on the MIPS are on the same continuum as the Negativistic/Passive-Aggressive and the Dependent personality disorders respectively.

TEST ADMINISTRATION

The MIPS can be administered in paper-and-pencil format or via computer with MIPS software (The Psychological Corporation, 1994). The questionnaire may be given individually or in groups. Examiners must ensure that conditions are suitable for examinees to complete the MIPS. This requires adequate lighting, seating arrangements, and work space. In addition, it is important to minimize auditory and visual distractions, as well as communication among test takers.

The MIPS administration is not timed. Most people take about 30 minutes to complete the questionnaire. College students may complete it in 20 to 25 minutes. Older individuals or those not accustomed to paperwork often take about 45 minutes. Rarely does anyone require an hour.

Testing Individuals With Special Needs

For individuals with special needs, examiners may choose to read the questions while they record their responses on the answer form. For individuals with severe disabilities, examiners may choose to read or sign the items as well as record the responses on the answer form. However, the examiner should avoid reviewing or commenting on individual responses while the examinee is completing the questionnaire. If a test taker asks for an explanation of the meaning of one of the questions, it is allowable for the examiner to define the unknown word or words in a neutral fashion, being careful not to influence the person's response.

SCORING THE MIPS

The MIPS can be administered, scored, and interpreted on a personal computer; administered in paper-and-pencil format and hand scored; or scanned on a desktop scanner. A mail-in scoring service is also available. Computer-generated reports provide either a single-page profile (i.e., graph) of the scores or a complete narrative interpretation of the profile pattern. The user's guide to the software includes a complete explanation of the logic that the computer program uses to analyze MIPS profiles and generate the Interpretive Reports (The Psychological Corporation, 1994).

To hand score the test, use the templates provided by the publisher. The first step is to calculate raw scale scores by summing the endorsed items, being sure to give the items their appropriate weight of 3, 2, or 1. In addition to the 24 substantive scales, there are three Validity Indicators called Positive Impression, Negative Impression, and Consistency. These do not have item weights. Positive Impression and Negative Impression contain 10 items each and have a maximum score of 10. Consistency is made up of five sets of paired items and has a maximum score of 5. A point is given whenever all items in a paired set are endorsed in the keyed direction. Higher scores on Positive Impression and Negative Impression indicate a stronger tendency to give an overly positive or negative impression. Higher scores on Consistency indicate greater consistency of responding.

In some settings, examiners may wish to assess a respondent's level of psychological adjustment or maladjustment. The MIPS Adjustment Index can be used for this purpose and is calculated as follows:

Adjustment raw score = (Enhancing prevalence score value + A) − (Preserving prevalence score value + B),

where A = the average of the prevalence score values for the Outgoing, Asserting, Conforming, Controlling, and Agreeing scales, and B = the average of the prevalence score values for the Retiring, Hesitating, Dissenting, Yielding, and Complaining scales.

The Adjustment raw score is then used in the following formula, which converts the raw score to a T score metric, which has a mean of 50 and a standard deviation of 10:

$$(RS - M) \ / \ SD \times 10 + 50$$

where RS = Adjustment raw score calculated above, and M and SD are the mean and standard deviation of the Adjustment raw score for the appropriate normative group found in Table 5.2. (For an example, see page 172 of the MIPS manual).

Once the raw scores for the substantive scales have been calculated, the second step is to transform them into prevalence scores. Six tables are pro-

Table 5.2 Adjustment Raw Score Means (M) and Standard Deviations (SD) for Each Normative Group.

Group	M	SD
Adult females	18.6	38.9
Adult males	19.9	37.9
General adult	18.9	38.1
College females	19.5	39.4
College males	17.6	39.0
General college	18.9	38.9

Note. Data and Table © 1994 Dicandrien, Inc. All Rights Reserved.

vided in the test manual for this purpose. Prevalence score transformations can be made using adult or college norms for men and women separately or for the sexes combined.

The final step is to plot the prevalence scores on the graph provided on the back of the MIPS answer sheet. This will make it easier to identify high and low scale scores and will facilitate test interpretation.

HOW TO INTERPRET THE MIPS

Examiners can interpret the MIPS themselves or use computerized interpretation. This section describes both practices.

Computerized Interpretation

Interpretive Reports are available with the computer version of the MIPS. The Interpretive Reports carry the flare, depth, and insightful wit for which Theodore Millon's writings have become widely known. Upon reviewing these works one has the feeling of reading carefully crafted prose rather than an automated psychological report.

More than 400 reports are built into the software. The reports differ from many computerized interpretations because the narratives do not follow a simplistic scale-by-scale procession of scores. The reports print a description of the individual as an integrated and holistic person. Practitioners often find the reports rich with discourse on the person's style that goes beyond a simple description of behavior and fosters a new understanding of and sensitivity toward the client.

The report requires a high reading level, and practitioners should exercise appropriate clinical judgment in deciding to give a report directly to the client. College-educated individuals easily understand the reports. Those with a good high school education grasp most of the report, although parts of it may be beyond their comprehension.

Most normally functioning adults easily recognize themselves in these narratives and favorably receive the message. Individuals whose interpersonal styles occasionally cause some life problems, however, may need to have the reports placed in appropriate context for them. Practitioners should review each report carefully before deciding whether it is appropriate for the client to read.

Step-by-Step Procedures for Test Interpretation

Five general steps, described below, should be followed when interpreting MIPS results.

Step 1: Check Validity Indicators
Check the Consistency, Negative Impression, and Positive Impression scale scores before beginning the content interpretation. If these scale scores are within acceptable ranges, then interpretation of the content scales can begin.

Step 2: Interpret Motivating Aims Scales
After reviewing the Validity Indicators, interpretation of the content scales can proceed. The Motivating Aims Scales have broad implications for the overall stance a person takes toward life. The three polarities considered in this group of scales are Enhancing-Preserving, Modifying-Accommodating, and Individuating-Nurturing; also important is to examine the possible patterns that exist among these polarities.

Step 3: Interpret Cognitive Modes Scales
The eight scales that make up the Cognitive Modes Scales are best thought of as four pairs: Extraversing-Introversing, Sensing-Intuiting, Thinking-Feeling, and

≡ Rapid Reference 5.3

Correlations Between the MIPS and the MBTI

Correlations of the MIPS Cognitive Modes scales with scales on the Myers-Briggs Type Indicator are very high, ranging from $r = .71$ to $r = .75$.

Systematizing-Innovating. They correspond closely to Jungian typology, as popularized in the MBTI (Myers & McCaulley, 1985) (see Rapid Reference 5.3). Interpretation differs from the MBTI, however, in that it is focused more on how one handles information than how one deals with others. Are examinees predisposed toward collecting information from external or internal sources (Extraversing-Introversing), and are they predisposed to attend to information that is more tangible or intangible (Sensing-Intuiting)? Similarly, when processing that information, do they rely more on intellective or affective resources in making sense of the information (Thinking-Feeling), and do they generally seek to assimilate the incoming information with existing knowledge or imagine novel interpretations and uses of that new information (Systematizing-Innovating [referred to as Judging-Perceiving in the MBTI]). The close link to the MBTI notwithstanding, the MIPS Cognitive Modes Scales make a unique contribution to personality assessment by addressing one's style of seeking and reconstructing information that is so much a part of life—not to mention being integral to larger life decisions as well as one's occupational functioning.

Step 4: Interpret Interpersonal Behaviors Scales

The 10 scales that constitute the Interpersonal Behaviors Scales may best be conceptualized as five pairs: Retiring-Outgoing, Hesitating-Asserting, Dissenting-Conforming, Yielding-Controlling, and Complaining-Agreeing. Because of the large number of possible profile combinations among this group of scales, the best approach to interpreting is to look for the highest two scales and blend an interpretation based on the individual scale descriptions (see the section Interpersonal Behaviors Scales on page 246). This approach, referred to as the 2-point code, has been widely used in interpreting the Minnesota Multiphasic Personality Inventory for several decades. As the research base on the MIPS expands over the next 10 years, examiners will likely be able to ascribe special meaning to some of the more common 2-point combinations.

Step 5: Integrate Findings With Other Information About the Respondent
Because the personality description developed up to this point is "blind" with respect to extratest data, it is imperative to take into account results of other tests, demographic information, and special knowledge of the respondent and his or her environment. MIPS test interpretation, then, should be altered to reflect knowledge of the respondent from other sources.

Validity Indicators

Consistency
Scores of 4 or 5 on the Consistency scale indicate the examinee responded consistently to the various items on the questionnaire. A score of 3 is of some concern though not especially uncommon. Scores of less than 3 are rare and may reflect significant reading difficulties or a lack of serious attention to the task on the part of the test taker. Such profiles may not be valid.

Positive Impression
The Positive Impression and Negative Impression scales measure the extent to which an individual's response style is characteristic of a Positive Impression or Negative Impression response set. For the Positive Impression scale, scores of 5 or greater are considered high for individuals with 2 years of college education or less; scores of 4 or greater are considered high for those with more than 2 years of college. Interpretation of individual Positive Impression scores is partly an empirical process and partly a matter of professional judgment. Certainly, there are some highly conscientious individuals who pride themselves on always doing the right thing and who are unable to admit, even to themselves, that they are prone to many of the same human foibles as other people. For example, as part of our research study on impression management, subjects were asked to complete the MIPS, "putting their best foot forward." One subject appeared confused and responded that he always does so. For such individuals, the motivation to create a positive impression may be so ingrained that they are not aware of it.

Negative Impression
For the Negative Impression scale, scores of 6 or greater are considered high for individuals with 2 years of college education or less; scores of 5 or greater

≡Rapid Reference 5.4

Validity Indicators Scores

Consistency scores of 4 or 5 indicate consistent responding.

Consistency scores of 3 are of some concern but are not especially uncommon.

Consistency scores below 3 are rare and suggest inconsistent or invalid responding.

Positive Impression scores of 5 or above are high for individuals with ≤ 2 years of college.

Positive Impression scores of 4 or above are high for individuals with > 2 years of college.

Negative Impression scores of 6 or above are high for individuals with ≤ 2 years of college.

Negative Impression scores of 5 or above are high for individuals with > 2 years of college.

are considered high for those with more than 2 years of college. As with the Positive Impression scale, interpretation of individual Negative Impression scores is partly empirical and partly judgment. A high Negative Impression score never should be considered conclusive evidence of a feigned profile even in the presence of an external motive to create a negative impression. This is because of the possibility of false-positive findings combined with the content of the Negative Impression items, and the high correlation of the Negative Impression scale with measures of pathology, such as the Beck Depression Inventory, reported in the MIPS manual.

Proper interpretation of high Negative Impression scores in the presence of a motive to create an unfavorable impression involve drawing a hypothesis of malingering, which then must be confirmed through other test data and clinical impression. On the other hand, low Negative Impression scores in the presence of a motive to create an unfavorable impression can be viewed as evidence that refutes a hypothesis of malingering.

In the absence of a motive to create an unfavorable impression, a high Negative Impression score may be considered to indicate possible psychological problems outside the scope of the MIPS, especially when the Negative Impression score is 8 or greater. In this case, administration of clinical-range instruments should be considered in order to investigate the possibility of a psychological disorder, such as depression or anxiety. At present, little is known about how the Negative Impression scale functions in a clinical population. Further research is needed concerning the relationship of the Negative Impression scale to measures of psychopathology in clinical samples. Alternatively, high Negative Impression scores could suggest reading difficulties or random responding. In such cases, the Negative Impression and Positive Impression scales both may be elevated. Scores of less than 3 on the MIPS Consistency scale would support this interpretation of high Negative Impression scores. (For a concise summary of acceptable ranges for the MIPS Validity Indicators, see Rapid Reference 5.4.)

Motivating Aims Scales

Enhancing-Preserving

Those who score high on the Enhancing side of the Enhancing-Preserving polarity possess attitudes and behaviors designed to foster and enrich life; to generate joy, pleasure, contentment, and fulfillment; and thereby to strengthen their capacity to remain competent physically and mentally. These individuals are likely to assert that human existence calls for more than life preservation and pain avoidance alone. Moreover, very high scorers are driven by the desire to seek invigorating experiences and challenges, to venture and explore, all to the end of magnifying if not escalating their vitality and viability.

Among people scoring high on the Preserving scale is a significant tendency to focus attention on potential threats to their emotional and physical security; they also display an expectation of and heightened alertness to the signs of potential negative feedback that can lead them to disengage from everyday relationships and pleasurable experiences. Most are successful in avoiding unnecessary risks and dangers, although it is often at the price of narrowing the range of their positive emotions and joyful experiences. As a consequence, they tend to be inhibited and restrained, worrisome and pessimistic, overly concerned with the difficulties of life.

Modifying-Accommodating

Those who score high on the Modifying scale are at the active end of the Modifying-Accommodating polarity and are best characterized by their alertness, vigilance, liveliness, vigor, forcefulness, stimulus-seeking energy, and drive. Some individuals plan strategies and scan alternatives to circumvent obstacles or avoid the distress of punishment, rejection, and anxiety. Others are impulsive, excitable, rash, and hasty, seeking to elicit pleasures and rewards. Although their specific goals vary and change from time to time, actively modifying individuals seek to alter their lives and to intrude on passing events by energetically and busily shaping their circumstances.

Those who are passively oriented, reflective, and deliberate often score high on the Accommodating scale. They employ few overt strategies to gain their ends. They display a seeming inertness, a phlegmatic quality, a tendency toward acquiescence, and a restrained attitude in which they initiate little to modify events, instead waiting for circumstances to take their course before making accommodations. Some may be temperamentally ill equipped to rouse or assert themselves; perhaps past experience has deprived them of opportunities to acquire a range of competencies or confidence in their ability to master the events of their environments. Equally possible is that they possess a naive confidence that things will come their way with little or no effort on their part. From a variety of diverse sources, then, people at the passive end of the bipolarity appear merely to sustain their existence, engaging in few direct activities to intercede in life events or to generate change. They seem suspended, quiescent, placid, immobile, restrained, and listless, waiting for things to happen and reacting only after events occur.

Individuating-Nurturing

People scoring high on the Individuating side of the Individuating-Nurturing polarity tend to be self-focused. These individuals often make up their own minds and reach their own decisions, without perceiving the need to seek input or gain approval from others. At their best, they are self-starting, self-actualizing, and strive to overcome obstacles that could be serious checks to fulfilling their potential, as they perceive it. These persons appear to others to have a strong sense of self-identity in which they seem to be in control of their lives, regulating their experiences and future with little external prompting or interference. In addition to being self-assured, striving, enterprising, and independent, those who score high on the Individuating scale seek to become what they believe they were intended to be. When their behavior is not appropriately channeled, however, they may become self-centered and self-absorbed, caring little about the needs and priorities of others and focusing largely on their own interests.

Those scoring high on the Nurturing scale seek to satisfy belonging and social needs. They establish intimate and caring relationships with significant

others in which it is just as important to give love as it is to receive it.
There is a warm relating with others and a capability of easily displaying intimacy and love for a par-
ent, child, spouse, or close friend.
Here they manifest a sense of one-

> **DON'T FORGET**
> ....
> When interpreting the Motivating
> Aims Scales, look for one of eight
> possible profile types to interpret.

ness with the other and a deep concern for his or her welfare. They often attend to the needs of significant others before considering their own needs.
Beyond their intimate family and friends, there is often an extension of
warmth toward humankind at large, an understanding of the human condition, and a feeling of kinship with most people.

There are three pairs of Motivating Aims Scales and only eight possible
profile patterns in this group.

1. Enhancing, Modifying, Individuating
2. Enhancing, Modifying, Nurturing
3. Enhancing, Accommodating, Individuating
4. Enhancing, Accommodating, Nurturing
5. Preserving, Modifying, Individuating
6. Preserving, Modifying, Nurturing
7. Preserving, Accommodating, Individuating
8. Preserving, Accommodating, Nurturing

By far, the first two profiles are the most common overall, with men being more likely to score high on Individuating (Profile 1) and women being
more likely to score high on Nurturing (Profile 2). But either of these two
profiles reflect a positive (Enhancing) and active (Modifying) stance toward
life, which is both ordinary and healthy. In fact, there are some early research
data (see the section Managerial Performance on page 255) to suggest that
individuals who are more successful in business-management jobs tend to
score higher on Enhancing and Accommodating than others. These are individuals who anticipate positive rewards in life and actively set out to
achieve them. One wonders, however, if particularly high scores on these
scales (prevalence score above 89) would create problems. (See Rapid Reference 5.5 for a look at how to view prevalence scores when interpreting the
MIPS.)

Rapid Reference 5.5

Interpreting Prevalence Scores

When interpreting the MIPS, individuals are assumed to possess the trait measured by the particular scale when the prevalence score is 50 or above. Prevalence score values of 69 are considered high, and prevalence score values of 89 are considered very high.

Individuals scoring very high on Preserving may have more difficulty with overall adjustment because they are so focused on avoiding problems and other painful experiences that they might have difficulty appreciating the good things and enjoying life. This is especially true if the Accommodating scale is also very high, such as in Profiles 7 and 8. This could suggest a somewhat fearful (Preserving) and passive (Accommodating) stance toward life. In combination with a high score on the Nurturing scale (Profile 8), these individuals may be at risk for being taken advantage of in various ways by others. In combination with high scores on the Individuating scale, these persons could be at risk for living a lonely and unfulfilled life. In either of these cases, it may be wise to check the MIPS Adjustment Index. If the Adjustment Index is T 35 or below, the examiner should consider further testing with a clinical-range instrument such as the MCMI-III.

Cognitive Modes Scales

Extraversing-Introversing

To understand the differences between Extraversing and Introversing styles of handling information, consider Jung's (1936/1971b) descriptions of extraverts and introverts:

Extraversion is characterized by interest in the external object, responsiveness, and a ready acceptance of external happenings, a desire to influence and be influenced by events, a need to join in and get "with it," the capacity to endure bustle and noise of every kind, and actually find them enjoyable. . . .

The introvert is not forthcoming, he is as though in continual retreat before the subject. He holds aloof from external happenings, does not join in. For him self-communings are a pleasure. His own world is a safe harbor, a carefully tended and walked-in garden, closed to the public and hidden from prying eyes. His own company is the best. He feels at home in his world, where the only changes are made by himself. His best work is done with his own resources, on his own initiative and in his own way. (pp. 550–551)

Those who obtain elevated Extraversing scores are outward looking; they seek information, stimulation, and attention from others. They value others' ideas and opinions, seek the company of people they respect, and feel uncomfortable when left on their own. Individuals who score high on the Introversing scale are inward looking; they strongly prefer information obtained from their own thoughts and feelings. Not only do they value their own cognitions over those offered by others, they feel most comfortable and relaxed when by themselves.

Sensing-Intuiting individuals who score high on Sensing favor tangible, structured, and well-defined sources of information that call on their five senses. These correlate with a wide range of associated behaviors, such as choosing actions of a pragmatic and realistic nature, preferring events in the here and now, and attending to matters that call for facts and quantitative precision. As Jung (1936/1971) conceived it, "There are people for whom the accent falls on sensation, on the perception of actualities, and elevates it into the sole determining and all-overriding principle. These are the fact-minded men, in whom intellectual judgment, feeling, and intuition are driven into the background by the paramount importance of actual facts" (p. 554).

In contrast, those who score high on Intuiting prefer the intangible, unstructured, and ambiguous. This is likely to be associated with actions inspired by possibilities, challenges, potentials, and thoughts of an abstract, complex, connotative, and symbolic character, as well as by matters that depend on novelty, mystery, and speculation. To quote Jung (1936/1971), "On intuition actual reality counts only in so far as it seems to harbour possibilities which then become the supreme motivating force, regardless of the way things actually are in the present" (p. 554).

....

Thinking-Feeling

The intellective pole of the Thinking-Feeling scales reflects a preference for interpreting experience in light of reason and logic. Although life events may derive from internal or external sources, and may be of a tangible or intangible nature, the interpretive and evaluative process is inclined toward the objective and impersonal, as events are analyzed by means of critical reason and the application of rational and judicious thought. By increasing affective detachment, reducing the unruly emotional input of others and the upsetting effects of one's own emotional state, it may be possible to sustain a high degree of cognitive cohesion and continuity. Objective analysis and affective detachment protect against unwanted incursions upon cognitive stability, but often at the price of promoting behavior that is rigid, overcontrolled, and unyielding.

In contrast, experiences processed affectively will activate subjective states such as liking versus disliking, feeling good versus feeling bad, comfort versus discomfort, attracted versus repelled, valuing versus devaluing, and so on. For those scoring high on the Feeling scale, the route of affectivity inclines the individual to record not so much what other people think but rather how he or she feels about matters. The individual who inclines toward the Feeling pole uses "psychic vibrations" to learn more from the emotional tone words convey than from their content or logic. The usual modality for those who exhibit an affective style is that of subjective reality, a more or less "gut" reaction composed of either global or differentiated positive or negative moods. There are, of course, individuals who are notably introspective, inclined to pursue inner affective states with an intellective cognitive style. These individuals are not merely psychological-minded; they may exhibit an obsessive search for self-insight. For the most part, however, the affective transformational style indicates individuals who evince modest introspective analysis, combined with an open and direct empathic response to others and a subconscious susceptibility to the emotional facets of experience in as pure a manner as possible.

Systematizing-Innovating

In the MIPS schema, Systematizers are akin in certain features to those who exhibit the "Judgment preference," which Katherine Briggs and Isabel Briggs Myers abstracted from Jung's notions (Myers, 1962). Both Systematizing and having a Judgment preference indicate persons with well-structured memory systems, to which they routinely attach new cognitive experiences. Disposed to operate within established perspectives, systematizers assimilate new information to previous points of view, exhibiting thereby a high degree of dependability and consistency, if not rigidity, in their functioning. Typically, such people are predictable, conventional, orderly, planful, decisive, methodical, exacting, formal, disciplined, conscientious, faithful, loyal, and devoted. Hence, in evolutionary terms, the assimilative polarity leads to continuity and tradition or to the maintenance of existing levels of cognitive entropy; this cognitive style promotes an architectural cohesion that remains unchallenged by risky variations that could potentially diminish established levels of order.

In contrast, those at the Innovating pole, or with a Perceiving preference, are characterized by an openness to forming new and imaginative cognitive constructions of an impromptu character. They are inclined to search for creative ideas and solutions, to find novel ways to order information, and to accumulate negative entropy, so to speak, by stepping outside of what is known and given so as to establish a new or higher level of cognitive organization. Innovators stretch beyond confirmed perspectives, seeking to broaden interpretations of experience, and are not concerned with demonstrating their reliability. The imaginative mode is typically associated with being open-minded, spontaneous, extemporaneous, informal, adaptable, flexible, resilient, impressionable, creative, inventive, and resourceful.

There are 16 possible combinations of the four bipolar Cognitive Modes Scales:

1. Extraversing, Sensing, Thinking, Systematizing
2. Extraversing, Sensing, Thinking, Innovating
3. Extraversing, Sensing, Feeling, Systematizing
4. Extraversing, Sensing, Feeling, Innovating
5. Extraversing, Intuiting, Thinking, Systematizing
6. Extraversing, Intuiting, Thinking, Innovating
7. Extraversing, Intuiting, Feeling, Systematizing
8. Extraversing, Intuiting, Feeling, Innovating
9. Introversing, Sensing, Thinking, Systematizing
10. Introversing, Sensing, Thinking, Innovating
11. Introversing, Sensing, Feeling, Systematizing

12. Introversing, Sensing, Feeling, Innovating
13. Introversing, Intuiting, Thinking, Systematizing
14. Introversing, Intuiting, Thinking, Innovating
15. Introversing, Intuiting, Feeling, Systematizing
16. Introversing, Intuiting, Feeling, Innovating

> **DON'T FORGET**
> ··
> When interpreting the Cognitive Modes Scales, look for 1 of 16 possible profile types to interpret.

There are important gender differences to be aware of when interpreting these scales. The most common patterns among women are Profile 8 (15.8%), Profile 3 (14.4%), and Profile 1 (12.8%). For men, the most common pattern by far is Profile 1; 24% of men fell in this category whereas 12.8% of women did so.

There may also be important trends in terms of occupations. Table 5.3 shows MIPS percentages for each of the Cognitive Modes types by occupational group. As shown in the table, there are interesting differences in profile types by occupation. For example, approximately 18% of those in technical occupations were classified as Introversing, Sensing, Thinking, and Systematizing, compared with about 7% of salespersons. Although this information may be useful in career decision making or vocational counseling, this table should be used with caution because these data do not imply a connection between profile type and superior job performance in that occupation.

Interpersonal Behaviors Scales

Retiring-Outgoing

People scoring higher on the Retiring scale, that is, displaying more features of aloofness than gregariousness, evince few social or group interests. Their needs to give and receive affection and to show feelings tend to be minimal. They are inclined to have few relationships and interpersonal involvements and do not develop strong ties to other people. They may be seen by others as calm, placid, untroubled, easygoing, and possibly indifferent. Rarely expressing their inner feelings or thoughts to others, they seem most comfortable when left alone. They tend to work in a slow, quiet, and methodical manner, almost always remaining in the background in an undemanding and unobtrusive way.

Table 5.3 MIPS Percentages for Each of the 16 Cognitive Modes Types by Occupational Group

	ISTZ	ISFZ	INFZ	INTZ
Upper management	10.1	2.3	1.5	3.2
Clerical/Secretarial	8.7	9.7	1.0	1.0
Sales	7.2	4.5	1.8	0.9
Technical	18.2	1.8	1.8	3.6
General labor	10.7	10.7	0.0	0.0
Air force recruits	9.4	3.1	3.6	1.6
Police applicants	9.2	0.3	0.3	1.4

	ISTV	ISFV	INFV	INTV
Upper management	3.9	3.1	1.5	0.7
Clerical/Secretarial	2.9	1.9	7.8	1.0
Sales	0.9	1.8	9.0	6.3
Technical	9.1	0.0	1.8	7.3
General labor	1.8	8.9	10.7	7.1
Air force recruits	1.0	4.2	8.3	3.6
Police applicants	1.7	0.3	1.4	0.0

	ESTV	ESFV	ENFV	ENTV
Upper management	12.5	0.8	7.8	13.2
Clerical/Secretarial	1.0	3.9	11.7	2.9
Sales	1.8	7.2	15.3	7.2
Technical	9.1	0.0	7.3	5.5
General labor	10.7	5.4	8.9	3.6
Air force recruits	5.2	4.2	6.8	3.1
Police applicants	5.6	2.0	1.4	3.4

(continued)

Table 5.3   (continued)

	ESTZ	ESFZ	ENFZ	ENTZ
Upper management	22.0	10.2	0.8	6.2
Clerical/Secretarial	16.5	18.4	10.7	1.0
Sales	20.7	7.2	2.7	5.4
Technical	20.0	7.3	0.0	7.3
General labor	10.7	7.1	3.6	0.0
Air force recruits	21.9	7.8	8.3	7.8
Police applicants	58.0	3.6	3.4	8.1

Note. The sizes of the samples are as follows: Upper management (N = 130); Clerical/Secretarial (N = 103); Sales (N = 111); Technical (N = 55); General labor (N = 56); Air force recruits (N = 206); and Police applicants (N = 349). E = Extraversing; F = Feeling; I = Introversing; S = Sensing; T = Thinking; V = Innovating; W = Intuiting; Z = Systematizing. Data and table © 1994. Dicandrien, Inc. All Rights Reserved.

Comfortable working by themselves, they are not easily distracted or bothered by what goes on around them. Being somewhat deficient in the ability to recognize the needs and feelings of others, they may be seen as socially awkward, if not insensitive, as well as lacking in spontaneity and vitality.

High scorers on the Outgoing scale display attributes opposite from the above constellation. These individuals go out of their way to be popular with others, have confidence in their social abilities, feel they can readily influence and charm others, and possess a personal style that makes people like them. Most enjoy engaging in social activities and like meeting new people and learning about their lives. Talkative, lively, socially clever, they are often dramatic attention-getters who thrive on being the center of social events. Many become easily bored, especially when faced with repetitive and mundane tasks. Often characterized by intense and shifting moods, these gregarious individ-

> **DON'T FORGET**
> ....
> When interpreting the Interpersonal Behaviors Scales, look for the highest two scales to interpret.

uals are sometimes viewed as fickle and excitable. However, their enthusiasms often prove effective in energizing and motivating others. Inclined to be facile and enterprising, outgoing people may be highly skilled in manipulating others to meet their needs.

Hesitating-Asserting

The Hesitating scale represents attributes of social inhibition and withdrawal. Those scoring high on the Hesitating scale have a tendency to be sensitive to social indifference or rejection; feel unsure of themselves; and be wary in new situations, especially those of a social or interpersonal character. Somewhat ill at ease and self-conscious, these individuals anticipate running into difficulties in interrelating and fear being embarrassed. They may feel tense when they have to deal with persons they do not know, expecting that others will not think well of them. Most prefer to work alone or in small groups where they know that people accept them. Once they feel accepted, they can open up, be friendly, cooperative, and participate with others productively.

An interpersonal boldness, stemming from a belief in themselves and their talents, characterize those scoring high on the Asserting scale. Competitive, ambitious, and self-assured, they naturally assume positions of leadership, act in a decisive and unwavering manner, and expect others to recognize their special qualities and cater to them. Beyond being self-confident, those with an Asserting profile often are audacious, clever, and persuasive, having sufficient charm to win others over to their own causes and purposes. Problematic in this regard may be their lack of social reciprocity and their sense of entitlement. On the other hand, they are often successful in achieving their ambitions and they typically prove to be effective leaders.

Dissenting-Conforming

The degree to which persons flout tradition or are tradition oriented undergirds the third polarity. The Dissenting versus Conforming dimension recognizes that some individuals act in a notably autonomous fashion; are not social-minded; and are not inclined to adhere to conventional standards, cultural mores, and organizational regulations. At the other pole, individuals are highly compliant and responsible, as well as conscientious and diligent about fulfilling their duties. High scorers on the Dissenting scale include unconventional persons who seek to do things their own way and are willing to take the consequences of doing so. They act as they see fit regardless of how others judge them. Inclined at times to elaborate on or shade the truth, as well as to ride close to the edge of the law, they are not conscientious; that is, they do not assume customary responsibilities. Rather, they frequently assert that too many rules stand in the way of people who wish to be free and inventive, and they prefer to think and act in an independent and often creative way. Many believe that people in authority are too hard on subordinates who do not conform. Dissenters dislike following the same routine day after day and at times act impulsively and irresponsibly. They will do what they believe to be best without much concern for the effects of their actions on others. Skeptical about the motives of most people, and refusing to be fettered or coerced, they exhibit a strong need for autonomy and self-determination.

At the other extreme of this Dissenting-Conforming polarity are those who score high on the Conforming scale. Conformers are notably respectful of tradition and authority and act in a responsible, proper, and conscientious way. They do their best to uphold conventional rules and standards, following given regulations closely, and they tend to be judgmental of those who do not. Well organized and reliable, prudent and restrained, they may appear to be overly self-controlled, formal, and inflexible in their relationships; intolerant of deviance; and unbending in their adherence to social proprieties. Diligent about their responsibilities, they dislike having their work pile up, worry about finishing things, and come across to others as highly dependable and industrious.

Yielding-Controlling

There is a clear and marked contrast between persons who are docile, obedient, subservient, and self-demeaning and those who are dominating, willful, forceful, and power oriented. The Yielding scale on the MIPS conveys more than cooperativeness and amicability; it involves a disposition to act in a subservient and self-abasing manner. Placing themselves in an inferior light or abject position, those high on the Yielding scale allow, even encourage, others to take advantage of them. They are unassertive and deferential, if not servile. Often viewing themselves as their own worst enemies, they behave in an unpresuming, self-effacing, even self-derogating manner, and tend to avoid displaying their talents and aptitudes. Obsequious and self-sacrificing in their interactions with others, they can be depended on to adhere to the expectations of those they follow. Most people in this category possess abilities far in excess of those they lay claim to.

Those scoring high on the Controlling scale enjoy the power to direct and intimidate others, and to evoke obedience and respect from them. They tend to be tough and unsentimental, as well as gain satisfaction in actions that dictate and manipulate the lives of others. Although many sublimate their power-oriented tendencies in publicly approved roles and vocations, these inclinations become evident in occasional intransigence, stubbornness, and coercive behaviors. Despite these periodic negative expressions, controlling types typically make effective leaders, being talented in supervising and persuading others to work for the achievement of common goals.

Complaining-Agreeing

The Complaining-Agreeing polarity takes up social negativism or "discontent"—a Complaining style—versus social amenability or "congeniality," which is named an Agreeing style. The former dimension extreme signifies a general displeasure both with oneself and others, combined with a tendency to act in a petulant, resentful, irritable, and oppositional manner. The latter pole represents a general inclination to be pleasant in relationships, and to act in a consenting, affable, and peaceable way (without the self-demeaning and self-abasing tendencies seen in the Yielding personality).

Those scoring high on the Complaining scale often assert that they have been treated unfairly, that little of what they have done has been appreciated, and that they have been blamed for things they did not do. Opportunities seem not to have worked out well for them, and they "know" that good things do not last. Often resentful of what they see as unfair demands placed on them, they may be disinclined to carry out responsibilities as well as they could. Ambivalent about their lives and relationships, they may get into problematic wrangles and disappointments as they vacillate between acceptance one time and resistance the next. When matters go well, they can be productive and constructively independent-minded, willing to speak out to remedy troublesome issues.

Quite another picture is seen among those who score high on the Agreeing scale. This bipolar extreme is akin to a cooperative stance toward others, representing an accommodating, participatory, compromising, and agreeing pattern of behavior. High scorers on this scale convey a self-respecting concordance with others and a congenial obligingness that is voluntary rather than coerced or a product of self-derogation. Those who fit the Agreeing pattern are notably cooperative and amicable. Disinclined to upset others, they are willing to adapt their preferences to be compatible with those of others. Trusting others to be kind and thoughtful, they are also willing to reconcile differences and to achieve peaceable solutions, as well as to be considerate and to concede when necessary. Cordiality and compromise characterize their interpersonal relationships.

One of the most common 2-point codes is Asserting and Controlling. This reflects a somewhat strong, perhaps domineering stance. The extent to which the individual's approach is overbearing versus adaptive and motivational is reflected in the magnitude of the scores. When moderately high, this is a very common profile pattern among managers and executives. When these scores exceed prevalence score values of 89, however, this style may lead to more problems than it solves. Another common 2-point code is Outgoing and Asserting. This code also reflects a strong stance toward life, but one that is more characterized by a general sense of active engagement with life than domineering behavior.

It is useful to consider how high scores on the Interpersonal Behaviors Scales relate to Motivating Aims and Cognitive Modes profiles. For example, individuals with moderately high scores on the Dissenting scale may, because of their tendency to question standard operating procedures, be creative and novel problem solvers. This is especially true if high scores on this scale are combined with a Cognitive Modes profile that includes high scores on Intuiting and Innovating. If they are also high on Enhancing and Modifying, then this dissenting energy may be well channeled in socially appropriate ways. However, when combined with high scores on Complaining or Preserving, these individuals behavior may be problematic in settings requiring conformity, especially if the Dissenting scale is very high.

A less common, but more troublesome, 2-point code is Retiring and Hesitating, especially when combined with high scores on Yielding (see the section Illustrative Case Report on page 262). This reflects an anxious stance toward life, and when combined with a Motivating Aims profile that includes Preserving and Accommodating these individuals may have considerable difficulty achieving a satisfactory adjustment to life demands.

STRENGTHS AND WEAKNESS OF THE MIPS

Strengths

1. *Theory, Integration, and Utility.* The main strength of the MIPS lies in the theoretical undergirding of its scales, the integration of information-processing styles into personality understanding, and the insightfulness and usefulness of the automated reports. Unlike many newer personality scales, which are largely atheoretical and empirically derived, the constructs measured by the MIPS scales have a rich theoretical background and are well grounded in traditional psychological thought. The Motivating Aims are broad and powerful constructs that have an important history in the field of psychology. In brief, the Enhancing-Preserving (pleasure-pain) dimension is related to drive theory, the Modifying-Accommodating (active-passive) dimension to ego psychology, and the Individuating-Nurturing (self-other) dimension to self psychology and object relations theory. As observed above, the Cognitive Modes Scales are related to the model formulated by Jung (1921/1971) and latter popularized in the MBTI. Dr. Millon has made an important contribution to normal-range personality assessment by reformulating these constructs in terms of their influence on one's cognitive style of dealing with the voluminous influx of information required for modern daily living. Further, the Interpersonal Behaviors Scales are normal-range variations of Millon's 10 personality disorders. As a group, the MIPS scales have a rich theoretical foundation in a model of personality that is deeply rooted in biosocial and evolutionary theory (Millon, 1969/1983, 1990, 1991).

2. *Inoffensive Instrument.* The MIPS test questions will not offend normally functioning adults in the way that questions from diagnostic instruments often do. Normal individuals entering counseling for common life stressors do not like to be asked if they hear voices or believe that people are following them—and the negative impact on therapeutic rapport created by use of such instruments is often underestimated.

3. *Assesses Individuals' Motivations.* The MIPS is capable of yielding a rich understanding of what motivates individuals, as well as their style of dealing with information and relating to others—something that di-

agnostic instruments can not do very well because they do not ask these types of questions.

Weaknesses

1. *Lack of MCMI-III Correlational Studies.* The lack of studies examining the relationship among the MIPS and the other Millon inventories, particularly the MCMI-III, is perhaps the most obvious weakness. How do the personality disorder scales on the MCMI-III relate to the personality styles measured by the MIPS? Where is the line between normality and abnormality?

CLINICAL APPLICATIONS OF THE MIPS

The MIPS is primarily for use with normally functioning adults. Appropriate applications of the MIPS include settings in which counselors seek to identify, understand, and assist adults who do not have DSM-IV diagnoses. Such settings include employee-assistance programs, vocational guidance and career-development programs, university counseling centers, marriage and family counseling centers. Also appropriate are independent and group practice settings in which reasonably functional individuals seek assistance with life problems such as divorce, child management, drinking, work stress, and so forth.

The MIPS is especially useful in organizational settings. One important application is to screen employees for general adjustment. This is particularly relevant for employees in high-risk fire and safety occupations. The MIPS is also frequently used to assist in identifying managerial potential or as developmental feedback to improve existing managerial talent. The MIPS also can be used to help form or project teams and to improve the effectiveness with which teams make decisions and work together. Feedback of MIPS results can be integrated into many team-building exercises and other organizational training and development programs. Practitioners using the MIPS in organizational settings should be aware of relevant legal and ethical issues regarding testing of job applicants. A brief discussion of applied organizational research with the MIPS follows. Further details of these studies can be found in the MIPS manual (Millon, Weiss, et al., 1994, Chapter 5).

Managerial Performance

The MIPS was administered to a sample of middle-level managers in a large telecommunications firm in the southeastern United States ($N = 51$). These were mostly White and well-educated men in the third tier of the corporation's management structure. The subjects participated in a 3-day management-assessment center that included two simulated board meetings with different agendas: one meeting involved a competitive resource-allocation decision, and the other involved a cooperative organizational problem-solving discussion. Other activities included an in-basket exercise; a formal presentation of a business plan to a superior, based on the review of a standardized packet of information; a counseling session with a disgruntled subordinate; and the preparation of a written business plan, based on the review of another standardized packet of information. Each manager's performance was rated by three trained assessors on 10 dimensions of managerial performance.

The mean MIPS profile for the managers is quite interesting. The profile suggests that these men actively seek positive reinforcement from their world by modifying surrounding circumstances and asserting themselves interpersonally in a socially confident and poised manner. The highest mean MIPS scores are on the MIPS Enhancing (prevalence score = 80.6), Asserting (prevalence score = 72.9), Outgoing (prevalence score = 70), Modifying (prevalence score = 68.5), and Extraversing (prevalence score = 68.5) scales. A Moderate elevation is observed on the MIPS Controlling scale (prevalence score = 55.1).

Several a priori hypotheses about the relationship of the MIPS scales to the 10 dimensions of managerial performance were supported. As predicted, Oral Communication was related to the MIPS Modifying, Extraversing, Outgoing, and Asserting scales. Oral Defense, or the ability to offer persuasive verbal responses in the face of challenges and criticism, was positively related to the MIPS Outgoing, Asserting, and Controlling scales and inversely related to the Yielding scale. Strategic Analysis was related to the MIPS Modifying and Controlling scales. Interactive Problem Solving was positively correlated with the MIPS Extraversing, Outgoing, and Asserting scales and inversely with the Hesitating scale. Team Management was related to the MIPS Controlling scale.

Although not anticipated, the MIPS Intuiting and Innovating scales were correlated significantly with several dimensions of managerial performance, including Strategic Analysis, Interactive Problem Solving, Oral Defense, and Oral Communication. Because the business decisions and situations encountered at higher levels of management are both more complex and less structured, this finding may suggest that an ability to deal with novelty and ambiguity, which sensing and systematizing individuals often lack, may be helpful to effective managerial performance at the higher levels on management. Further research is needed on this topic.

Also not anticipated was a significant correlation between Team Management and the MIPS Preserving, Complaining, and Feeling scales. While a Feeling style of cognitive processing may relate to Team Management because of the tendency to attend to the views of others, the positive relationship of high ability in this dimension with the Preserving and Complaining scales is more difficult to interpret. According to MIPS theory, the Complaining scale represents a tendency to be discontented with situations in general, and the Preserving scale reflects a basic motivation to avoid negative reinforcement from the environment. If the current findings can be replicated, they may suggest that this increased alertness to negative feedback, if appropriately channeled, can be adaptive when managing a team.

The present findings are consistent with definitions of leadership as a process of interpersonal influence involving persuasion rather than dominance (Hogan, Curphey, & Hogan, 1993).

Law-Enforcement Performance

The relationship between the MIPS and police officer performance was studied in a predominantly Hispanic metropolitan city in the southwestern United States. The mean MIPS profile for those applicants offered admission to the training academy ($N = 47$) was noteworthy for the relatively moderate elevation on the Controlling (prevalence score = 47) scale, as well as the balance of scores on the Individuating (prevalence score = 41) and Nurturing (prevalence score = 41) polarity. The highest MIPS scores were observed on the Thinking (prevalence score = 71), Asserting (prevalence score = 74), and Enhancing (prevalence score = 81) scales. Also noteworthy is the mean score on the Adjustment Index ($T = 59$), which is almost 1 full standard deviation above average.

A structured job analysis was conducted to determine the personality traits that are considered essential to effective performance as an entry level patrol officer, with consensus ratings provided by five field-training officers. The results suggested that four personality dimensions were essential to effective performance: (a) Adherence to Work Ethic, (b) Thoroughness and Attentiveness to Details, (c) Sensitivity to the Interests of Others, and (d) Emotional Stability. The job analysis was conducted using a research version of *An Inventory of General Position Requirements* (Bowling Green State University, 1992), which was developed to provide an empirical basis for matching position requirements and personality traits in specific occupations (Guion, 1991).

MIPS composites were developed to measure each of the four dimensions identified in the job analysis. After 6 months of academy training, these composites were correlated with ratings on simulated tactical police exercises. The MIPS Emotional Stability composite was correlated with the use of secure police tactics during a barroom disturbance and with appropriately removing a suspect from the disturbance. Appropriate removal of the suspect was also correlated with the MIPS composite for Sensitivity to the Interests of Others and the MIPS composite for Adherence to Work Ethic. In another exercise the MIPS composite for Thoroughness and Attentiveness to Detail and the MIPS composite for Adherence to Work Ethic were both correlated with properly issuing a traffic citation.

After graduation from the academy, the cadets were followed through 4 months of field training. They were rated multiple times on Tasks, Attitude, Knowledge, and Appearance. The MIPS Controlling scale showed a pattern of medium to large inverse correlations with all areas of field performance measured in this study.

According to MIPS theory, individuals with moderately high scores on the MIPS Controlling scale demonstrate a pervasively forceful and domineering style of relating to others. Individuals with very high Controlling scores may be chronically combative, tending toward a contentious, even hostile, tone in their relationships. In the author's theory of personality disorders, these individuals are on the same continuum (although not as extreme) as those diagnosed with aggressive personality disorders. As written previously about these individuals, "Although many may cloak their more malicious and power-oriented tendencies in publicly approved roles and vocations, they give themselves away in their dominating, antagonistic, and frequent persecutory actions" (Millon, Millon, Davis, Choca, & Van Denburg, 1997, pp. 12–13).

On the polar MIPS scale, Yielding was uncorrelated with field performance. This suggests a nonlinear relationship between dominance and police performance in which either too little or too much of this trait is associated with problematic performance as a law enforcement officer. This finding is also consistent with the results of the job analysis in which the police department's field-training officers indicated that sensitivity to the interests of others is essential to effective performance of police duties. Overall, these results mirror the changing conceptualization of the police officers' role from "carrying a big stick" to a highly technical position requiring considerable interpersonal skill and judgment.

Screening for Psychological Adjustment

The MIPS was administered to 297 U.S. Air Force recruits during the 1st week of basic training as part of a routine screening program designed to identify individuals who are psychologically incapable of adjusting to military service. MIPS results were not available to the psychologists making these decisions. One hundred sixty-nine recruits passed the initial mass screening based on their responses to a structured life-history questionnaire. Ninety-five recruits were referred for further testing but were then cleared for duty based on the test results. Thirty-three recruits were recommended for discharge from the military after a complete psychological evaluation.

The mean MIPS profiles for these groups were dramatically different. Whereas the group that passed the initial screening was reasonably balanced on the pleasure-pain polarity, for example, the group found unfit for duty scored extremely high on pain (Preserving prevalence score = 98) and extremely low on pleasure (Enhancing prevalence score = 1).

The unfit for duty group scored more than 2.5 standard deviations below average on the Adjustment Index ($T = 23$). A T score less than or equal to 35 points on the Adjustment Index was identified as a cutoff score because it correctly classified 100% of recruits in the unfit for duty group while misclassifying less than 20% of recruits who were actually fit for duty. The correlation of the Adjustment Index with fit versus unfit designations was at the upper limit of the statistic. This study suggested that use of the Adjustment

Index in the screening program could have significantly reduced the caseload of the examining psychologists.

Although the cutoff score should be cross-validated in an independent sample, the MIPS Adjustment Index holds considerable promise in a wide variety of organizational settings in which screening for overall adjustment is considered job relevant, such as safety-sensitive positions or positions working with children or the elderly. Individuals who score below T 35 on this index should be administered a clinical-range instrument, such as the MCMI-III (Millon, Millon, Davis, Choca, & Van Denburg, 1997) to assess for psychopathology.

Absenteeism and Disciplinary Personnel Actions

The MIPS was administered to a sample of hourly workers employed by a medium-size municipal government in the southeastern United States (N = 41), and absenteeism and disciplinary records were obtained. These employees were predominantly laborers working in the city maintenance, landscape, and sanitation departments. The sample was largely male (76%) and African American (56%), with a high school education or less (70%). The median age was 35 years.

The mean MIPS Interpersonal Behaviors Scales for this sample were characterized by high scores on the Conforming (prevalence score = 60) and Agreeing (prevalence score = 61) scales. These employees tend to use more Sensing (prevalence score = 63) modes of gathering information and Systematizing (prevalence score = 55) strategies for processing information. In general, this sample of laborers was considerably more Introversing, Retiring, and Yielding, as well as less Enhancing and Modifying, than samples of managers and executives.

MIPS scores were correlated with personnel records for the preceding 12 months. The MIPS Controlling scale was inversely correlated with both disciplinary personnel action taken against an employee ($r = -.35, p < .01$) and absenteeism ($r = -.33, p < .01$). In addition, the MIPS Hesitating scale was positively related to absenteeism ($r = .32, p < .01$). Thus, we can speculate that employees with high scores on the Controlling scale and low scores on the Hesitating scale will have better attendance records than other employees. According to MIPS theory, individuals who score high on the Controlling scale seek to arrange and control the events in their lives in order to meet their schedules, needs, and priorities. In addition, individuals scoring low on the Hesitating scale tend to feel more secure about their personal worth and to be more decisive about taking action than those who score higher. Perhaps these employees take better command of potential conflict between their personal and work schedules than those who are absent more often.

Career Decision Making

Two studies examined the use of the MIPS in career decision making. In the first study the MIPS was administered to 70 clients participating in career-management counseling at a large nationally based firm that specializes in executive outplacement and management consulting to Fortune 500 companies. The sample consisted of all upper-level managers who had been displaced during corporate downsizing.

The mean MIPS profile for this sample suggested that on average these managers are people who actively seek positive reinforcement from the environment and who are assertive and outgoing in interpersonal relations. Their preferred information-gathering styles are Extraversing and Sensing, and their preferred information-processing styles are Thinking and Systematizing.

Correlations with the Strong Interest Inventory (Hansen & Campbell, 1985) show that a Systematizing style of processing information is significantly correlated with Conventional occupations involving methodical, organized, or clerical tasks. The polar MIPS scale, Innovating, is correlated with interest in Enterprising activities, which require entrepreneurial, persuasive, and political behaviors. The Strong Enterprising scale is also significantly correlated with the MIPS Modifying, Extraversing, Outgoing, Asserting, and Controlling scales.

An interest in Business Management on the Strong Enterprising scale was positively correlated with the MIPS Controlling and Asserting scales and negatively correlated with the MIPS Accommodating scale. By contrast, an interest in Office Practices on the Strong Enterprising scale was correlated with a Systematizing style of processing information and a Conforming and Agreeing style of interpersonal behavior. Further, an Outgoing style of relating, as measured on the MIPS, was correlated with an interest in both Sales and Merchandising, as expressed on the Strong Enterprising scale.

In the second study on career decision, the MIPS and the Strong Enterprising scales were administered to a sample of 100 community college students identified as expressing uncertainty about their career goals, and describing their uncertainty as troublesome and unresolved issue for them. A canonical analysis yielded three distinct patterns of relationships between the MIPS and Strong Enterprising scales labeled the Retreator, the Feeler, and the Conscientious Conformer. Retreators are characterized by the Hesitating and Agreeing scales on the MIPS. They do not trust others or take risks easily. They prefer disconnection from the world of work and may develop interpersonally defensive career intentions. For the Retreator, career indecision may reflect a lack of receptivity to the social relations that are part of most work settings. There was a hint at some compatibility with highly structured subordinate-follower roles in work.

The Feeler is characterized by the Nurturing, Feeling, and Agreeing scales on the MIPS. Although Retreators and Feelers both tend to have Agreeing personalities, they differ in their approach toward others. Retreators may use agreeing behavior as a way of avoiding more meaningful and, perhaps, threatening interpersonal communication. Feelers, on the other hand, are socially open, and their agreeing behavior lacks the defensive quality shown by Retreators. Feelers show a pattern of being people oriented and avoiding activities that are highly regulated and involve calculation or the use of standardized procedures to find solutions.

The Conscientious Conformer is characterized by the MIPS Conforming, Sensing, and Systematizing scales. These students tend to express interest in Office Practice, Domestic Activities, Social Service, and Religious Activities.

General negative affectivity—the propensity to focus on and experience painful emotional states—may provide a framework for understanding chronic career indecision. Perhaps the strong need for systems, which is characteristic of the Conscientious Conformer, and the willingness to defer to the wishes of others, which is characteristic of both the Retreator and Feeler, represent two methods of avoiding possible negative stimulation from the work environment. Students who exhibit pervasive career indecision present unique challenges for counselors in traditional vocational guidance programs. The common career-counseling techniques of exploration, job shadowing, and placement assistance may be inadequate for these clients. To remediate chronic career indecision, counselors may need to address the underlying personality issues (Super, 1983; Tango & Dziuban, 1984).

The studies reviewed in this section provide empirical support for many of the applications of the MIPS suggested earlier in this chapter.

ILLUSTRATIVE CASE REPORT

Figure 5.1 illustrates a computer-generated Interpretive Report for J. D., a 30-year-old administrative assistant with a ninth grade education who was referred for testing by her supervisor because of trouble at work.

According to the supervisor, J. D. works in a small department of six people. In addition to serving as a receptionist and typist, she organizes and schedules meetings and runs errands. J. D. is known for being conscientious and careful in carrying out her duties. She tends not to socialize much, preferring instead to spend time by herself. She is typically pleasant if somewhat distant from colleagues, accepts new work assignments without hesitation, and places few demands on those around her. In the past few weeks coworkers have noticed that she has become quite irritable and withdrawn. She has been rude to a few people on the telephone and has made serious mistakes in scheduling appointments and deadlines. When coworkers approached her to find out what the problem was, she avoided the discussion by apologizing for her behavior and saying that "soon" everything would be better. Things did not improve, and the referral for evaluation came after she stormed out of a meeting where several people were upset with her because she did not properly prepare some important documents.

During an initial interview, J. D. acknowledged her recent trouble. She reported that she was having marital difficulties and this was distracting her from her work. She admitted that she had become overloaded with duties and simply "lost control" of the situation. Nevertheless, in her opinion her coworkers were "insensitive" to her plight, and she felt that it was becoming "unbearable" for her to assist people whom she felt were unconcerned about her needs.

Turning to her MIPS results, the Validity Indicators suggest that she was conscientious and careful in answering the test items, did not accentuate or downplay her positive qualities, but may have exaggerated personal problems and difficulties. The Interpretive Report notes a consistent pat-

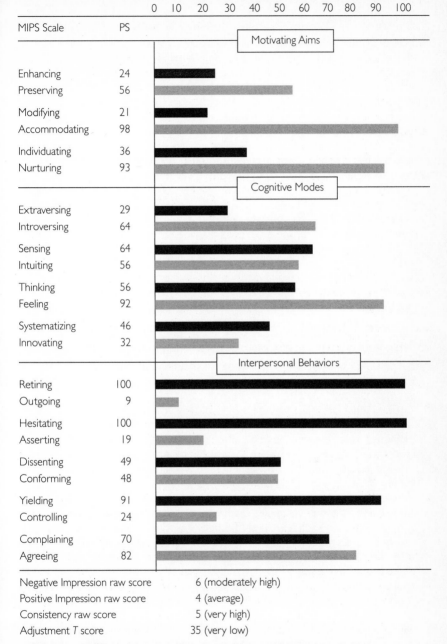

Prevalence Scores (Adult Female Norms)

MIPS Scale	PS

Motivating Aims

Enhancing	24
Preserving	56
Modifying	21
Accommodating	98
Individuating	36
Nurturing	93

Cognitive Modes

Extraversing	29
Introversing	64
Sensing	64
Intuiting	56
Thinking	56
Feeling	92
Systematizing	46
Innovating	32

Interpersonal Behaviors

Retiring	100
Outgoing	9
Hesitating	100
Asserting	19
Dissenting	49
Conforming	48
Yielding	91
Controlling	24
Complaining	70
Agreeing	82

Negative Impression raw score	6 (moderately high)
Positive Impression raw score	4 (average)
Consistency raw score	5 (very high)
Adjustment T score	35 (very low)

Figure 5.1 MIPS Interpretive Report for J. D., a 30-year-old Female Administrative Assistant With a Ninth Grade Education

Note. © 1994 by Dicandrien, Inc. and The Psychological Corporation. All Rights Reserved.

J. D.'s balance on the enhancing versus preserving polarity moderately indicates that she is disposed to be cautious, to avoid problematic situations and troublesome relationships, to find a niche that maximizes security, and to arrange her affairs to ensure a measure of social and interpersonal predictability. Often upset by disappointments, she evinces a concern that the better things of life rarely last and that its pleasures and joys often are ephemeral, neither genuine nor durable. Hence, she judges it wise to minimize social discomforts and to work at making sure that mistakes not be a function of her actions. She tries to make life most gratifying by being prudent and sensible and by acting in a level-headed and judicious way, not by seeking to generate personal pleasures or by engaging in social risks.

On the modifying and accommodating continuum, J. D.'s scores suggest that she is very inclined not to act until she knows what others are likely to do and to wait for events to transpire before deciding what should be done. She takes an inactive role for the most part, reacting to the passing scene, evincing little initiative, engaging in few direct actions to change her life circumstances, and being quiescent or restrained in seeking to effect the ends she may desire. Willing at times to submit to whatever life presents, she appears to accommodate obligingly to her "destiny," behaving in a manner that suggests that she believes that her life is determined essentially by external forces that are beyond her control. Why bother expending much effort toward an end that others can do either better or achieve by force of their greater will?

The balance on the individuating versus nurturing polarity indicates strongly that J. D.'s lack of initiative and dependence on the good faith of others are not the only factors that account for her genuine warmth and caring for their welfare and needs. Despite her somewhat concerned outlook on life, she has concluded that closeness to others can not only improve her own circumstances but may generate an atmosphere conducive to the welfare of all. Platitudinous though this may be as a philosophy of life, it appears to guide her to a more satisfying and secure state than would otherwise be the case. Feeling best and judging oneself worthy as a person when providing solace to others appears to validate this philosophy for her.

Although J. D. draws energy and gains security primarily from sources within herself, she is nevertheless quietly accommodating, showing a high degree of concern for the welfare of others. Responsible and conscientious in her endeavors, she prefers to deal with the factual, tangible, and realistic rather than the abstract or hypothetical. In general, she is passively inclined to follow established guidelines pertaining to practical matters that focus on details and order. She tends to be self-effacing and is ill-disposed to be assertive. Nor is she willing to take credit for her efforts, especially those carried out on behalf of others. Painstaking and highly organized in approaching tasks and routines, often adhering religiously to the "tried and true," she will try to fulfill the expectations set down by tradition, typically meeting what she

Figure 5.1 (continued)

sees as worthy goals in a quietly efficient and timely manner. Rarely expressing her inner thoughts and feelings to others, she usually keeps private ideas and reactions well in check. This surface reserve often cloaks strong inner emotions, which she regards as intrusive and problematic in that they might undermine the efficiency and propriety she seeks to exhibit publicly.

Systematically arranging her affairs, finishing her labors before relaxing, persevering and being serious-minded, J. D. readily accepts responsibilities, especially in tasks where patience and mastery of details can be demonstrated. Rarely acting on impulse, she is more likely to approach a task slowly and methodically, overlearning its particulars perhaps to the point of inflexibility. Similarly, she strives to organize things in her own distinctive fashion, one that she has found to be both suitable and comforting. In all likelihood, she will feel out of sorts should things be in disarray or events occur out of her accustomed order. Despite these inflexibilities and preoccupations with details and procedures, she is also oriented toward others. Few activities result in as much security for her as those in which she can provide desired services for family or employers. Acting in a dutiful and accommodating manner, her energies are devoted in part to a concern for others, albeit expressed in a practical and down-to-earth manner.

Praiseworthy as these traits may be, however, note should be made of some possibly undesirable consequences. Focusing excessively on the details of the here-and-now may result in a narrowing of perspective, a slowness to grasp the larger picture of alternative and innovative possibilities. Frequently stuck in the rut of traditional thinking, she may have some difficulty recognizing new and more effective solutions to unanticipated problems. In another domain, her commitment to the welfare of those to whom she is close may lead them to take advantage of her, resulting in her feeling disappointment and resentment. Similarly, owing to her passive and self-denying style, she may come to feel discontentment and pessimism, especially when her efforts go unappreciated by significant others, perhaps resulting in a tendency to become even more retiring and self-absorbed.

Although J. D. may assume a quietly passive if not peripheral role in social activities, she has a strong need to connect to others, but not in a joyful, lively, and high-spirited fashion. Rather, her social attachments are of a calm and well-mannered sort, harmonious, subdued, and controlled. Emotionally close to if not dependent on those few to whom she is attached, she keeps her distance from the unknown, be it persons or situations. Feeling a measure of strain and self-consciousness when faced with new acquaintances, she favors the well-known and unthreatening, persons whose styles of behavior are established and predictable. She has learned that it is best to follow a relatively uneventful and repetitive life pattern where she can avoid self-assertion, competition, and unanticipated responsibilities. Having some doubts concern-

(continued)

Figure 5.1 (continued)

ing her ability to function autonomously and effectively, she attempts to follow the rules and guidelines set down by persons whom she respects and admires. Beyond this, she has a noticeable adherence to social conventions and proprieties and a feeling of security in settings and relationships that are conducted in accord with traditional principles and formalities. She prefers to see herself as trustworthy and compliant, even devoted and perfectionistic. However, beneath her surface composure, she is not as sure of these virtuous self-appraisals as she would like to be.

Despite her best efforts, an individual with this profile often experiences considerable difficulty in forming a satisfactory adjustment to life. More in-depth assessment of J. D.'s social and emotional functioning should be considered.

Figure 5.1 (continued)

tern of traits. J. D. is cautious, tends to avoid conflicts, is passive and accommodating of others, is introverted and feelings oriented, tends to wall herself off when faced with trouble, and may have a poor view of her personal abilities and coping skills. Given her presenting problem, J. D.'s marital problems probably caused enough emotional distress to overwhelm her coping resources. Unable to retreat safely into herself, she exaggerated her usual methods of keeping others at arm's length. She became less communicative and more self-absorbed after her marital conflicts escalated. At the same time her sense of disappointment in herself was evident to others in her irritability and tendency to lash out when pushed beyond her limits. Not accustomed to managing problem situations interpersonally, she did not effectively communicate her distress or seek help to reduce her workload.

J. D.'s sense of disappointment that her colleagues did not recognize her plight signals an impasse that can be very difficult to resolve without professional intervention. Her low Adjustment Score of 35 additionally suggests that she has problems in many areas of her life that she is not able to resolve. Based on this assessment a referral for additional testing and counseling is appropriate. Until she obtains some emotional relief and is able to resume her usual duties, she may also be considered for lighter duties or transferred temporarily to a site where she can have more privacy and control over the flow of work.

✒ TEST YOURSELF ✒

1. **The MIPS is most appropriate for use with**
   (a) psychiatric inpatients.
   (b) patients with personality disorders.
   (c) astronauts.
   (d) normal people.

2. **The MIPS is appropriate for**
   (a) teenagers.
   (b) adults.
   (c) both a and b.

3. **The MIPS content scales are divided into how many sections?**
   (a) 8
   (b) 16
   (c) 5
   (d) 3

4. **Which pair of MIPS scales is not part of the Motivating Aims Scales?**
   (a) Enhancing and Preserving
   (b) Modifying and Accommodating
   (c) Individuating and Nurturing
   (d) Extraversing and Introversing

5. **When interpreting the Motivating Aims Scales, how many possible profile types are there?**
   (a) 8
   (b) 16
   (c) 2
   (d) 6

6. **Which MIPS scale is not part of the Cognitive Modes Scales?**
   (a) Extraversing and Introversing
   (b) Sensing and Intuiting
   (c) Thinking and Feeling
   (d) Individuating and Nurturing
   (e) Systematizing and Innovating

(continued)

7. **When interpreting the Cognitive Modes Scales, how many possible profile types are there?**
   - (a) 8
   - (b) 16
   - (c) 24
   - (d) 2

8. **The MIPS Cognitive Modes Scales measure the same Jungian construct as which other popular test?**
   - (a) MCMI-III
   - (b) WAIS-III
   - (c) Rorschach
   - (d) MBTI
   - (e) 16 PF

9. **When interpreting the Cognitive Modes Scales of the MIPS, how would your interpretation differ for two individuals who obtain the following profiles?**

   Extraversing, Sensing, Thinking, Systematizing

   Introversing, Intuiting, Feeling, Innovating

10. **What Motivating Aims profile would you expect to see for an individual whose highest two scales on Interpersonal Behaviors are Asserting and Outgoing? Why?**

Answers: 1. d; 2. b; 3. d; 4. d; 5. a; 6. d; 7. b; 8. d; 9. The former would look for inspiration from others, focus on tangible facts, and process information logically and in an organized fashion. The latter would look within him- or herself for inspiration and utilize intuition and feelings to process information in novel ways; 10. Enhancing, Modifying, and Individuating.

References

Chapter I

American Psychiatric Association. (1987). *Diagnostic and statistical manual of mental disorders* (3rd ed., rev.). Washington, DC: Author.

American Psychiatric Association. (1994). *Diagnostic and statistical manual of mental disorders* (4th ed.). Washington, DC: Author.

Ben-Porath, Y. S., Hostetler, K., Butcher, J. N., & Graham, J. R. (1989). New subscales for the MMPI-2 Social Introversion (Si) scale. *Psychological Assessment, 1,* 169–174.

Butcher, J. N., Dahlstrom, W. G., Graham, J. R., Tellegen, A., & Kaemmer, B. (1989). *MMPI-2: Manual for administration and scoring.* Minneapolis: University of Minnesota Press.

Choca, J. P., & Van Denburg, E. (1996). *Interpretive guide to the Millon Clinical Multiaxial Inventory* (2nd ed.). Washington, DC: American Psychological Association.

Craig, R. J. (Ed.). (1993a). *The Millon Clinical Multiaxial Inventory: A clinical research information synthesis.* Hillsdale, NJ: Erlbaum.

Craig, R. J. (1993b). *Psychological assessment with the Millon Clinical Multiaxial Inventory (II): An interpretive guide.* Odessa, FL: Psychological Assessment Resources.

Craig, R. J. (1997). A selected review of the MCMI empirical literature. In T. Millon (Ed.), *The Millon inventories: Clinical and personality assessment* (pp. 303–326). New York: Guilford.

Cronbach, L. J. (1951). Coefficient alpha and the internal structure of tests. *Psychometrica, 16,* 297–334.

Exner, J. E., Jr. (1993). *The Rorschach: A comprehensive system: Vol. 1. Basic foundations* (3rd ed.). New York: Wiley.

Harris, R. E., & Lingoes, J. C. (1955). *Subscales for the MMPI: An aid to profile interpretation.* San Francisco, CA: University of California at San Francisco, Department of Psychiatry.

Jankowski, D. (2002). *Beginner's guide to the MCMI-III.* Washington, DC: American Psychological Association.

Loevinger, J. (1957). Objective tests as instruments of psychological theory. *Psychological Reports, 3,* 635–694.

McCann, J., & Dyer, F. J. (1996). *Forensic assessment with the Millon inventories.* New York: Guilford Press.

Millon, T. (1983a). *Millon Clinical Multiaxial Inventory manual* (3rd ed.). Minneapolis, MN: National Computer Systems.

Millon, T. (1983b). *Modern psychopathology.* Prospect Heights, IL: Waveland Press. (Original work published 1969)

Millon, T. (1987). *Millon Clinical Multiaxial Inventory–II manual* (2nd ed.). Minneapolis, MN: National Computer Systems.

Millon, T. (1990). *Toward a new personology.* New York: Wiley.

Millon, T. (1997a) *Millon Clinical Multiaxial Inventory–III manual* (2nd ed.), Minneapolis, MN: National Computer Systems.

Millon, T. (Ed.). (1997b). *The Millon inventories: Clinical and personality assessment.* New York: Guilford.

Millon, T., & Davis, R. (1996). *Disorders of personality* (2nd ed.). New York: Guilford.

Retzlaff, P. (1995). *Tactical psychotherapy for the personality disorders: An MCMI-III-based approach.* Boston: Allyn & Bacon.

Schlenger, W. E., & Kulka, R. A. (1987, August). *Performance of the Keane-Fairbank MMPI scale and other self-report measures in identifying post-traumatic stress disorder.* Paper presented at the meeting of the American Psychological Association, New York, NY.

Strack, S. (1987). Development and validation of an adjective check list to assess the Millon personality types in a normal population. *Journal of Personality Assessment, 51,* 572–587.

Chapter 2

American Psychiatric Association. (1994). *Diagnostic and statistical manual of mental disorders* (4th ed.). Washington, DC: Author.

Antoni, M. H., Millon, C., & Millon, T. (1997). The role of psychological assessment in health care: The MBHI, MBMC, and beyond. In T. Millon (Ed.), *The Millon inventories* (pp. 409–448). New York: Guilford.

Harper, R. G., Chacko, R. C., Kotik-Harper, D., Young, J., & Gotto, J. (1998). Self-report evaluation of health behavior, stress vulnerability, and medical outcome of heart transplant recipients. *Psychosomatic Medicine, 60,* 563–569.

Loevinger, J.(1957). Objective tests as instruments of psychological theory. *Psychological Reports, 3,* 635–694.

Millon, C., & Meagher, S. E. (1999). Essentials of MBHI assessment. In S. Strack (Ed.), *Essentials of Millon inventories assessment,* pp. 52–91. New York: Wiley.

Millon, T. (1969). *Modern psychopathology: A biosocial approach to maladaptive learning and functioning.* Philadelphia: W.B. Saunders.

Millon, T. (1990). *Toward a new personology: An evolutionary model.* New York: Wiley.

Millon, T., Antoni, M., Millon, C., Meagher, S., & Grossman, S. (2001). *MBMD manual.* Minneapolis, MN: National Computer Systems.

Millon, T., & Davis, R. (1996). *Disorders of personality: DSM-IV and beyond.* New York: Wiley.

Millon, T., Green, C., & Meagher, R. (1982). *Millon Behavioral Health Inventory manual* (3rd ed.). Minneapolis, MN: National Computer Systems.

Regier, D. (1994). Health care reform: Opportunities and challenge. In S. Blumenthal, K. Mathews, & S. Weiss (Eds.), *New research frontiers in behavioral medicine: Proceedings of the National Conference* (NIH Publication No. 94-3772, pp. 19–24). Washington, DC: U.S. Government Printing Office.

Chapter 3

American Psychiatric Association. (1994). *Diagnostic and statistical manual of mental disorders* (4th ed.). Washington, DC: Author.

Bagby, R. M., Gillis, J. R., & Rogers, R. (1991). Effectiveness of the Millon Clinical Multiaxial Inventory validity index in the detection of random responding. *Psychological Assessment, 3,* 285–287.

Campbell, D. T., & Fiske, D. W. (1959). Convergent and discriminant validation by the multitrait-multimethod matrix. *Psychological Bulletin, 56,* 81–105.

Hiatt, M. D., & Cornell, D. G. (1999). Concurrent validity of the Millon Adolescent Clinical Inventory as a measure of depression in hospitalized adolescents. *Journal of Personality Assessment, 73,* 64–79.

Loevinger, J. (1957). Objective tests as instruments of psychological theory. *Psychological Reports, 3,* 635–694.

McCann, J. T. (1997). The MACI: Composition and clinical applications. In T. Millon (Ed.), *The Millon inventories: Clinical and personality assessment* (pp. 363–388). New York: Guilford.

McCann, J. T. (1999). *Assessing adolescents with the MACI.* New York: Guilford.

Millon, T. (1969). *Modern psychopathology.* Philadelphia: Saunders.

Millon, T. (1981). *Disorders of personality: DSM-III: Axis II.* New York: Wiley.

Millon, T. (1987). *Millon Clinical Multiaxial Inventory–II manual* (2nd ed.). Minneapolis, MN: National Computer Systems.

Millon, T. (1990). *Toward a new personology.* New York: Wiley.

Millon, T. (1993). *Millon Adolescent Clinical Inventory manual.* Minneapolis, MN: National Computer Systems.

Millon, T. (1995). [Factor analytically derived content scales for the MACI]. Unpublished raw data.

Millon, T., & Davis, R. D. (1993). The Millon Adolescent Personality Inventory and the Millon Adolescent Clinical Inventory. *Journal of Counseling and Development, 71,* 570–574.

Millon, T., & Davis, R. D. (1996). *Disorders of personality* (2nd ed.). New York: Guilford.

Millon, T., Green, C., & Meagher, R. B. (1982). *Millon Adolescent Personality Inventory manual.* Minneapolis, MN: National Computer Systems.

Millon, T., Millon, C., & Davis, R. (1994). *Millon Clinical Multiaxial Inventory–III manual.* Minneapolis, MN: National Computer Systems.

Murrie, D. C., & Cornell, D. G. (2000). The Millon Adolescent Clinical Inventory and psychopathy. *Journal of Personality Assessment, 75,* 110–125.

Romm, S., Bockian, N., & Harvey, M. (1999). Factor-based prototypes of the Millon Adolescent Clinical Inventory in adolescents referred for residential treatment. *Journal of Personality Assessment, 72,* 125–143.

Chapter 4

American Psychiatric Association. (1980). *Diagnostic and statistical manual of mental disorders* (3rd ed). Washington, DC: Author.

American Psychiatric Association. (1987). *Diagnostic and statistical manual of mental disorders* (3rd ed., rev.). Washington, DC: Author.

American Psychiatric Association. (1994). *Diagnostic and statistical manual of mental disorders* (4th ed.). Washington, DC: Author.

Costa, P. T., & McCrae, R. R. (1985). The NEO Personality Inventory manual. Odessa, FL: Psychological Assessment Resources.

Derogatis, L. R. (1994). *SCL-90-R: Administration, scoring, and procedures manual* (3rd ed.). Minneapolis, MN: National Computer Systems.

Guevara, L. F., & Strack, S. (1998). An examination of Millon's dimensional and stylistic descriptions of normal personality. *Journal of Personality Assessment, 71,* 337–348.

Hyer, L., & Boyd, S. (1996). Personality scales as predictors of older combat veterans with posttraumatic stress disorder. *Psychological Reports, 79,* 1040–1042.

Loevinger, J. (1957). Objective tests as instruments of psychological theory. *Psychological Reports, 3,* 635–694.

Millon, T. (1974). *Millon Personality Inventory.* Philadelphia: Saunders.

Millon, T. (1977). *Millon Multiaxial Clinical Inventory manual.* Minneapolis, MN: National Computer Systems.

Millon, T. (1981). *Disorders of personality.* New York: Wiley.

Millon, T. (1983a). *Millon Clinical Multiaxial Inventory manual* (3rd ed.). Minneapolis, MN: National Computer Systems.

Millon, T. (1983b). *Modern psychopathology.* Prospect Heights, IL: Waveland Press. (Original work published 1969)

Millon, T. (1986a). Personality prototypes and their diagnostic criteria. In T. Millon & G. L. Klerman (Eds.), *Contemporary directions in psychopathology: Toward the DSM-IV* (pp. 639–670). New York: Guilford.

Millon, T. (1986b). A theoretical derivation of pathological personalities. In T. Millon & G. L. Klerman (Eds.), *Contemporary directions in psychopathology: Toward the DSM-IV* (pp. 639–670). New York: Guilford.

Millon, T. (1987). *Millon Clinical Multiaxial Inventory–II manual* (2nd ed.). Minneapolis, MN: National Computer Systems.

Millon, T. (1990). *Toward a new personology.* New York: Wiley.

Millon, T. (1994). *Millon Index of Personality Styles manual.* San Antonio, TX: Psychological Corporation.

Millon, T. (1996). *Disorders of personality* (2nd ed.). New York: Guilford.

Millon, T. (1997). *Millon Clinical Multiaxial Inventory–III manual* (2nd ed.). Minneapolis, MN: National Computer Systems.

Millon, T., & Davis, R. D. (1994). Millon's evolutionary model of normal and abnormal personality: Theory and measures. In S. Strack & M. Lorr (Eds.), *Differentiating normal and abnormal personality* (pp. 79–113). New York: Springer.

Millon, T., Green, C., & Meagher, R. B. (1982a). *Millon Adolescent Personality Inventory manual* (3rd ed.). Minneapolis, MN: National Computer Systems.

Millon, T., Green, C., & Meagher, R. B. (1982b). *Millon Behavioral Health Inventory manual* (3rd ed.). Minneapolis, MN: National Computer Systems.

Robbins, B. (Ed.) (1998a). *AUTOPACL user's guide (version 2.0).* South Pasadena, CA: 21st Century Assessment.

Robbins, B. (Ed.) (1998b). *WinPACL user's guide (version 2.0).* South Pasadena, CA: 21st Century Assessment.

Strack, S. (1981). *Development and preliminary validation of the Personality Adjective Check List.* Unpublished manuscript.

Strack, S. (1987). Development and validation of an adjective checklist to assess the Millon personality types in a normal population. *Journal of Personality Assessment, 51,* 572–587.

Strack, S. (1991a). *Comparison of PACL PI scale elevations in samples of psychiatric patients and normal adults.* Unpublished manuscript.

Strack, S. (1991b). Computer administration of the PACL and test interpretation. In B. Robbins (Ed.), *AUTOPACL user's guide (version 1.0)* (pp. 15–20). South Pasadena, CA: 21st Century Assessment.

Strack, S. (1991c). *Manual for the Personality Adjective Check List (PACL)* (Rev.). South Pasadena, CA: 21st Century Assessment.

Strack, S. (1992). Profile clusters for men and women on the Personality Adjective Check List. *Journal of Personality Assessment, 59,* 204–217.

Strack, S. (1993). Measuring Millon's personality styles in normal adults. In R. J. Craig (Ed.), *The Millon Clinical Multiaxial Inventory: A clinical research information synthesis* (pp. 253–278). Hillsdale, NJ: Erlbaum.

Strack, S. (1994). Relating Millon's basic personality styles and Holland's occupational types. *Journal of Vocational Behavior, 45,* 41–54.

Strack, S. (1997). The PACL: Gauging normal personality styles. In T. Millon (Ed.), *The Millon inventories: Clinical and personality assessment* (pp. 477–497). New York: Guilford.

Strack, S. (1999). Millon's normal personality styles and dimensions. *Journal of Personality Assessment, 72,* 426–436.

Strack, S., & Guevara, L. F. (1999). Relating PACL measures of Millon's basic personality styles and MMPI-2 scales in patient and normal samples. *Journal of Clinical Psychology, 55,* 895–906.

Strack, S., & Lorr, M. (1990a). Item factor structure of the personality adjective check list (PACL). *Journal of Personality Assessment, 55,* 86–94.

Strack, S., & Lorr, M. (1990b). Three approaches to interpersonal behavior and their common factors. *Journal of Personality Assessment, 54,* 782–790.

Strack, S., Lorr, M., & Campbell, L. (1989, August). *Similarities in Millon personality styles among normals and psychiatric patients.* Paper presented at the annual convention of the American Psychological Association, New Orleans, LA.

Strack, S., Lorr, M., & Campbell, L. (1990). An evaluation of Millon's circular model of personality disorders. *Journal of Personality Disorders, 4,* 353–361.

Chapter 5

Bowling Green State University. (1992). *An inventory of general position requirements.* Bowling Green, OH: Author.

Guion, R. M. (1991, May). *Matching position requirements and personality traits.* Paper presented at the annual convention of the Society of Industrial and Organizational Psychology, Montreal, Quebec, Canada.

Hansen, J. C., & Campbell, D. P. (1985). *Manual for the Strong Interest Inventory* (4th ed.). Palo Alto, CA: Consulting Psychologists Press.

Hogan, R., Curphy, G. J., & Hogan, J. (1993, April). *What we know about leadership: Effectiveness and personality.* Paper presented at the annual convention of the Society for Industrial and Organizational Psychology, San Francisco.

Jung, C. G. (1971a). Psychological types (R. F. C. Hull, Rev. trans.). *The collected works of C. G. Jung* (Vol. 6). Princeton, NJ: Princeton University Press (Original work published in 1921)

Jung, C. G. (1971b). Psychology typology. *Psychological types* (R. F. C. Hull, Rev. trans.). Princeton, NJ: Princeton University Press. (Original work published in 1936)

Loevinger, J. (1957). Objective tests as instruments of psychological theory. *Psychological Reports, 3,* 635–694.

Millon, T. (1983). *Modern psychopathology.* Prospect Heights, IL: Waveland Press. (Original work published 1969)

Millon, T. (1990). *Toward a new personology.* New York: Wiley.

Millon, T. (1991). Normality: What may we learn from evolutionary theory? In D. Offer & M. Sabshin (Eds.), *The diversity of normal behavior.* New York: Basic Books.

Millon, T., Millon, C., Davis, R., Choca, J., & Van Denburg, E. (1997). *Manual for the Millon Clinical Multiaxial Inventory–III* (2nd ed.). Minneapolis, MN: National Computer Systems.

Millon, T., Weiss, L., Millon, C., & Davis, R. (1994). *Millon Index of Personality Styles manual.* San Antonio, TX: The Psychological Corporation.

Myers, I. B. (1962). *The Myers-Briggs Type Indicator.* Palo Alto, CA: Consulting Psychologists Press.

Myers, I. B., & McCaulley, M. H. (1985). *Manual: A guide to the development and use of the Myers-Briggs Type Indicator.* Palo Alto, CA: Consulting Psychologists Press.

The Psychological Corporation. (1994). *User's Guide for the Millon Index of Personality Styles computer program.* San Antonio, TX: Author.

Super, D. E. (1983). Assessment in career guidance: Toward truly developmental counseling. *The Personnel and Guidance Journal, 61,* 555–562.

Tango, R. A. & Dziuban, C. D. (1984). The use of personality components in the interpretation of career indecision. *Journal of College Student Personnel, 25,* 509–512.

Annotated Bibliography

Antoni, M. H., Millon, C., & Millon, T. (1997). The role of psychological assessment in health care: The MBHI, MBMC, and beyond. In T. Millon (Ed.), *The Millon inventories* (pp. 409–448). New York: Guilford.

This chapter gives a persuasive argument for the need of assessment tools such as the MBMD in an effort to control skyrocketing costs of health care. It argues for the psychosocial factors that play a role in health maintenance and the clinical utility of the MBMD to provide this information in a systematic and synthesized format. The chapter also presents a comprehensive literature review of relevant research done on health care delivery and psychosocial characteristics that influence medical patients.

Choca, J. P., & Van Denburg, E. (1996). *Interpretive guide to the Millon Clinical Multiaxial Inventory* (2nd ed.). Washington, DC: American Psychological Association.

The only MCMI-III source book that provides comprehensive information about test development, interpretation, and research. The interpretations provided are somewhat at variance from those suggested by Millon. The Choca group believes the scales are measuring personality styles and hence provides more attenuated interpretations. One chapter provides interpretations for the more frequently appearing MCMI-III code types along with treatment recommendations. The book contains up-to-date research on a variety of selected populations.

Craig, R. J. (Ed.). (1993a). *The Millon Clinical Multiaxial Inventory: A clinical research information synthesis.* Hillsdale, NJ: Erlbaum.

This book provides an overview of current information on the MCMI and presents such topics as a literature review, factor studies, applications to special populations (schizophrenia, affective disorders, substance abusers, eating disorders, post-traumatic stress disorder, and anxiety disorders), its correspondence with DSM disorders, computer interpretation of the MCMI, and new developments in the use of this instrument, including the development of special scales for the MCMI, measuring Millon's personality styles in normal adults and integrating the MCMI with the MMPI.

Craig, R. J. (1993b). *Psychological assessment with the Millon Clinical Multiaxial Inventory (II): An interpretive guide.* Odessa, FL: Psychological Assessment Resources.

This book is clinically focused and designed to be a "hands-on" companion for clinical interpretation of the MCMI. Interpretation of each personality and clinical syndrome scale is provided, as well as the interpretation of 2-point, 3-point, and high-ranging code types. The final chapter presents case illustrations of combining the MCMI with other objective personality tests, including the Minnesota Multiphasic Personality Inventory, the Adjective Check List, the 16 Personality Factors, and the California Psychological Inventory.

Craig, R. J. (1997). A selected review of the MCMI empirical literature. In T. Millon (Ed.). *The Millon inventories: Clinical and personality assessment* (pp. 303–326). New York: Guilford.

This reference provides an up-to-date summary with the MCMI, dealing with reliability and validity; it also shows how various clinical populations have tended to score on the MCMI.

McCann, J. T. (1997). The MACI: Composition and clinical applications. In T. Millon (Ed.), *The Millon Inventories: Clinical and personality assessment* (pp. 363–388). New York: Guilford.

This chapter provides an overview of the MACI. The scale interpretations are excellent and the section on the "poor-fit" profile is especially instructive.

McCann, J. T. (1999). *Assessing adolescents with the MACI.* New York: Guilford.

This is the first book devoted to the MACI. It is comprehensive in its scope, thorough and detailed, and provides excellent case illustrations. A must-read for clinicians who use the MACI in their assessments.

McCann, J., & Dyer, F. J. (1996). *Forensic assessment with the Millon inventories.* New York: Guilford.

This book provides the reader with seminal information on the use of the MCMI in forensic settings. It details case laws that have sanctioned the use of the MCMI in court as it applies to a variety of forensic uses, such as custody evaluations, termination of parental rights, assessment of fitness to stand trial, insanity, and so on. The authors recommend using the MCMI-II in court since it has more empirical support than the MCMI-III.

Millon, T. (1983). *Modern psychopathology.* Prospect Heights, IL: Waveland Press. (Original work published 1969)

The text that introduced Millon's biosocial learning theory to the world. The text outlines Millon's perspective regarding personality and mental disorders. Comprehensive in its scope, it addresses innumerable theories and concepts.

Millon, T. (1981) *Disorders of personality: DSM-III: Axis II.* New York: Wiley.

The follow-up to Modern Psychopathology, *this text focuses more specifically on the personality disorders and illustrates how they could be theoretically derived from the three-polarity model. An excellent text that provided an enlightening historical context for each of the personality disorders as well as outstanding descriptions of the personality disorders.*

Millon, T. (1990). *Toward a new personology.* New York: Wiley.

This 200-page book contains a scholarly elucidation of the author's theory of evolutionary psychology and how it relates to his schema of personality classification that runs through the Millon family of instruments. The following topics are discussed: scientific creativity and theoretical integration, evolutionary foundations of physical and biological science, concordance of evolutionary polarities and psychological science; deriving a classification for personological science; and assessments of personality polarities, domains, and disorders.

Millon, T. (1993). *Millon Adolescent Clinical Inventory manual.* Minneapolis, MN: National Computer Systems.

This is the most comprehensive resource regarding the MACI's development, validation, scoring, and interpretation.

Millon, T. (1997a) *Millon Clinical Multiaxial Inventory–III manual* (2nd ed.). Minneapolis, MN: National Computer Systems.

This test manual provides detailed information on the theory on which the test is based, validating strategies, internal and external validity data, administration and scoring considerations, test interpretation, a sample automated MCMI-III report, applications of the test, and future directions. There are extensive tables presented in the appendices providing additional information dealing with such things as conversion tables and psycometric data. The manual is a "must purchase" for anyone who seriously plans to use the MCMI-III for clinical or research purposes.

Millon, T. (Ed.). (1997b). *The Millon inventories: Clinical and personality assessment.* New York: Guilford.

This edited volume presents a complete account of the MCMI as it currently exists, detailing Millon's theory, test development, use with special populations, and applications of the instrument. There is a selected review of the research literature as well as a discussion of integrating the test with the MMPI-2. Future applications are also considered.

Millon, T., Antoni, M., Millon, C., Meagher, S., & Grossman, S. (2001). *MBMD manual.* Minneapolis, MN: National Computer Systems.

Indispensible for users of the MBMD, this manual gives detailed information on every aspect of test development and validation, including item content of each scale, as well as information on how to score and interpret the measure. Particularly helpful are the validation study reports, correlations with other measures, and profiles of different patient groups.

Millon, T., & Davis, R. D. (1993). The Millon Adolescent Personality Inventory and the Millon Adolescent Clinical Inventory. *Journal of Counseling and Development, 71,* 570–574.

This article describes the rationale for the development of the MACI and the changes that it represents from the MAPI.

Millon, T., & Davis, R. D. (1994). Millon's evolutionary model of normal and abnormal personality: Theory and measures. In S. Strack & M. Lorr (Eds.), *Differentiating normal and abnormal personality* (pp. 79–113). New York: Springer.

This chapter gives a comprehensive overview of Millon's model of personality and available measurement instruments, including the PACL. It is helpful in showing how the various Millon instruments extend from, and are integrated with, the theoretical model.

Millon, T., & Davis, R. (1996). *Disorders of personality* (2nd ed.). New York: Guilford.

This is the most comprehensive book on personality disorders. It covers all the disorders in DSM-IV plus those emanating from Millon's theory. A thorough history is given for each disorder, along with its defining characteristics and comorbidities.

Millon, T., & Davis, R. D. (1997). The MCMI-III: Present and future directions. *Journal of Personality Assessment, 68,* 69–88.

This article is the most recent one published by the test's author, which reports on theoretical and empirical developments that are being considered for possible revisions of the MCMI-III. For example, Millon theorizes that there may be subtypes of each personality disorder and has identified anywhere from three to five subtypes for each disorder. He is also considering trait subscales. Currently there is no way of ascertaining which of the many domain traits are saliently organized within a personality disorder. Identification of trait subscales would assist in this determination.

Millon, T., Green, C., & Meagher, R. (1982). *Millon Behavioral Health Inventory manual* (3rd ed). Minneapolis, MN: National Computer Systems.

This manual provides detailed information on development of the MBMD's predecessor, including item selection criteria, reliability data, and correlations of scales with several widely used assessment instruments.

Millon, T., Weiss, L. G., Millon, C, & Davis, R. (1994). *Millon Index of Personality Styles manual.* San Antonio: The Psychological Corporation.

This 182-page manual is an excellent source of information about the MIPS. Chapter 1 is a solid but brief introduction to the structure of the scales. Chapter 2 is an in-depth treatise on the theoretical underpinnings of the scales, which forms the basis of an interpretive approach. Chapters 3 and 4 handle the technical characteristics of the test in very easy to understand language, addressing development, standardization, reliability, and validity. Chapter 5 stands out as a compendium of six organizational validity studies conducted with the MIPS during its development at the Psychological Corporation.

Pincus, A. L., & Wiggins, J. S. (1990). Interpersonal problems and conceptions of personality disorders. *Journal of Personality Disorders, 4,* 342–352.

This empirical report shows how PACL scales are associated with MMPI personality disorder scales and self-reported personality problems in a large sample of college students. It demonstrates the utility of the PACL as a measure of normal personality styles, which are directly linked to their personality disorder counterparts.

Retzlaff, P. (1995). *Tactical psychotherapy for the personality disorders: An MCMI-III-based approach.* Boston: Allyn & Bacon.

This book applies Millon's theory and utilizes the MCMI to assess and plan treatment strategies from a variety of theoretical perspectives. How each therapy would address the functional and structural attributes for each personality disorder is accounted for in this edited text, and each author provides a case illustration of implementing the MCMI assessment and the therapy as applied to the case.

Robbins, B. (1998). *AUTOPACL user's guide* (version 2.0) and *WinPACL user's guide* (version 2.0). South Pasadena, CA: 21st Century Assessment.

Both guides give information on how to administer, score, and interpret the PACL by computer. They explain the various rules used to create Interpretive Reports and compare the computer and paper versions of the test.

Strack, S. (1987). Development and validation of an adjective check list to assess the Millon personality types in a normal population. *Journal of Personality Assessment, 51,* 572–587.

This article describes the development of the PACL and its theoretical foundation. Its fairly technical presentation can be difficult for novice assessment students to follow, but there is extensive information in its 16 pages that is of historical interest.

Strack, S. (1991). *Manual for the Personality Adjective Check List (PACL)* (Rev.) South Pasadena, CA: 21st Century Assessment.

This revised edition is essential for anyone who uses the PACL. This resource provides information on how to administer, score, and interpret the test. It summarizes the development of the checklist and gives extensive reliability and validity information.

Strack, S. (1992). Profile clusters for men and women on the Personality Adjective Check List. *Journal of Personality Assessment, 59,* 204–217.

This article presents nine PACL cluster profiles for men and women based on the normative sample. The study demonstrates that a handful of profiles can account for much of the variability in PACL scores. What this means is that although there are thousands of possible scale combinations for the PACL, most people give profiles that are statistically similar to those found here. Use these clusters as a comparison for profiles generated by persons in any clinical or research setting.

Strack, S. (1993). Measuring Millon's personality styles in normal adults. In R. J. Craig (Ed.), *The Millon Clinical Multiaxial Inventory: A clinical research information synthesis* (pp. 253–278). Hillsdale, NJ: Erlbaum.

This chapter gives an overview of the PACL and supporting research following a presentation of empirical evidence against using the MCMI in normal populations.

Strack, S. (1997). The PACL: Gauging normal personality styles. In T. Millon (Ed.), *The Millon inventories: Clinical and personality assessment* (pp. 477–497). New York: Guilford.

This chapter gives a concise overview of the PACL and a summary of research findings from 1987 to 1996.

Strack, S. (Ed.) (1999). Millon's evolving personality theory and measures. [Special series]. *Journal of Personality Assessment, 72,* 323–456.

A number of prominent personality psychologists offer insights into the history and development of Millon's comprehensive theory of personality and psychopathology, as well as his measures, from 1969 to 1999. Millon provides an original commentary reflecting on his vision for the future of personology in the 21st century.

Weiss, L. G. (1997). The MIPS: Gauging the dimensions of normality. In T. Millon (Ed.), *The Millon Inventories: Clinical and personality assessment.* New York: Guilford.

This 26-page chapter is an excellent summary of the material presented in the MIPS manual. In addition, the author proposes an extension to Millon's personality schema for normal range personality that includes the active-pleasure and passive-pleasure styles.

Weiss, L. G., & Lowther, J. (1995, March). *The factor structure of the Millon Index of Personality Styles.* Paper presented at the annual convention of the Society for Personality Assessment, Atlanta, GA.

This paper reports a five-factor structure for the MIPS that conforms to the Big Five personality scales. Factors are named Maladaption, Surgency, Conscientiousness, Disagreeableness, and Closed-Mindedness. The paper presents scoring rules and norms for these factors and shows how these factors perform in several occupational samples including managers, military recruits, police officers, hourly employees, and executives. Theoretical implications for the five-factor model are discussed.

Wiggins, J. S., & Pincus, A. L. (1990). Conceptions of personality disorders and dimensions of personality. *JCCP: Psychological Assessment, 1,* 305–316.

A companion to Pincus and Wiggins (1990), this report links the PACL and MMPI personality disorder scales to the five-factor model of personality.

INDEX

Numbers in *italics* indicate tables and figures.